IMAGES
of America

MICHIGAN CITY'S WASHINGTON PARK

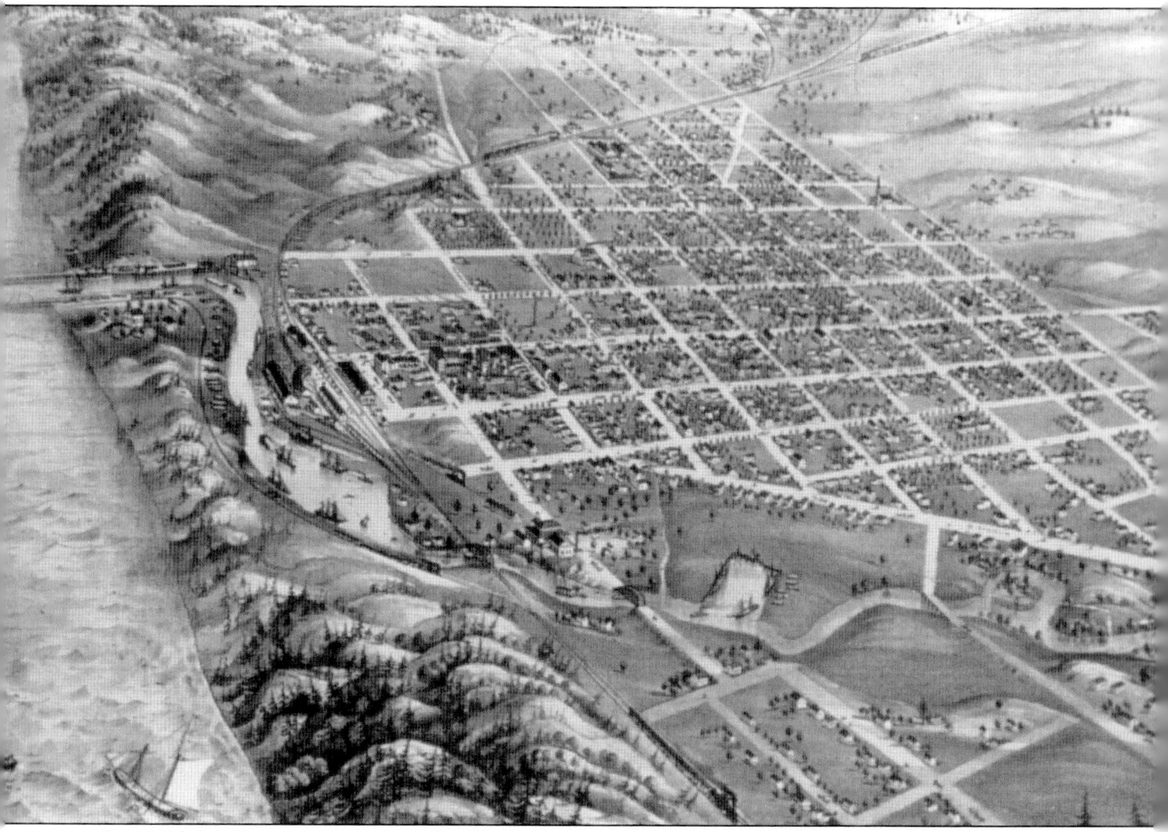

In 1865, Michigan City was a bustling commercial port and growing town. In just a few short years, that would change. Once the bustle abandoned the port, the lumber piles and remnants of industry were left behind. The homeless took up residence, using these materials to build temporary homes. Locals considered the area north of Trail Creek a skid row or shantytown. This map illustrates the town in 1869.

On the Cover: This is the entrance to Washington Park in 1911. Families would drive, walk, and take ferries from across Lake Michigan for a day of amusement in Washington Park. The monument greeting each visitor was and still is the Civil War Memorial donated by Michigan City resident John Winterbotham. (Courtesy Michigan City Historical Society.)

IMAGES
of America

MICHIGAN CITY'S WASHINGTON PARK

Jonita Davis

ARCADIA
PUBLISHING

Copyright © 2010 by Jonita Davis
ISBN 978-0-7385-8338-9

Published by Arcadia Publishing
Charleston, South Carolina

Printed in the United States of America

Library of Congress Control Number: 2010937731

For all general information, please contact Arcadia Publishing:
Telephone 843-853-2070
Fax 843-853-0044
E-mail sales@arcadiapublishing.com
For customer service and orders:
Toll-Free 1-888-313-2665

Visit us on the Internet at www.arcadiapublishing.com

To the park supporters and visionaries who go to the mat for their lakefront day after day.

Contents

ACKNOWLEDGMENTS

I began this project eager to discover how the park was created and was pleasantly surprised to unearth photographs of wooden roller coasters and carousels. The park documented in these images was one that I never knew. My mission became a discovery of how the park went from amusement to a complete green space. I would like to acknowledge my many assistants in this journey, the wonderful ladies in the Michigan City Library reference department for their help and accommodations. Also special thanks to the Michigan City Lighthouse Museum for allowing me access to their one-of-a-kind photograph collection. The Michigan City Lighthouse Museum was also the source of a book of speeches that proved invaluable in piecing together the history of Washington Park. Thanks to Michigan City clerk Thomas Fedder for unlocking the history underneath city hall. The many memories of Michigan City are being preserved in a climate-controlled room, just waiting for a curious soul to delve into them. A very special thanks goes to my family, especially my little helpers who loved going through the images as much as I did. Finally, thanks to Anna Wilson and John Pearson of Arcadia Publishing for their knowledge and unending supply of patience. Unless otherwise noted, all images within these pages appear courtesy of the Michigan City Library. Now, on with the story.

Introduction

The story begins at the lakefront, where the little river known as Trail Creek pours into the great Lake Michigan. The area has attracted attention from politicians, settlers, and businessmen, as well as those in need of a place to lay low for a little while. The massive dunes only added to the appeal—protection, beauty, and the money that would come from selling the sand. Surprisingly, the factors that attracted the future residents of Michigan City were the same factors that Washington Park's founder, Martin Krueger, had to overcome in establishing it.

Long before Michigan City was formed, before Indiana was even a state, the white-sand lakefront was fertile stomping grounds for the Miami, Iroquois, and Potawatomi Indian tribes. They hunted, fished, and lived among the dunes that lined the lake and the swamp that bordered Trail Creek. Kayaks and canoes were frequently used for transport despite the problem spots in the river that defied navigation. The sandbar at the river's mouth impeded direct travel to and from the lake. Trail Creek narrowed severely as it flowed south, preventing a complete trip inland as well. The river did harbor food for the tribes in the form of fox, rabbit, and other small game. It also invited fish from Lake Michigan, which became a large part of the local diet.

The trees along the south side of the sand dunes just along the creek provided the basis for shelter, fires, and weaponry for all tribes. The sand dunes and swampland in and around Trail Creek were used to protect the women and children during attacks between the tribes. During the French and Indian War, the area hosted secret meetings amongst the tribes, including one rumored to have been held by Pontiac, chief of the Ottawa and emissary of the French military. Pontiac's goal was to raise the ranks for a raid on Fort Detroit, the site of the current city of Detroit, Michigan. The Trail Creek area provided the perfect cover.

Actually, the French were no strangers to the area. Sometime around the beginning of the 17th century, French explorers roamed the Great Lakes region. Trail Creek was such an integral part of their travels that it was only one of a few tributaries included on a Franquelin map dated 1608. Jean Baptiste Louis Franquelin was a cartographer in the 17th century. He was charged with mapping New France, the area colonized by France in North America that included areas in northern Indiana and Michigan. Not long after the French explorers came and went, the fur traders arrived. Armed with ammunition, trinkets, good will, and a sales pitch, the fur traders made a name for themselves while buying furs from the local tribes. Famous visitors at that time included explorer and Jesuit priest Fr. Jacques Marquette. He reportedly arrived on what would become known as Washington Park Beach in Michigan City in 1675; Marquette was ill and in need of food and refuge. The Potawatomi sheltered and fed Marquette and the rest of his team. The cleric preached to those in the area, staying a few days before moving on. He died in Ludington, Michigan, just two months after his Michigan City visit.

In addition to tribal trading, the French left a lasting legacy on Michigan City's lakefront in the name of the river that would eventually lead to the start of the town. The French name Riviere du Chemin, or "River on the Trail," described the importance of Trail Creek as a navigational tool. The British fur traders, who later poured into the area after the French and Indian War, mispronounced the name. Trail Creek was incorrectly referred to as "Dysman" or "Dishmaw" in a failed attempt to Anglicize the French name. Even still, the area remained untamed with plenty of wild game to eat and trade. That seemed to be all the tribes and French and British traders cared about until the Revolutionary War broke out.

History is full of accounts about the colonies along the Atlantic Seaboard and their efforts during the Revolutionary War. Little recognition is given to the people living in what is now known as the Midwest. In fact, one famous battle took place near the site of Washington Park, known as the Battle of Trail Creek. The events began in Illinois, in a town named Cahokia, where American Lieutenant Tom Brady, along with 16 French and American soldiers, successfully attacked a British fort. They turned north and west, making their way to Fort Joseph in Niles, Michigan. According to historian Elizabeth Munger's *A History of the Trail Creek Region*, French fur trader and British sympathizer Etienne Champion met Brady and his cohorts at Trail Creek. The meeting was actually an ambush that became known as the Battle of Trail Creek on December 5, 1780. Champion was only a fur trader, but he used influence to rally the Potawatomi tribes along the lakefront and British soldiers in the area. The team of British soldiers and Potawatomi warriors overtook Brady, arresting him as he and his men tried to escape.

The beginning of the end for the untamed land and its inhabitants came in early 1828, when the State of Indiana sent scouts John McDonald, Chester Eliot, and John Neely to explore the area around the lakes. The residents described an area that was dense but backed by northern Indiana's large sand dunes. The river that poured into Lake Michigan was considered much more than the navigational tool that the French once saw. Upon returning to the Indiana State Legislature, McDonald, Eliot, and Neely presented their ideas about using the harbor at the Riviere du Chemin as Indiana's major shipping port on Lake Michigan. Incidentally, these three men were the first to properly translate the British mispronunciation of the river's name. Their report began the push to develop and maintain a shipping port located in the area that would eventually become Michigan City.

By 1816, Indiana had become a state when the Potawatomi had given up their rights to the land. The scouts' report had become big news for the state. Speculators arrived, none more eager than Maj. Isaac Elston of Crawfordsville, Indiana. Elston bought up all of the land from Lake Michigan's entrance to Trail Creek southward, measuring a quarter of a mile. Elston never intended to live on the land and bought it sight unseen. Elston's purchase was bolstered by the state's intended port in the area and a road that was being constructed to run from the state capital to Lake Michigan. The endpoint was Trail Creek. In those days of travel by foot, horse, and carriage, a cleared road meant traffic and, most importantly, significant trade potential. Michigan Road, known today as Highway 421, was commissioned in 1829. Elston purchased the endpoint of this road just a year later in 1830.

Michigan City had a name before Elston arrived, which was a shortened version of "the city by Lake Michigan." Immediately after it was settled, residents began working on a harbor. A shipping industry was created around the mouth of Trail Creek, and city businessman Samuel Miller was the first to build a warehouse along the channel. Fish, grain, salt, farm equipment, and other goods came in from Lake Michigan, and they were kept in warehouses before being transported throughout the state. Items like lumber were manufactured in Trail Creek, which were also warehoused and bound for other communities. The shipping industry boomed, bolstered by government funding to build the harbor and dredge the Trail Creek channel. By the late 1800s, lumber had taken over as the principal export, and mills and lumberyards lined the creek. The unanticipated result was the transformation of the beach and surrounding area into a less-than-desirable place to visit. That was the state of the harbor when Martin T. Krueger became mayor in 1890.

One

The Forsaken Land

"A curious freak of nature is the circumstances that people seldom want or provide for a public park when they can get one, in the best location and for a song. They usually wait until the most desirable land for that purpose have been denuded of their natural beauty or converted to other uses before they realize what they have lost. And this situation the people of Michigan City have escaped by a very narrow margin. " Martin Krueger spoke these words when describing the opposition he faced in creating a park for Michigan City. Krueger was understating things, however. The events that eventually led to Washington Park were much more complicated, expensive, and arduous.

Martin Krueger came to office with a vision for the land left abandoned along the Lake Michigan shore. By the time he took office, the bridge that connected the northern and southern sections of Trail Creek was gone. The campaign to develop the harbor required that the bridge be removed in the 1860s. The bridge was never replaced. The harbor was also deteriorated, as the city moved on from the dream of a shipping port. Several harbor enthusiasts made attempts to rebuild the bridge, but those plans were never realized.

Krueger described the lakefront as a "no man's land" full of "ex-convicts, dissolute men and women and every kind of human scum that has ever hung on to the skirts of civilized society." Fishermen who lived at the lakefront during fishing season built part of the shantytowns. The nets drying beside a few of the shacks evidenced this. According to Krueger, "No one cared and very few people knew who owned those lands." Many of the speculators who bought up the land in the 1830s, looking to cash in on the prospect of a commercial port, lost on the investment when such a port failed to fully materialize. In fact, neighboring city (across Lake Michigan), Chicago, Illinois, was granted the federal funding to develop such a port in the mid-1800s. When this happened, several of the speculators sold their lots to the first person willing to buy them. Many of the landowners did not live locally and harbored with no guilt about their dilapidated properties.

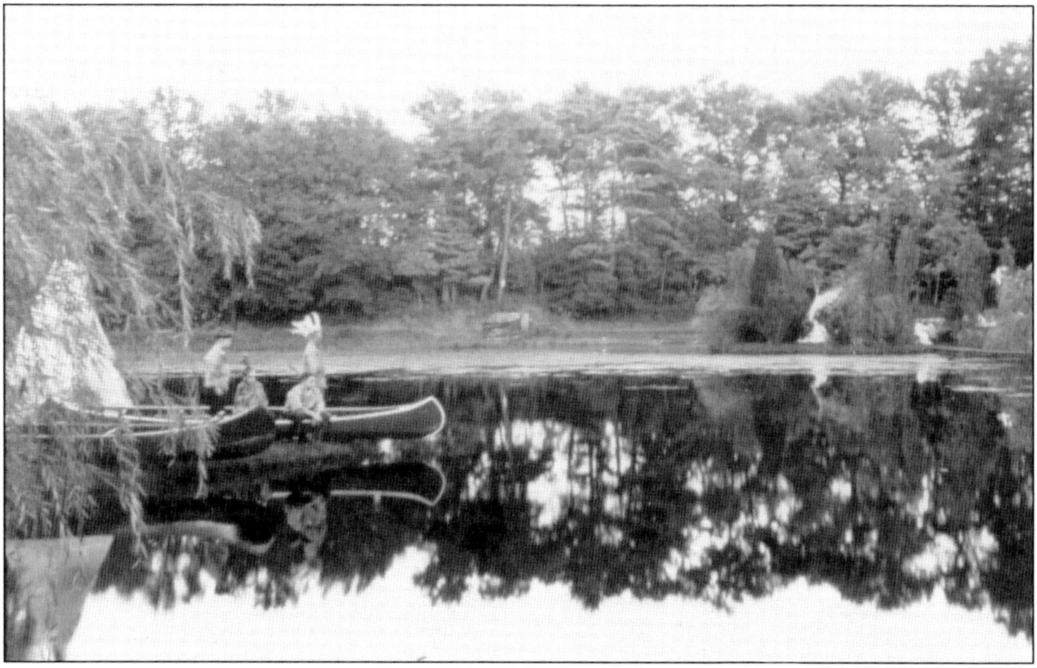

Fur traders and Native Americans did brisk commerce along Trail Creek, so it comes as no surprise that the settlers wanted to do the same once they established the area. In this photograph, canoers reenact Native Americans traveling along Trail Creek. This mode of transport was quickly adapted by the fur traders.

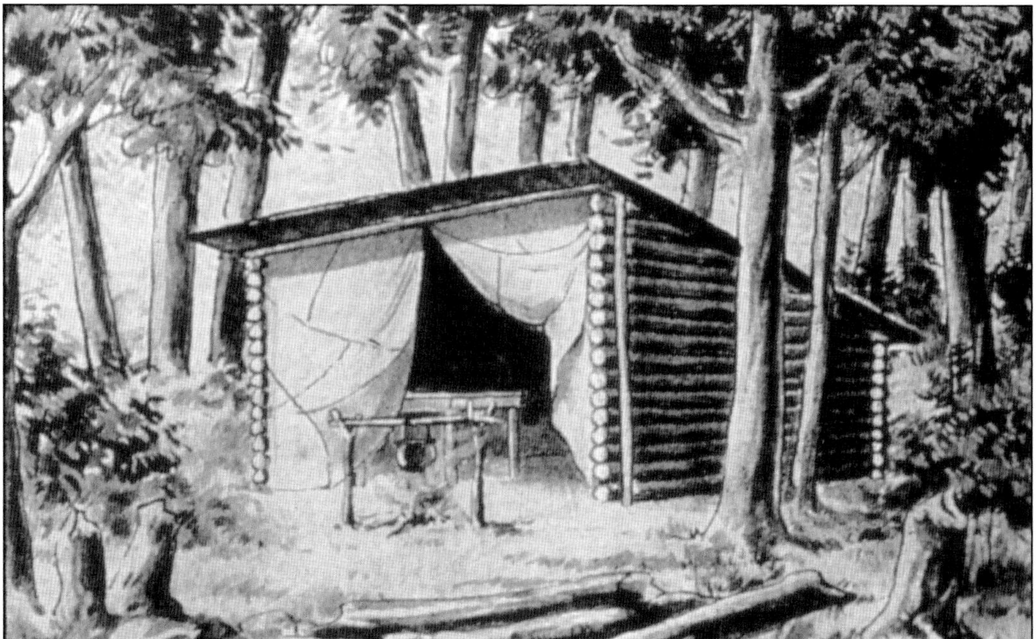

Log cabins were the norm, as can be seen here. Traders lived among the tribes, almost as their equals in an effort to promote and maintain successful trade business.

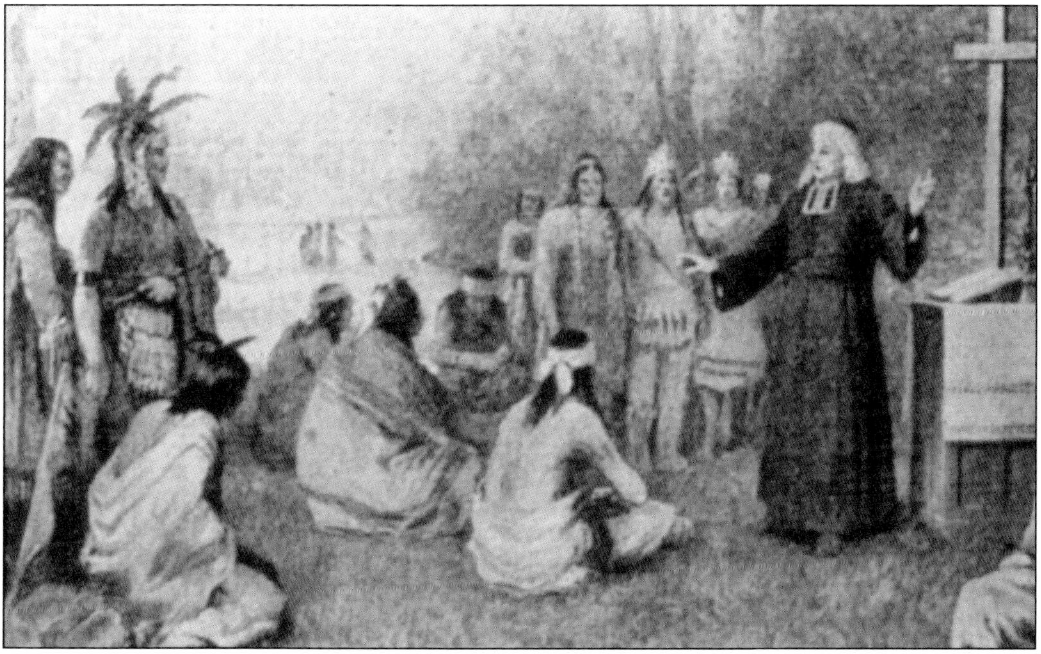

Friend to all beings, adventurer and priest Father Marquette made the Michigan City lakefront one of the last stops before his death in 1675. Missions to the area in an effort to convert the native people were not uncommon. The tribes that lived around Trail Creek did reportedly treat the missionaries with hospitality, but only if those religious groups were not seen as a threat.

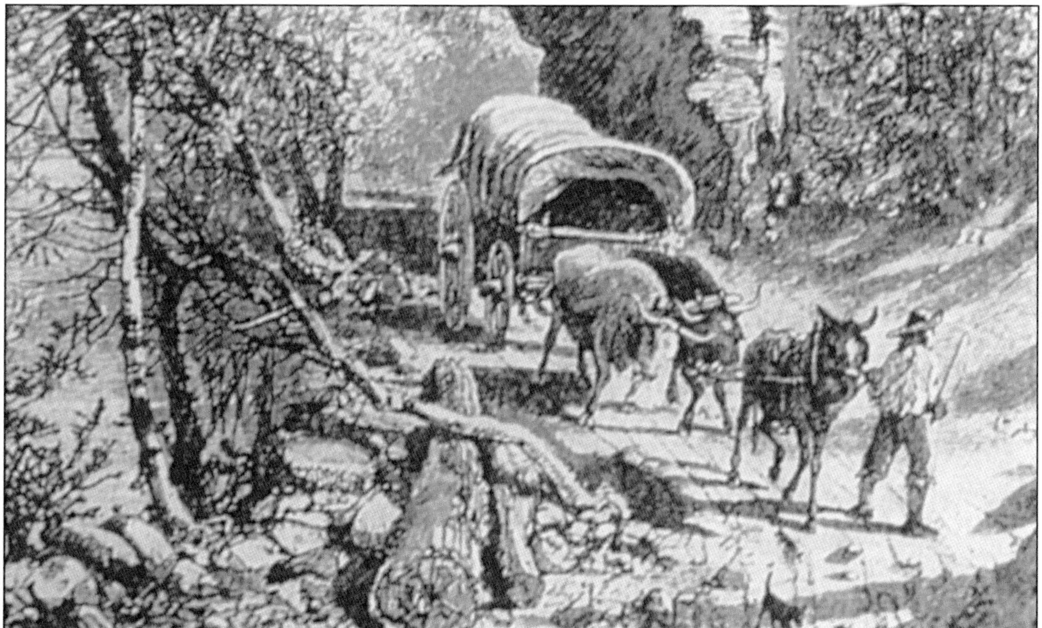

As settlers moved into the area, more space was cleared; the swamplands were eventually tamed. The construction of Michigan Road (a road from Indiana's state capital, through Michigan City, to Lake Michigan) made settling in Michigan City an even better prospect. As seen here, the vehicles at the time could not maneuver without a road.

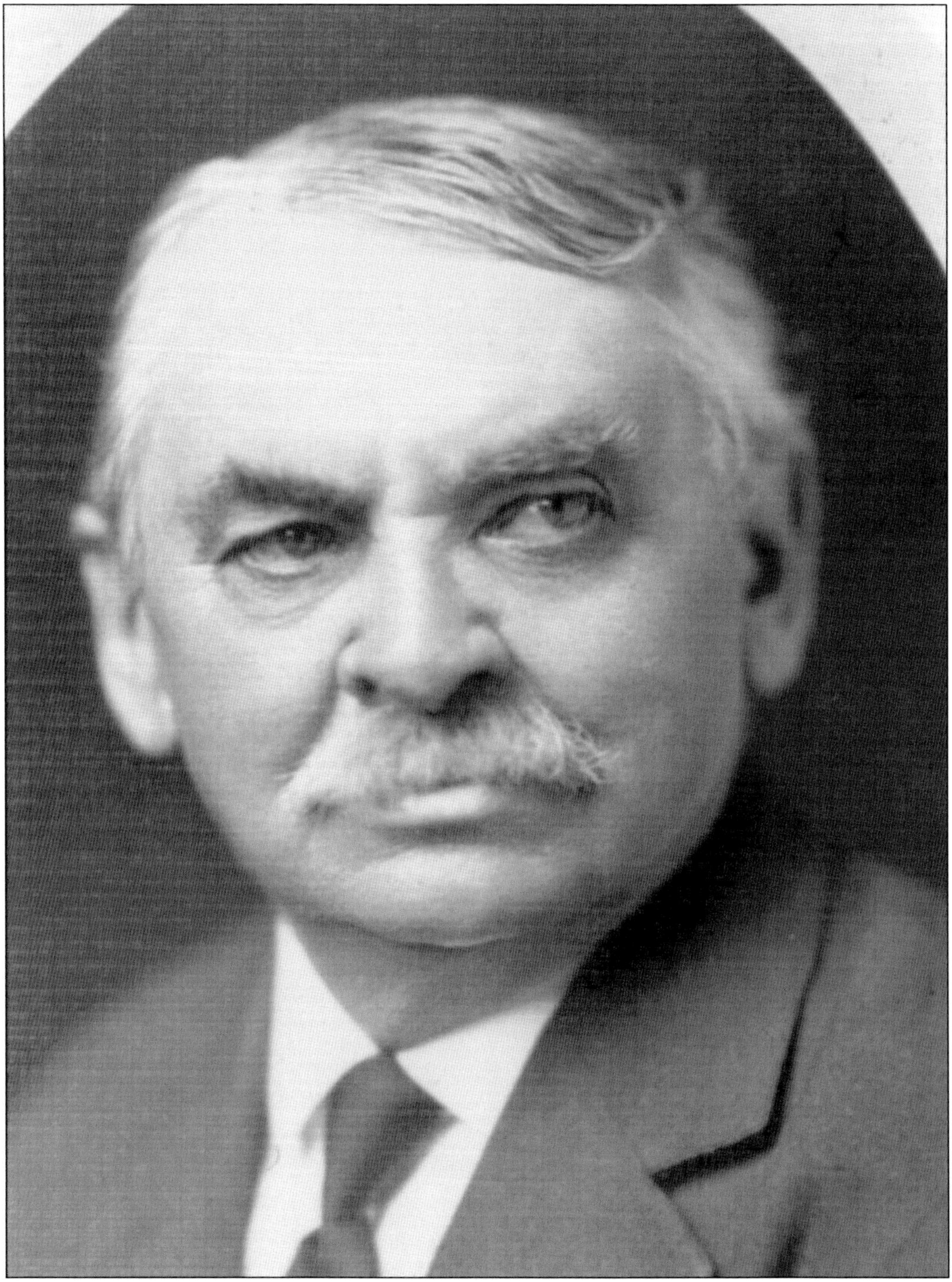

The state of the harbor was an obstacle to Martin Krueger's vision for the lakefront. The vision was cultivated before Krueger's tenure as mayor during a visit to Lincoln Park, Illinois, in 1883. There, Krueger, a city clerk at the time, saw what Michigan City's lakefront could become. He returned from the trip telling everyone about the idea of turning the lakefront into a park. Initially, his plans were largely ignored.

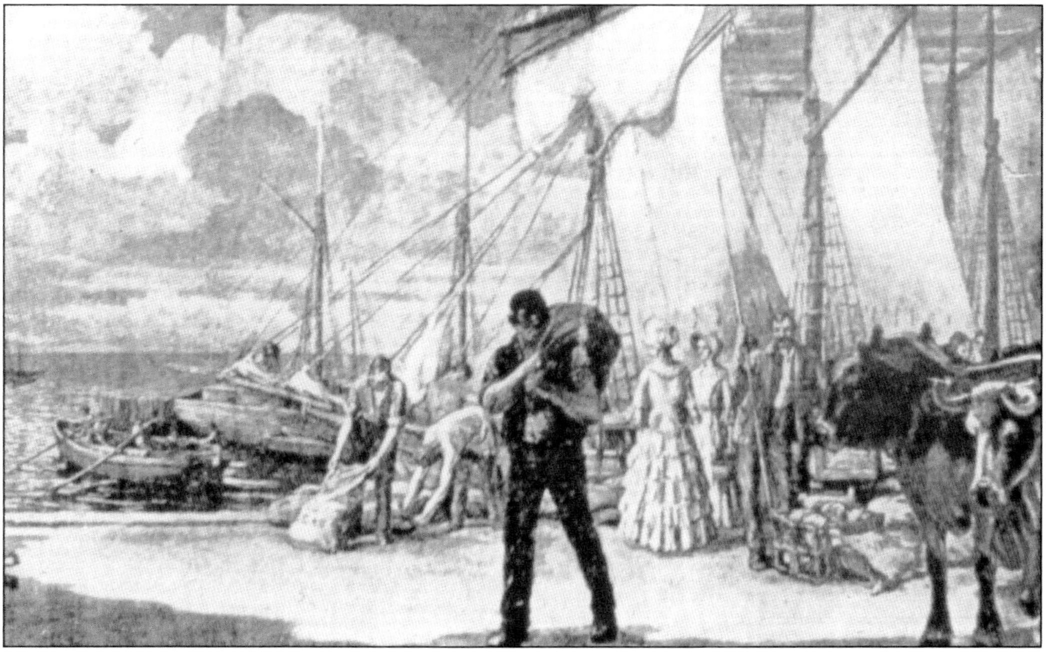

This image depicts Washington Park Beach, the area north of what would become Washington Park and across Trail Creek from the Hoosier Slide that was often a shallow dock as well. Traders and settlers found this to be convenient to receive provisions brought by ship across Lake Michigan. When Krueger gained control of the harbor, this area was filled with shanties and lumbers piles.

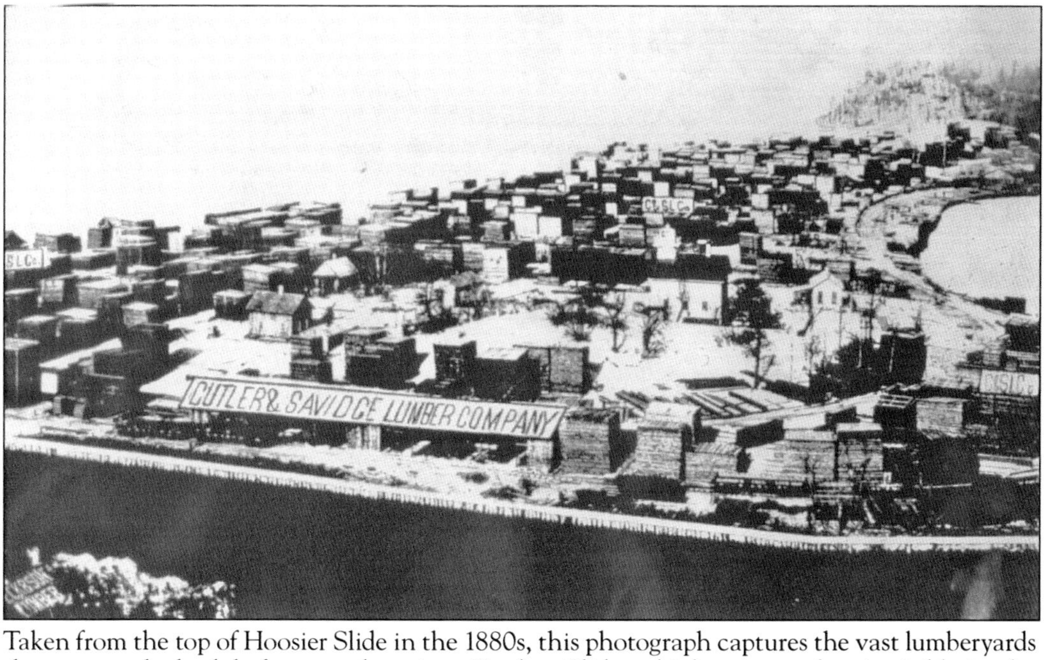

Taken from the top of Hoosier Slide in the 1880s, this photograph captures the vast lumberyards that overtook the lakefront at that time. Yankee Slide, which exists today, is visible in the background. The old lighthouse and a few homes can be seen. A closer look reveals a few of the shack homes Martin Krueger wished to eliminate.

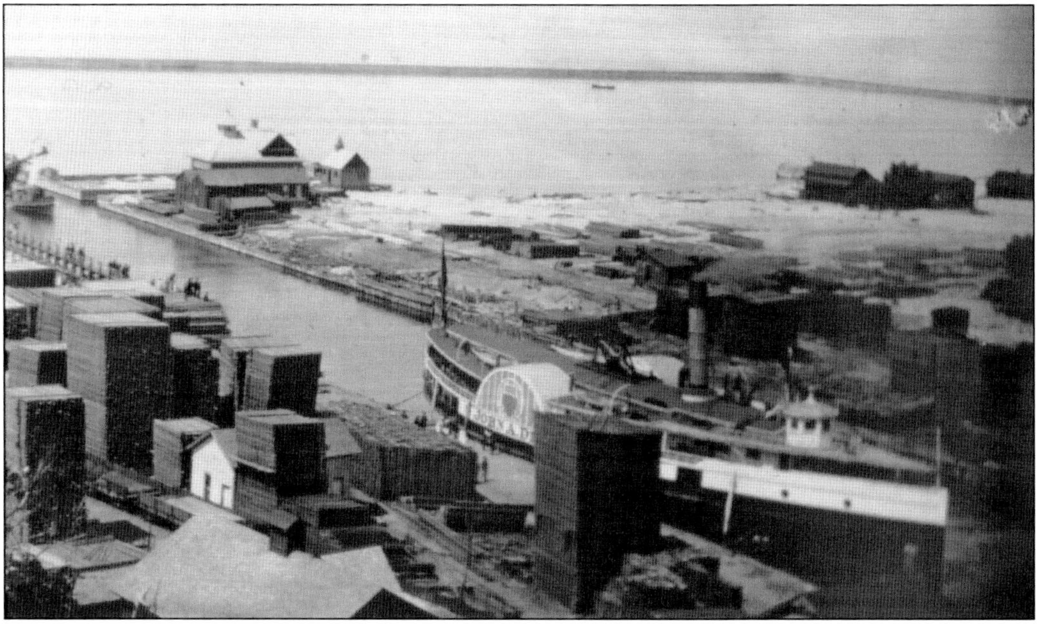

These images of the lakefront illustrate the extent to which the lumber industry had overtaken the shore. Residents of Michigan City began to view this area as separate from the section south of Trail Creek. Commercial traffic did not stop during this time; it simply crawled to a pace that was slower than when the harbor was first improved years earlier. In addition to losing harbor funding to Chicago, a short-lived economic depression hit the area in the 1860s, causing an even more significant drop in commercial freight. The recovery from that depression never fully restored commercial traffic to the area.

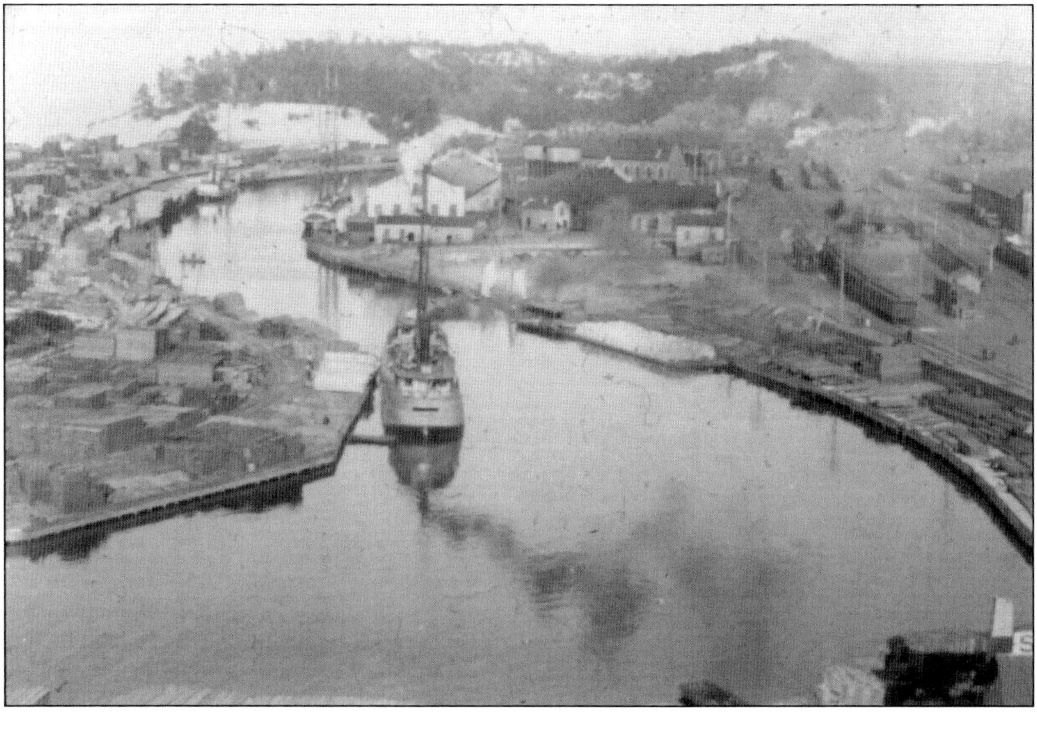

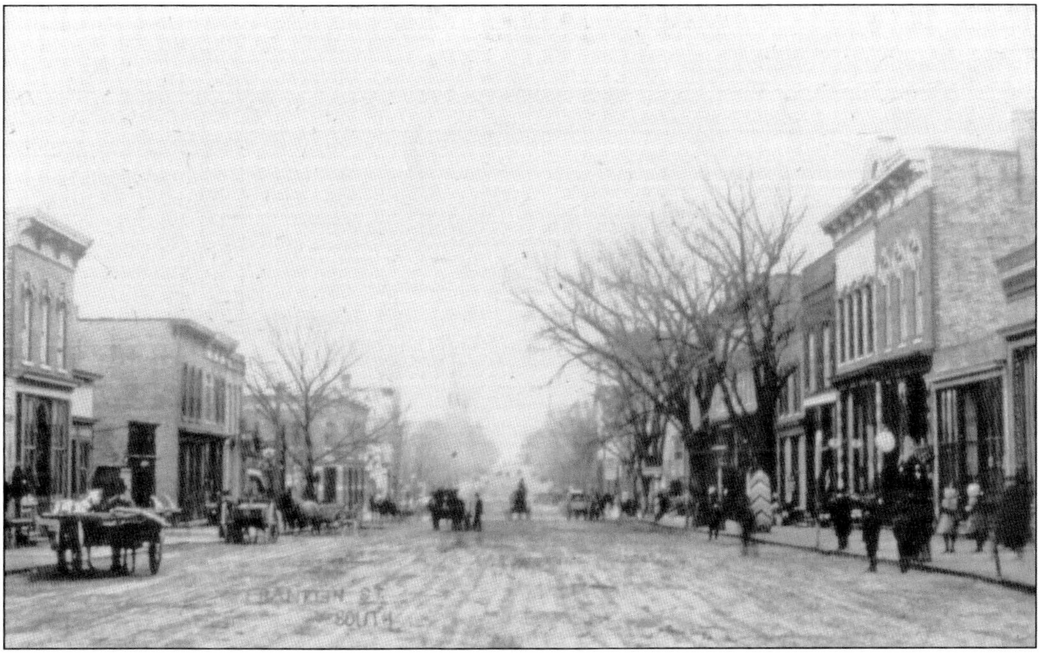

Martin Krueger consulted his good friend Harry Francis, founder of the *Michigan City Dispatch*, housed in one of the buildings pictured here. Both men agreed that a bridge must be constructed across Trail Creek at Franklin Street before the park could be a possibility. However, this posed a problem, as the topic of building a bridge polarized the people of Michigan City.

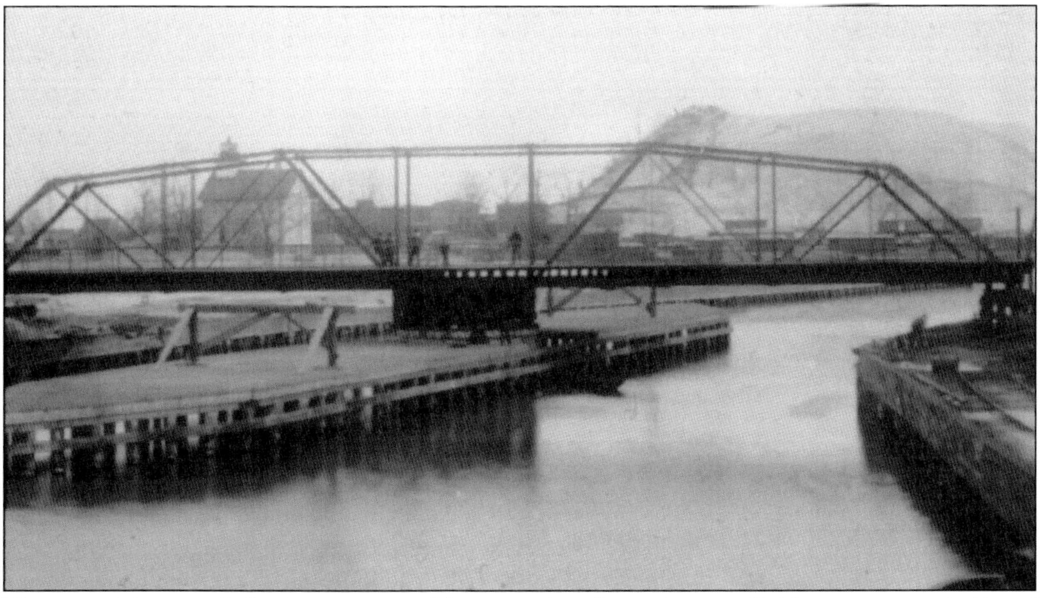

The opposition cited the importance of keeping the channel open. Bridge opponents believed that the structure would impede the commercial traffic that was still trickling into the city. The turnstile bridge pictured here was put into place to accommodate the traffic both overland and commercially. Many residents would be in denial of Michigan City's loss of a commercial shipping economy until the 1950s. Until then, many residents held out hope that the heavy commercial traffic would return.

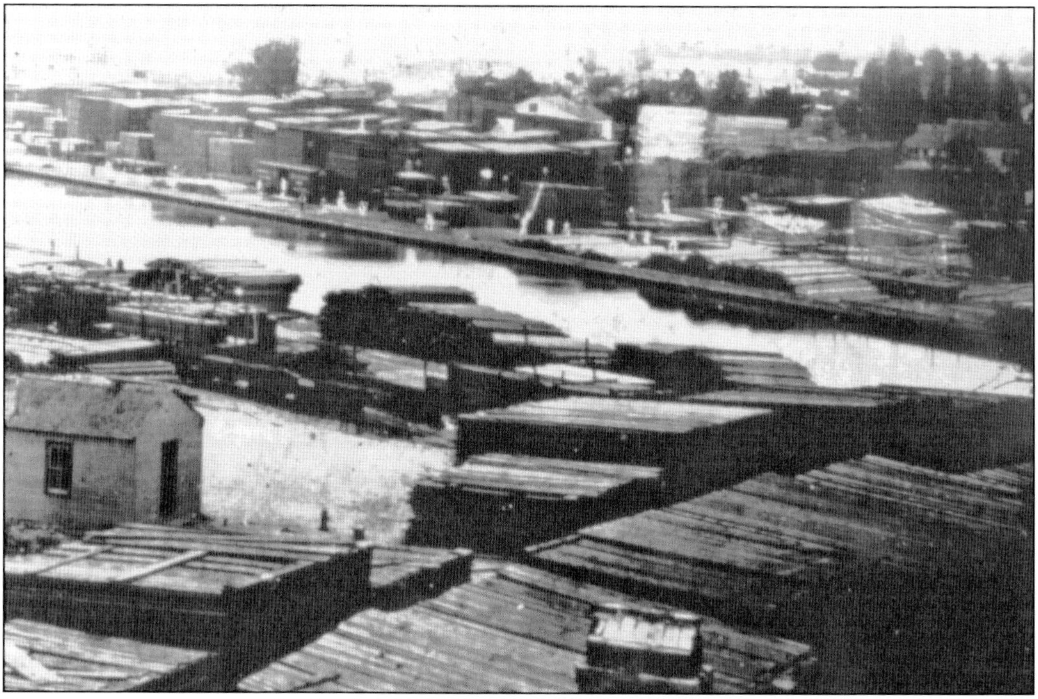

One argument against the bridge over Trail Creek was the state of the harbor itself. The opposition reasoned that no one would want to visit the neglected harbor and beach. There was no reason to interrupt the dwindling shipping traffic over a bridge to a place no one was interested in visiting.

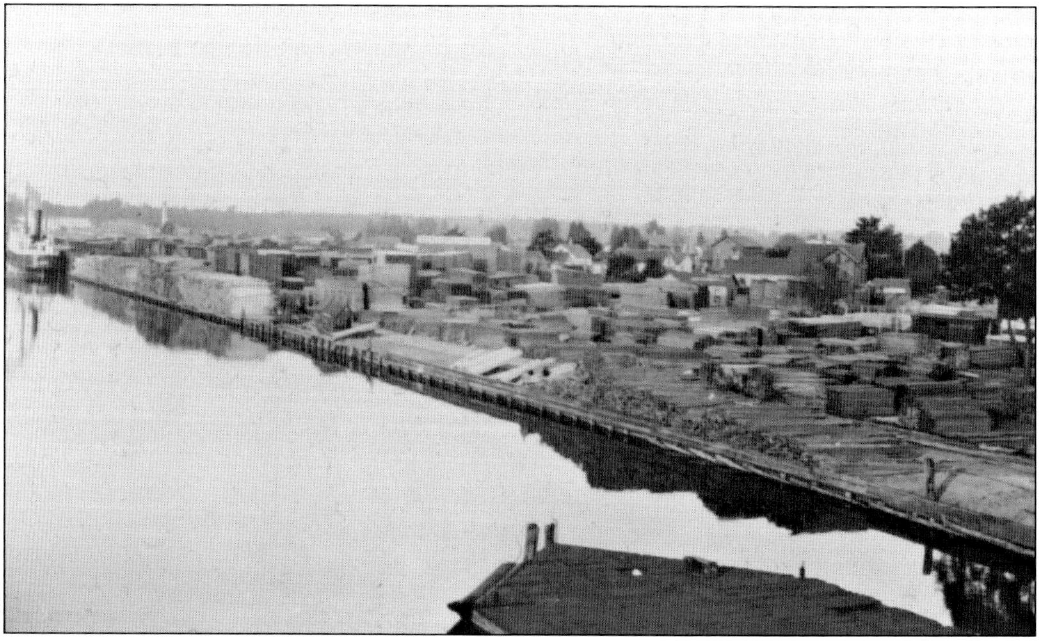

In a speech after his tenure as mayor, Krueger remembered a woman's statement on the subject: "I have lived in this city over 30 years and have never yet been on the shore of Lake Michigan, and I have not missed anything thereby." Many people in Michigan City shared a similar attitude.

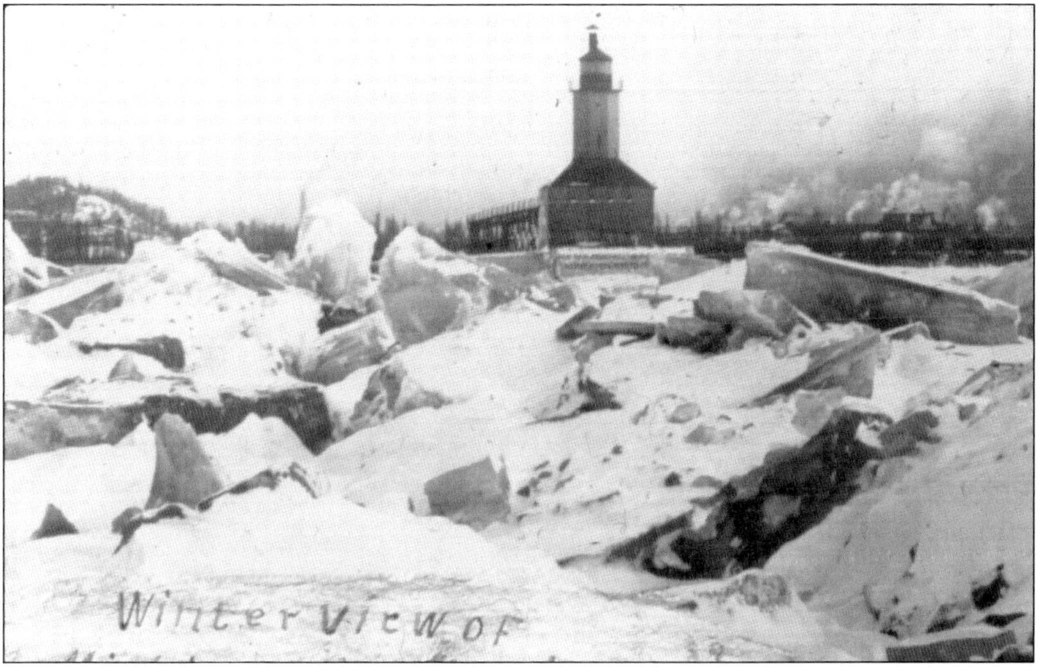

Another argument was the price tag. The bridge, parkland, and cleanup were all expensive costs that the city was not prepared to shoulder. Instead of letting the project wash away with the waves of Lake Michigan, Krueger decided to act. He attacked each obstacle one at a time.

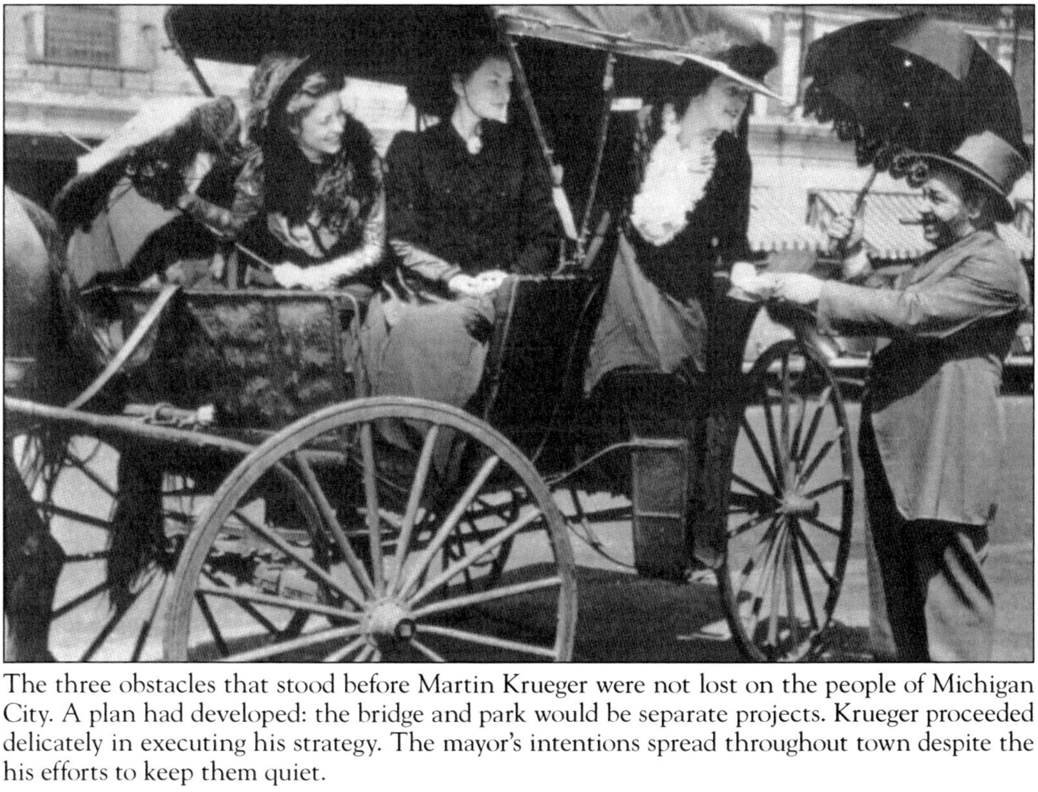

The three obstacles that stood before Martin Krueger were not lost on the people of Michigan City. A plan had developed: the bridge and park would be separate projects. Krueger proceeded delicately in executing his strategy. The mayor's intentions spread throughout town despite the his efforts to keep them quiet.

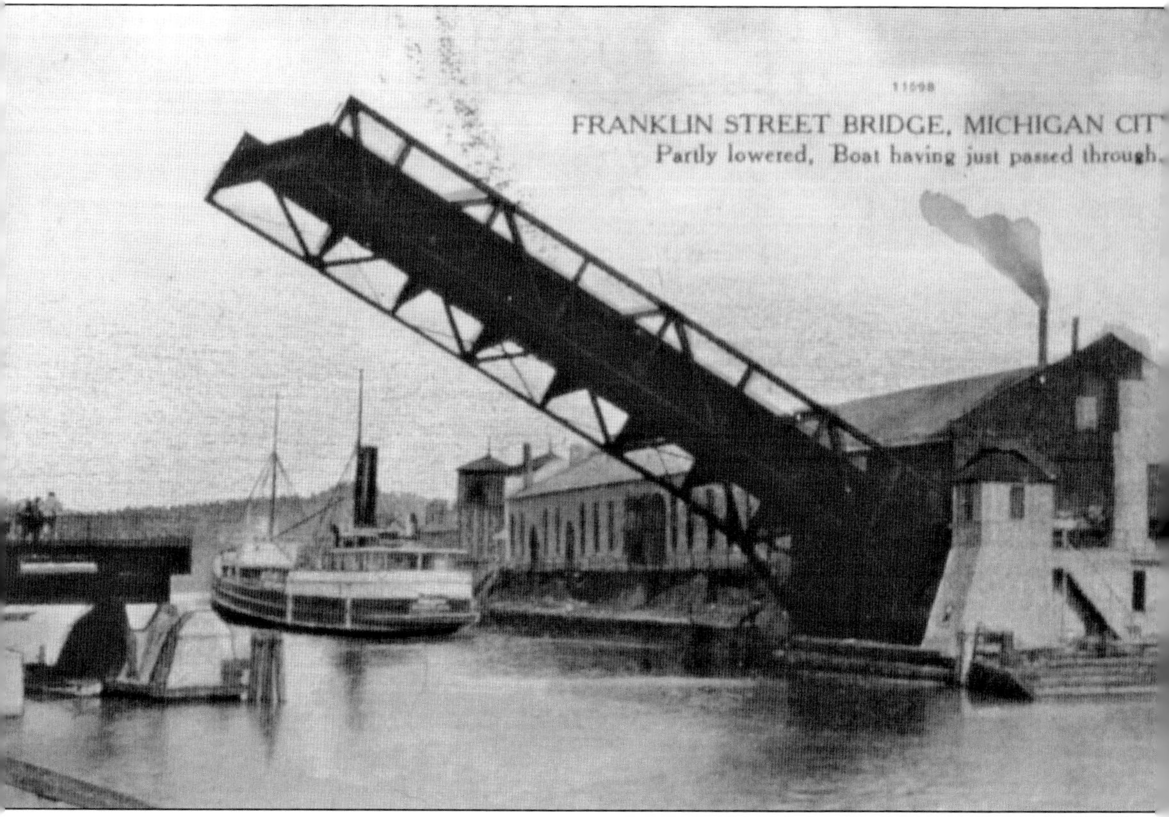

The bridge construction was tackled first. Krueger began a campaign to gain the town's interest. Harry Francis utilized his paper, the *Michigan City Dispatch*, to spread the word. His mission was to encourage townspeople to consider the possibilities that a bridge over Trail Creek, pictured here, could bring.

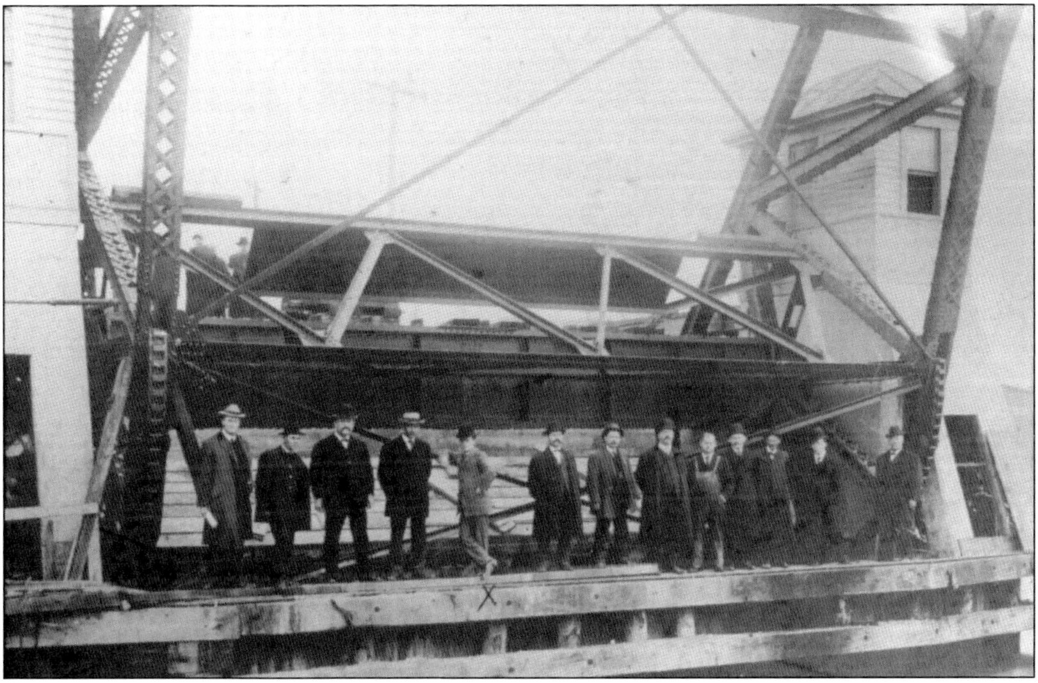

Krueger pushed through the legislation needed to get the bridge built. The now-repealed Indiana state law was created by Krueger and his supporters to enable city government the power to buy, sell, or trade public land for purposes of creating a municipal park. Instead of using the cash held by the city, bonds were issued, according to Michigan City City Hall records. Construction began before 1890 ended. The photographs on this page were actually taken after the second construction of the Franklin Street Bridge.

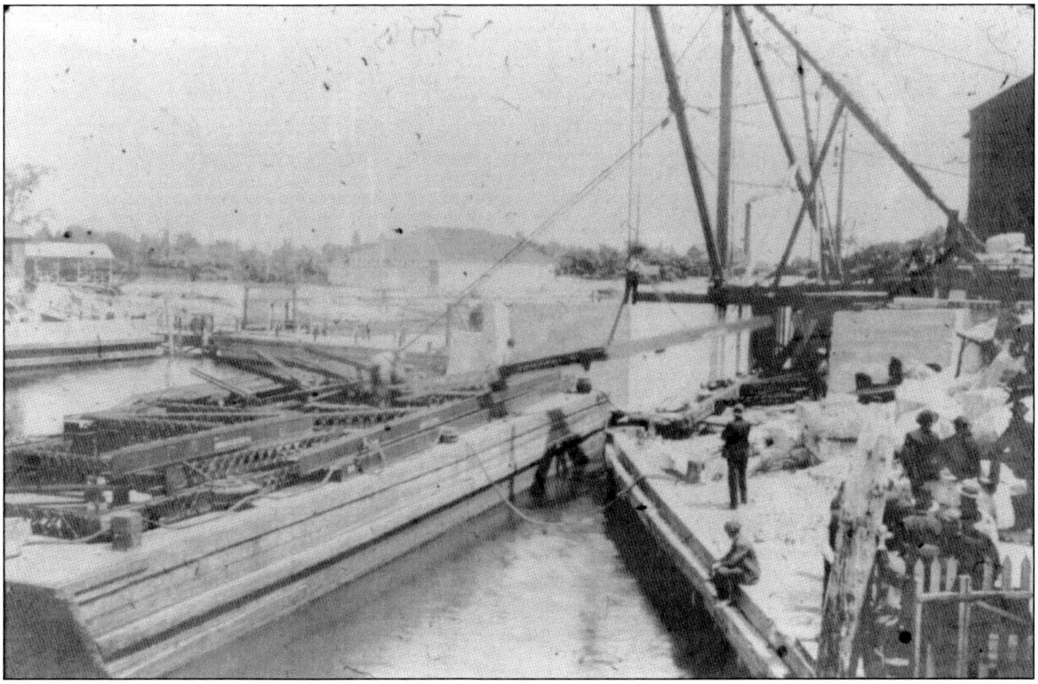

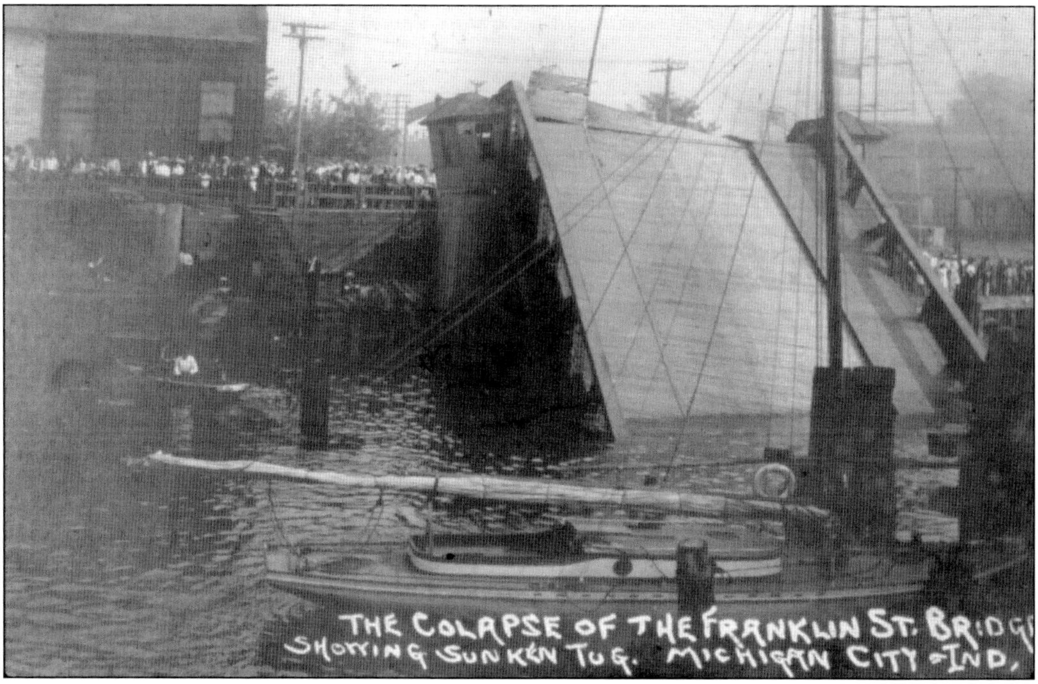

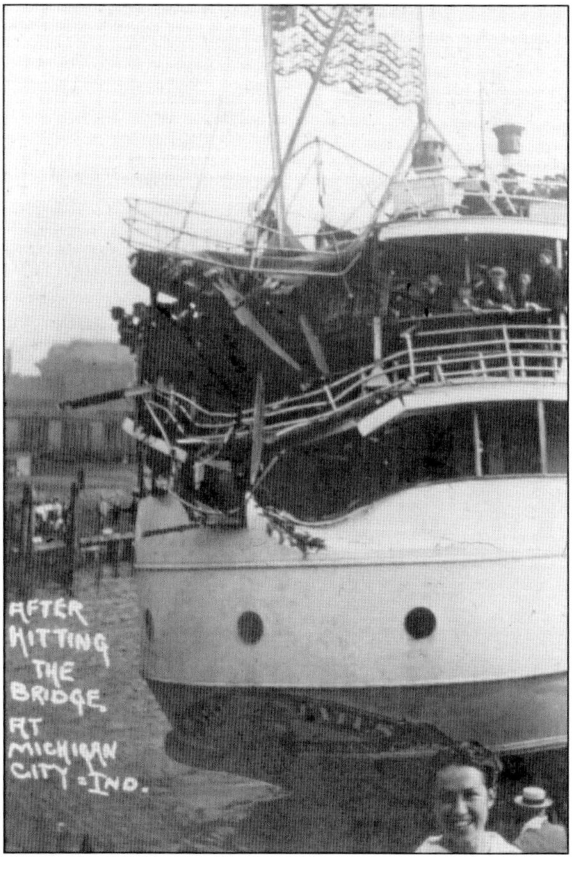

The first bridge over Trail Creek was destroyed but rebuilt in 1910 after the shipping vessel *City West* crashed into it. The *City West* was not alone. Other excursion ships that would regularly stop in Michigan City had close calls with the bridge. The *United States*, pictured at left, was one casualty. These wrecks, along with more fatal ones, would eventually lead to a collapse of the excursion boat market in Michigan City. The name Franklin Street Bridge was an unofficial one used by city residents for the street that ended at Trail Creek where the bridge stood.

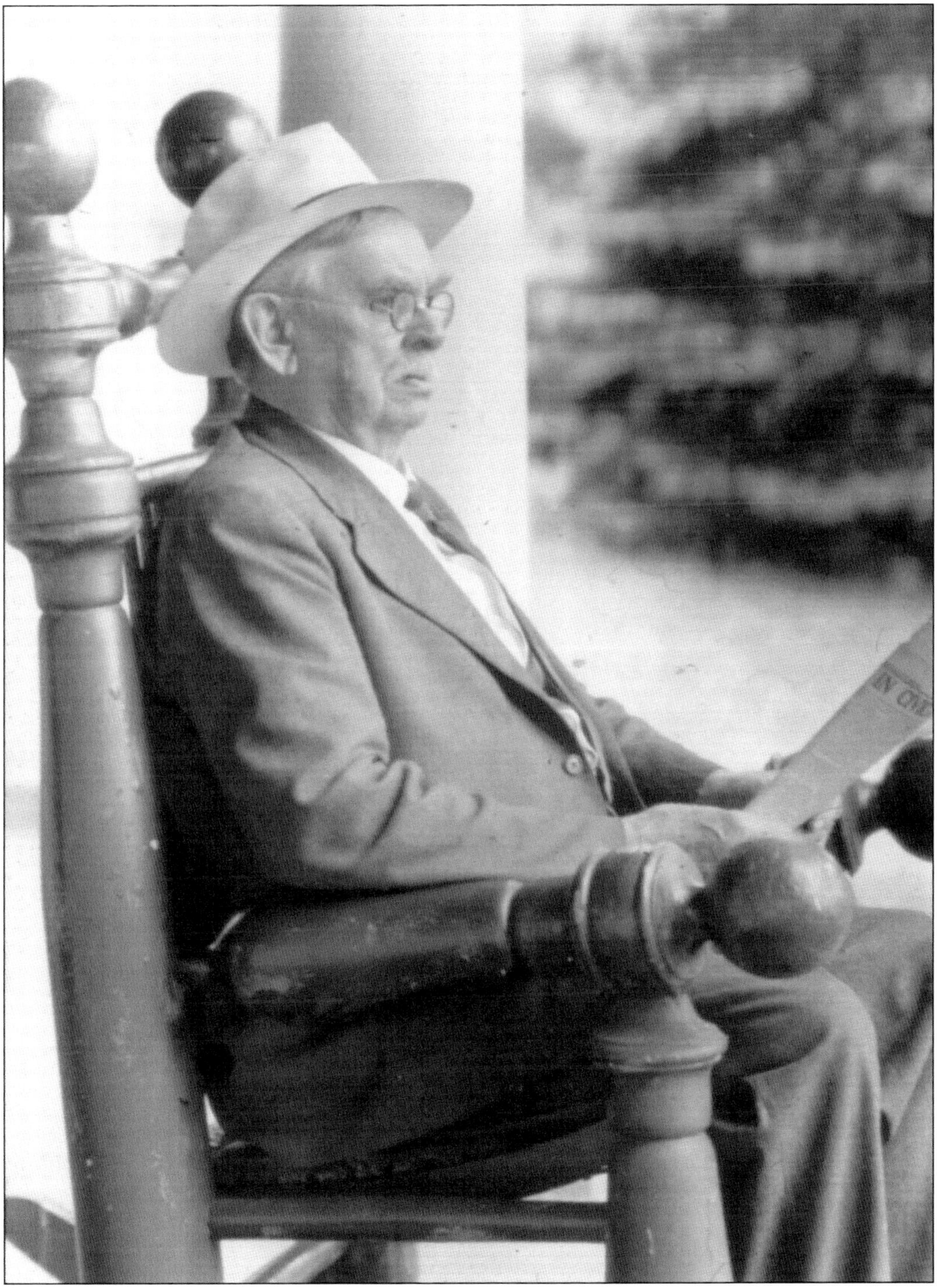

There was no mention of the park until the bridge project was complete. Martin Krueger could not make progress as the law stood at that time, which forbade local governments to buy or sell parklands. Krueger took the initiative by writing and submitting a bill to the Indiana State Legislature in 1891 that would allow him to do so.

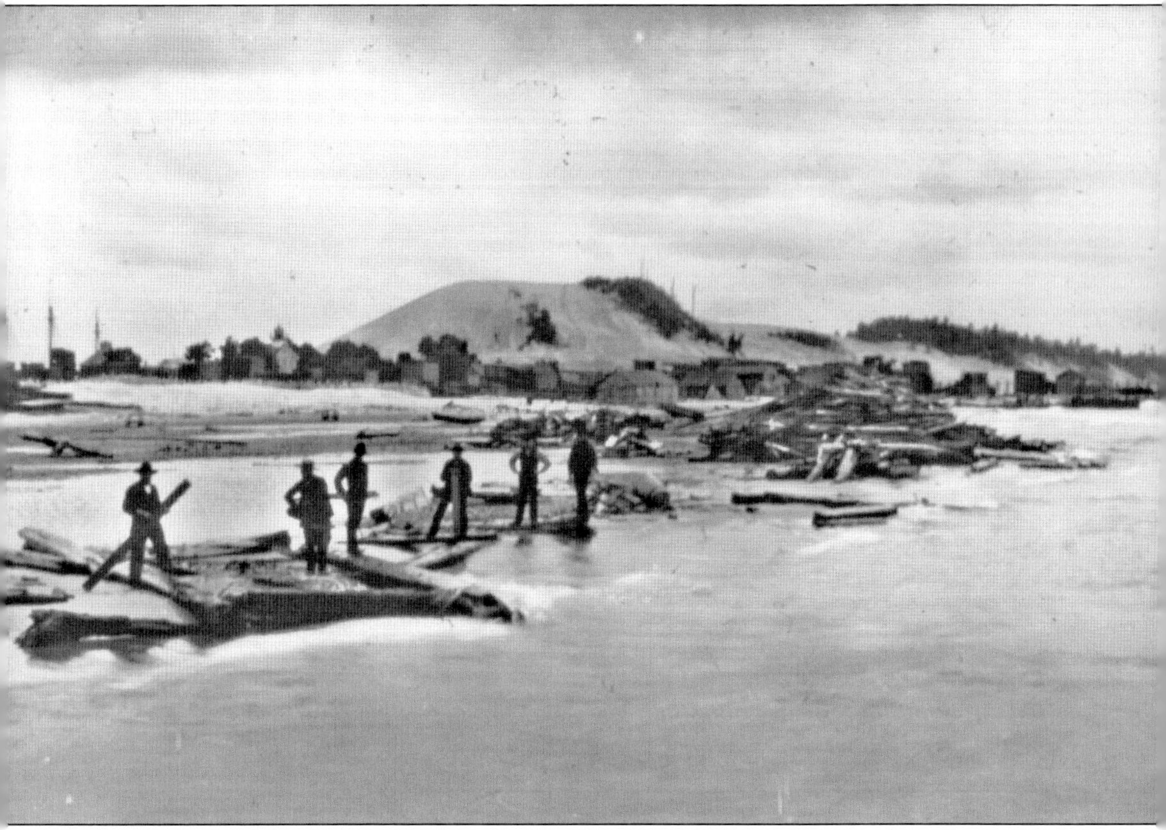

As a result of Krueger's bill, the city could purchase property or simply take possession of a property. The imminent domain clause was necessary in obtaining parklands. Ownership of the property along Trail Creek was difficult and sometimes impossible to determine. Later, Krueger would admit that this park-enabling law was akin to confiscation. The law was passed March 5, 1891. However, the shadowy land-grabbing tactics that the law granted municipalities the power to use led to its eventual repeal.

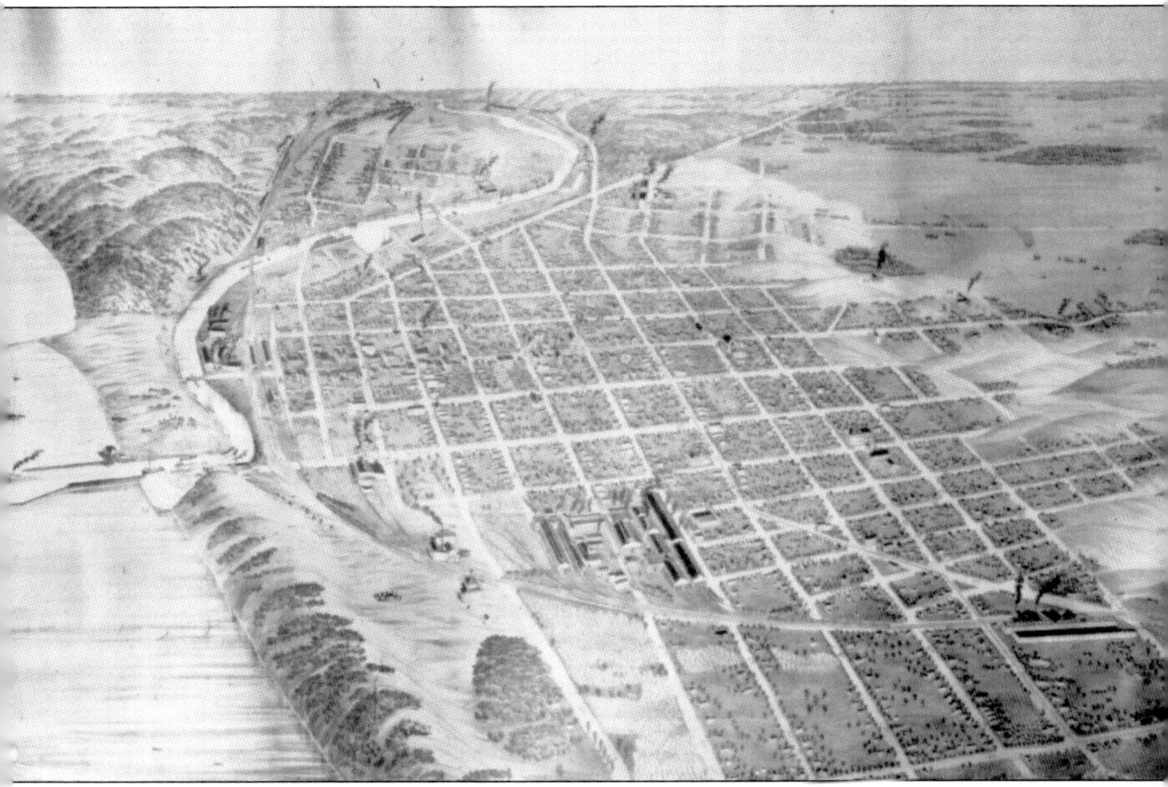

Before buying the land, the city needed money. Martin Krueger used his newly enacted law to sell off the town square located at the town center (Washington Street to the west, Franklin Street to the east, Fourth Street to the south, and Michigan Boulevard to the north). The decision to make these transactions possible did not easily gain approval. Krueger admits that he had to massage the city council for votes. He took an unnamed council member aside, and when the two men returned from a brief recess the law was passed to sell the town square. Krueger never revealed what it took to get his law passed. This image is a map of Michigan City in 1889. It illustrates that Krueger was trying to mold the city into a tourist attraction.

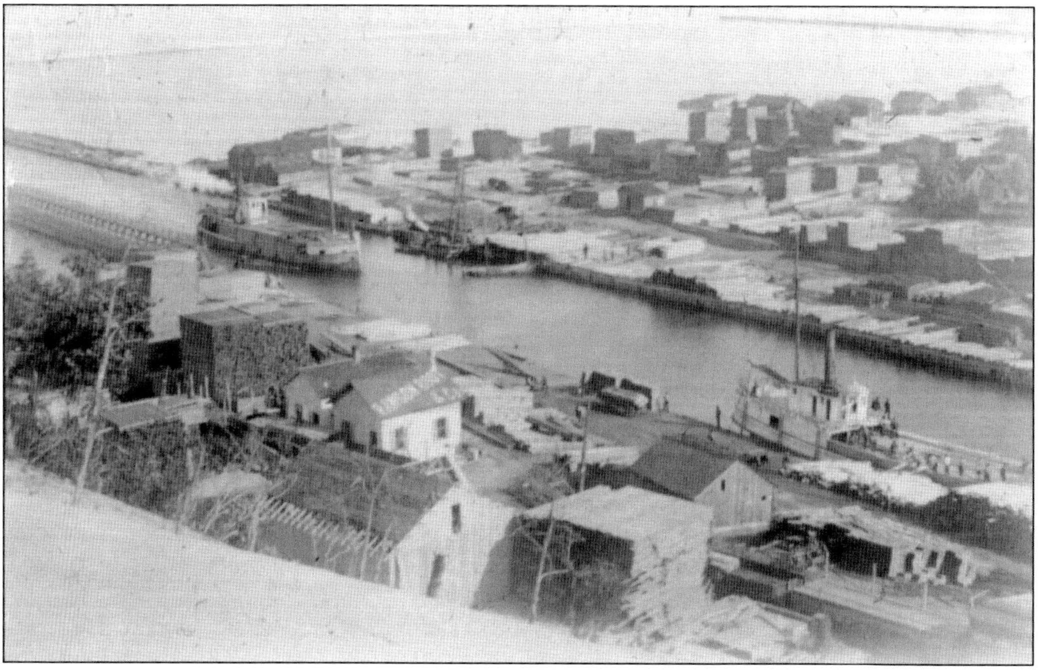

The town square sold for $10,675 at auction. Over 107 parcels of land were bought along the lakefront for $7,500. Most of the owners of the tracts of land lived too far away to care and had forgotten about the land. There were a few challenges: some owners held out for more money, while others never responded to the city's notices to acquire deeds. To park supporters, the most important condition on acquiring the land was that no tax funds were to be used in the purchase.

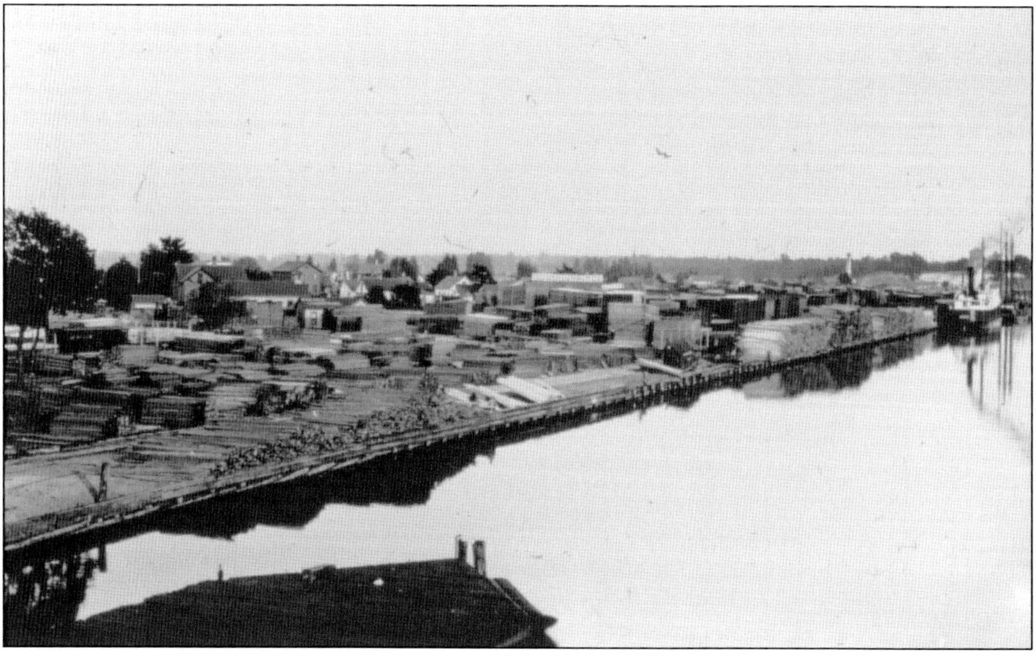

Two

Building a Park

The next decade would be spent creating a park out of the squalid district that was the neglected lakefront. The city government had the area graded and the debris removed. The only thing left was the sandy soil, a few trees, and a magnificent view. The city's enthusiasm for the area increased, and building the park became a group effort.

The open land did not go unnoticed by the business community in Michigan City, particularly Mayor Krueger's good friend John Barker, owner and operator of a successful railcar manufacturing company that originated in Michigan City in 1855. Barker saw potential on the lakefront, offering his pal Krueger enough money to pay off the city debts if Krueger would just open the land up to commercial development instead of reserving it for a park. Krueger turned down the $75,000 offer and moved forward with development. The first order of business was electing a board of commissioners for the new park; John Mott, Charles Porter, and William Schoenen were appointed.

Incidentally, Washington Park was not the official name of the park but the proposed name of the bridge that Krueger had built in order to make the park possible. One of the mayor's creative tactics in those days involved using the name of the bridge to coerce lawmakers into passing the needed legislation. Krueger invited federal, state, and local officials to the site of his proposed bridge, which he named the George Washington Memorial Bridge. Krueger later admitted that it would be a "treasonous act of criticizing or voting against any project that bore the name of the father of these United States of America" The park by Washington Bridge quickly became Washington Park, outliving Krueger's version of the bridge over Trail Creek by decades.

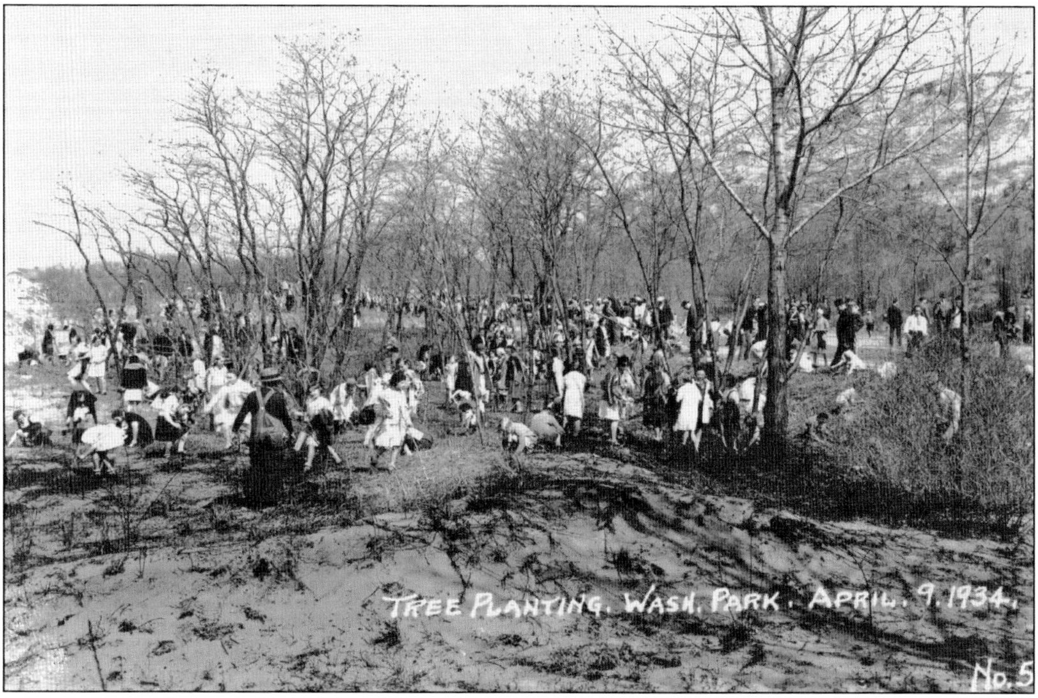

The newly graded area looked less like a park than it did before the lumber was removed. The commissioners remedied this by announcing a tree planting, asking everyone to pitch in. According Mayor Krueger, "Hundreds of trees were donated." Much of the town reportedly turned out to participate in the event. It was a way for each family to contribute a little part to the new park. The tree planting was repeated in 1934, after the park had undergone some renovations courtesy of the Works Progress Administration. These photographs from 1934 show the mass effort that took place during the plantings.

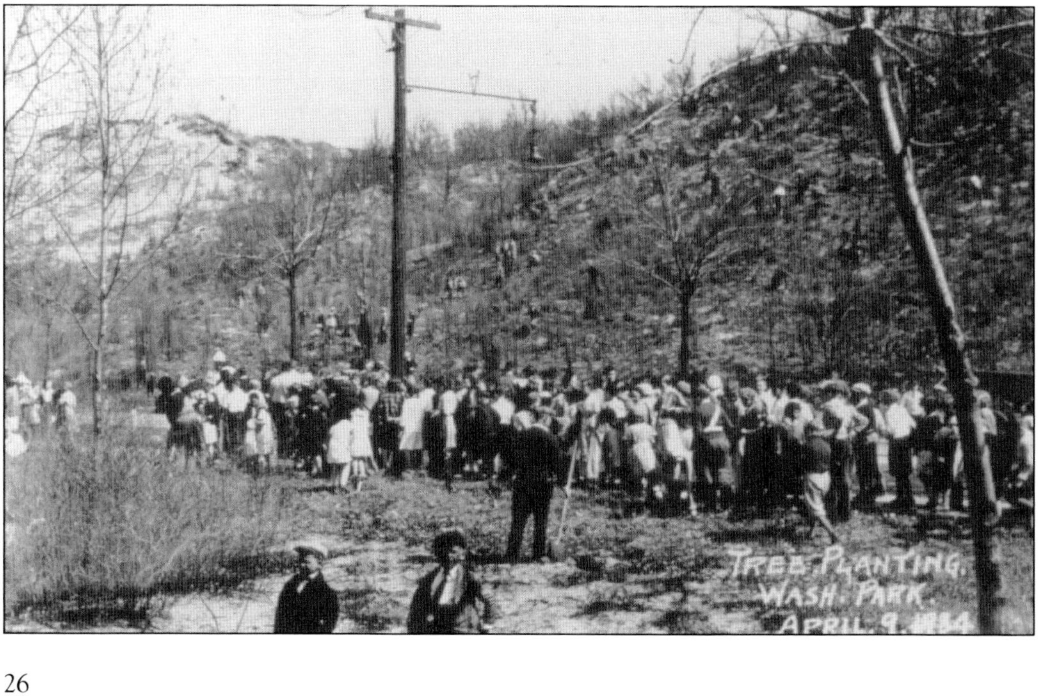

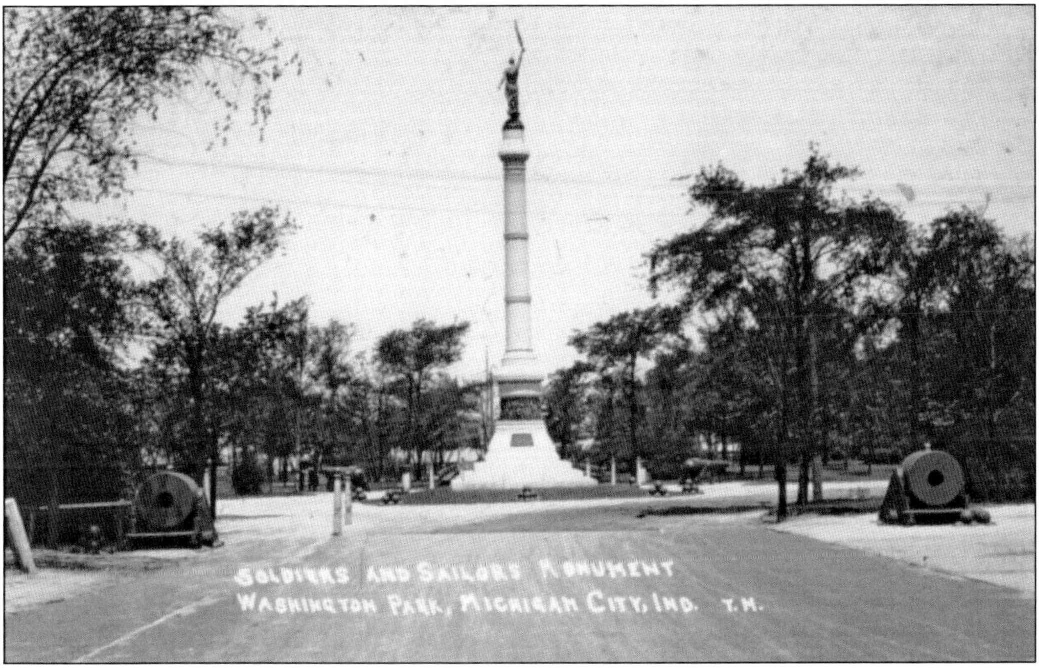

An area at the proposed entrance to the park was left unplanted to make room for a bathhouse and lodge. Such a structure was never built, but something else was used to fill the space. In 1893, John Winterbotham, a local businessman and politician, donated a monument to place at the park entrance. It was a tribute to the area Civil War veterans, dubbed *Victorious Peace.* The monument still stands 60 feet high today, overlooking the entrance at Washington Park. The brass peace figure was designed by New York sculptures William O'Donovan and Jonathan Hartley.

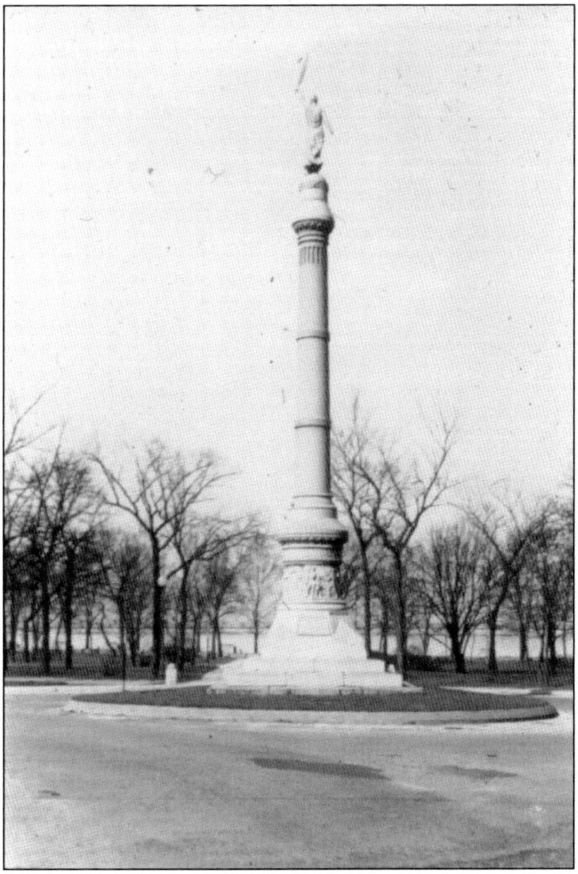

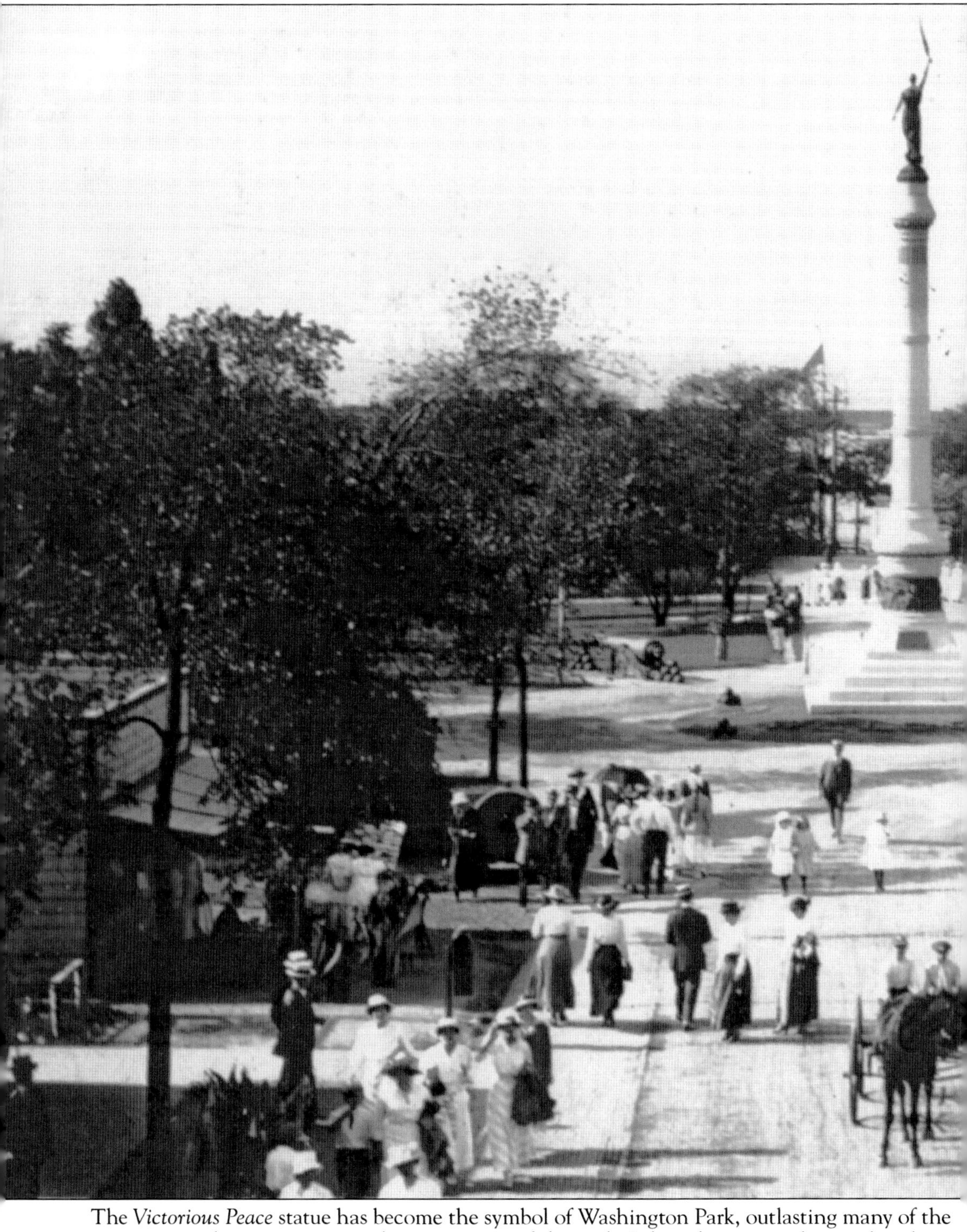

The *Victorious Peace* statue has become the symbol of Washington Park, outlasting many of the structures and overseeing several incarnations of the park. It has also survived several parking pattern redesigns, which always seems to lead park visitors past the monument, whether they are

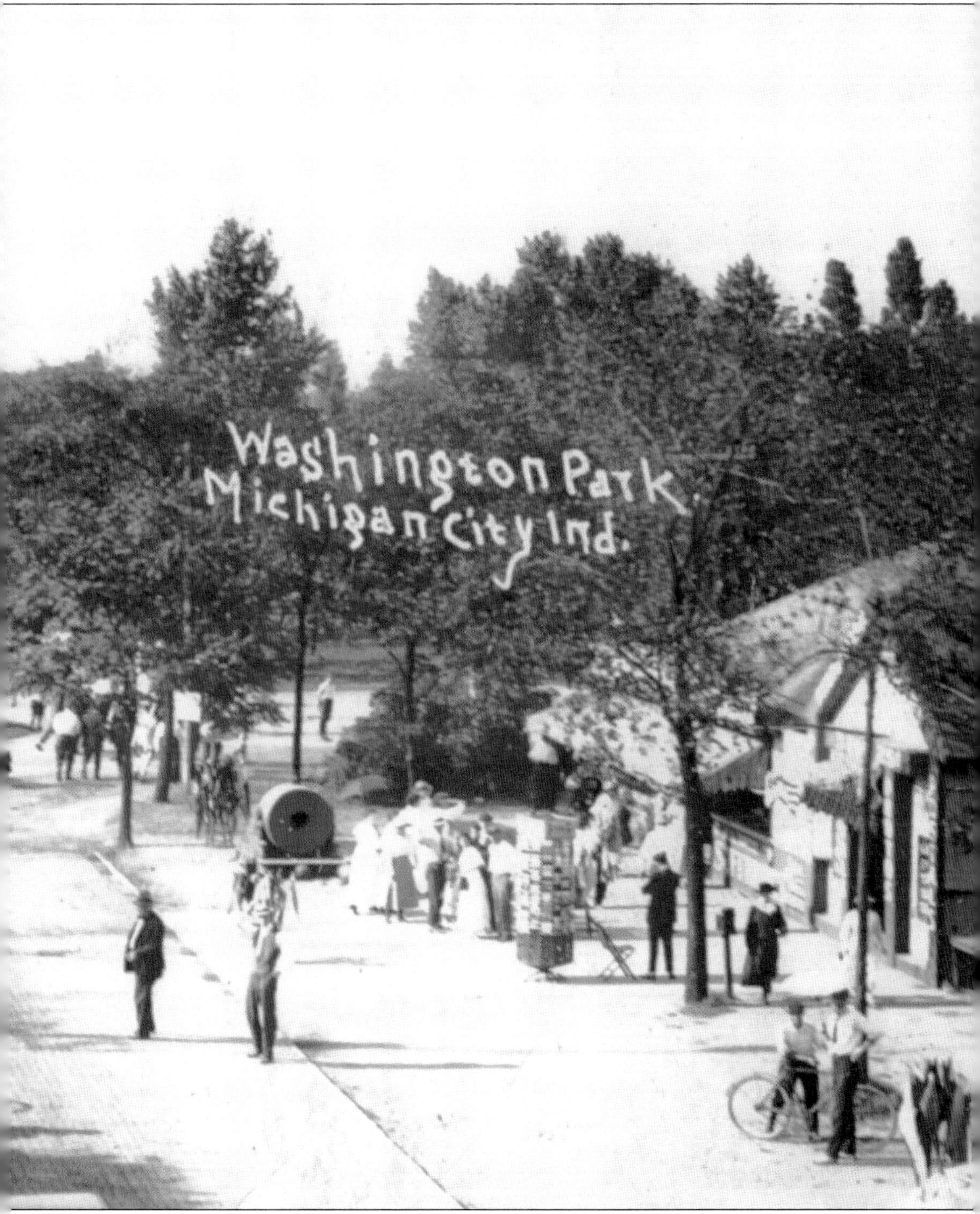

coming or going. This aerial photograph, taken sometime in the early 1900s, shows how *Victorious Peace* towers over guests. Interestingly, the monument faces the lake, away from Michigan City.

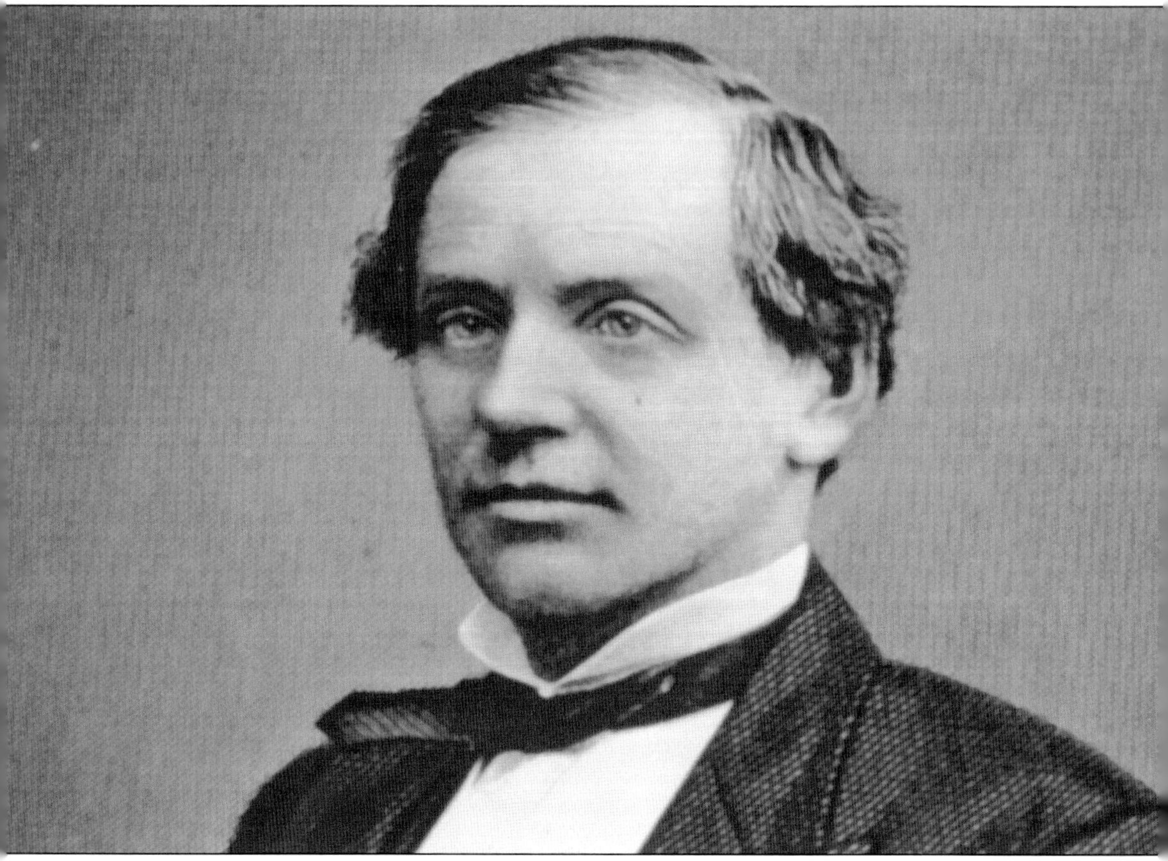

John Winterbotham was not the only person to help with the decor of the early park. John Barker (pictured), satisfied that the lakefront would not become an industrial area, donated two structures for use in the park. In addition to being a philanthropist, he was a business tycoon. Barker had a peristyle and bandstand built and sent to the new park.

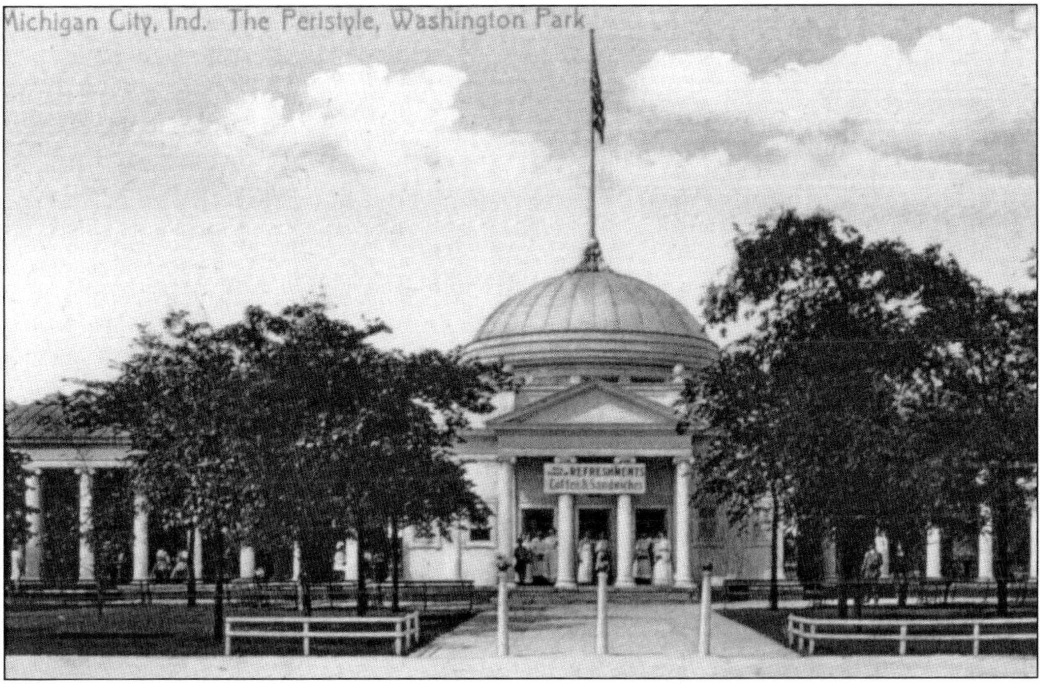

The peristyle was used for picnics and special events in the park, and the city displayed artwork within the structure. It was a dry place for those caught in the park on a rainy night, especially if there was a concert going on in the bandstand. The peristyle was the symbol for Washington Park for more than half a century.

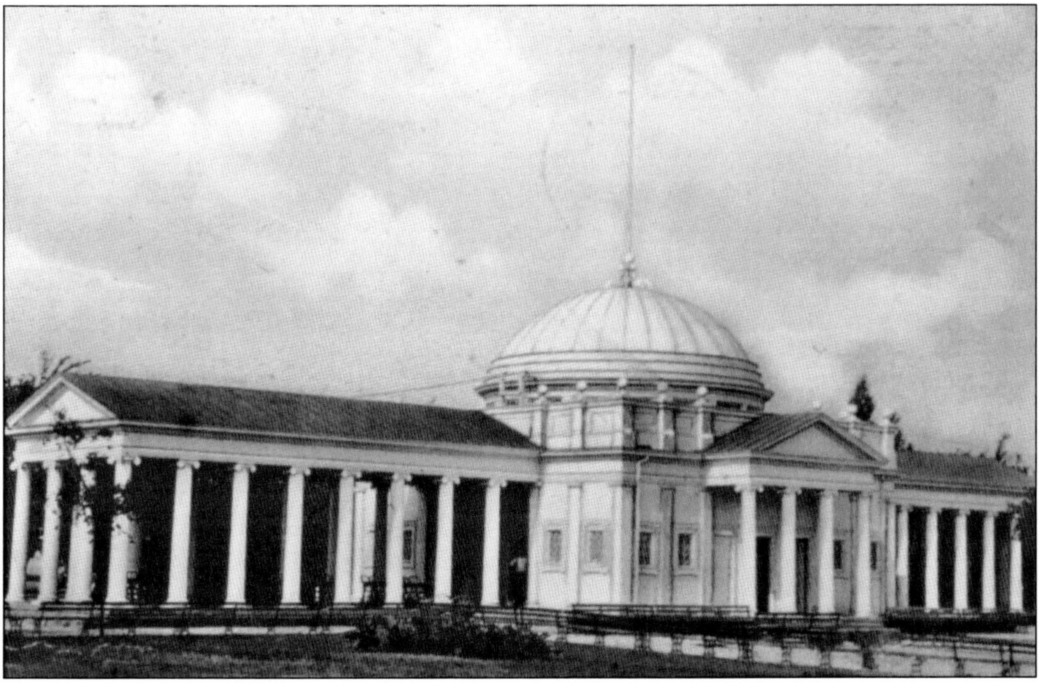

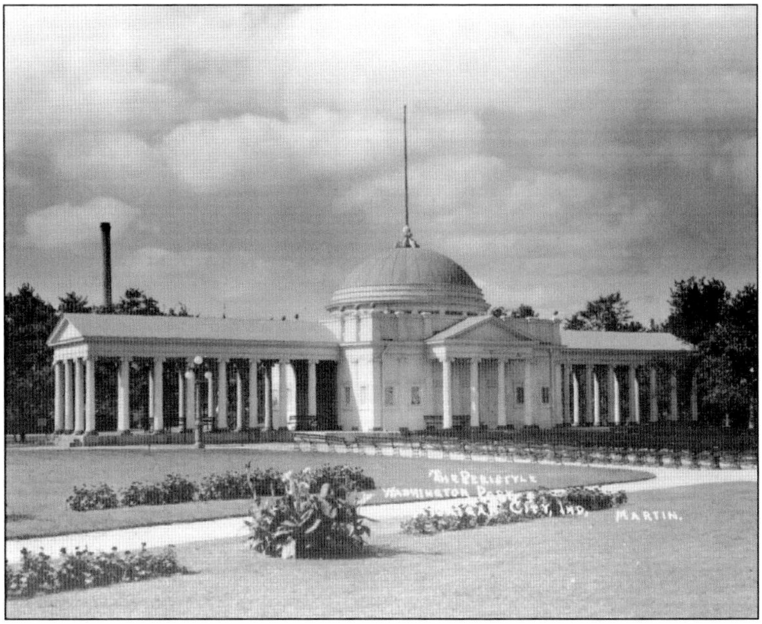

The peristyle was modeled after the Greek structures that were little more than porches or colonnades. There was plenty of room to sit and reflect, host outdoor functions, or enjoy impromptu picnics. It was remodeled in 1924 and again in 1931. John Barker's daughter Catherine Barker Hickox funded the latter remodel at a time when the city was ill equipped to do so. The peristyle was demolished for good in 1972.

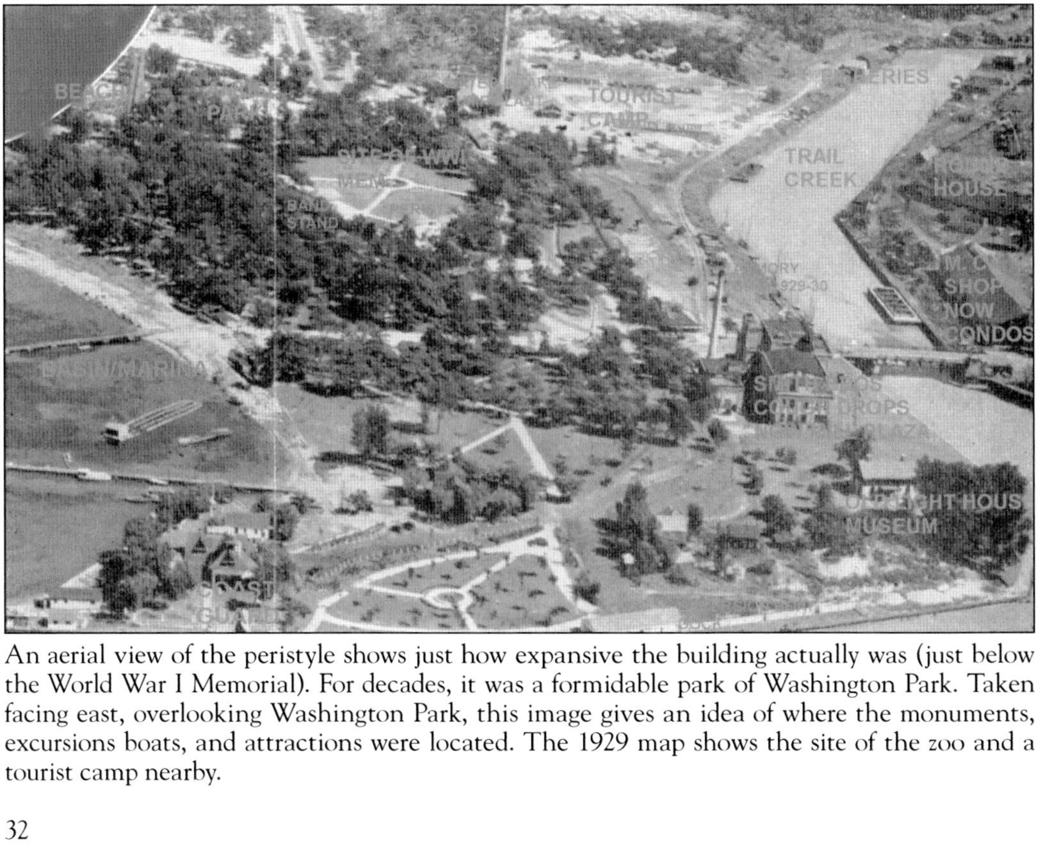

An aerial view of the peristyle shows just how expansive the building actually was (just below the World War I Memorial). For decades, it was a formidable park of Washington Park. Taken facing east, overlooking Washington Park, this image gives an idea of where the monuments, excursions boats, and attractions were located. The 1929 map shows the site of the zoo and a tourist camp nearby.

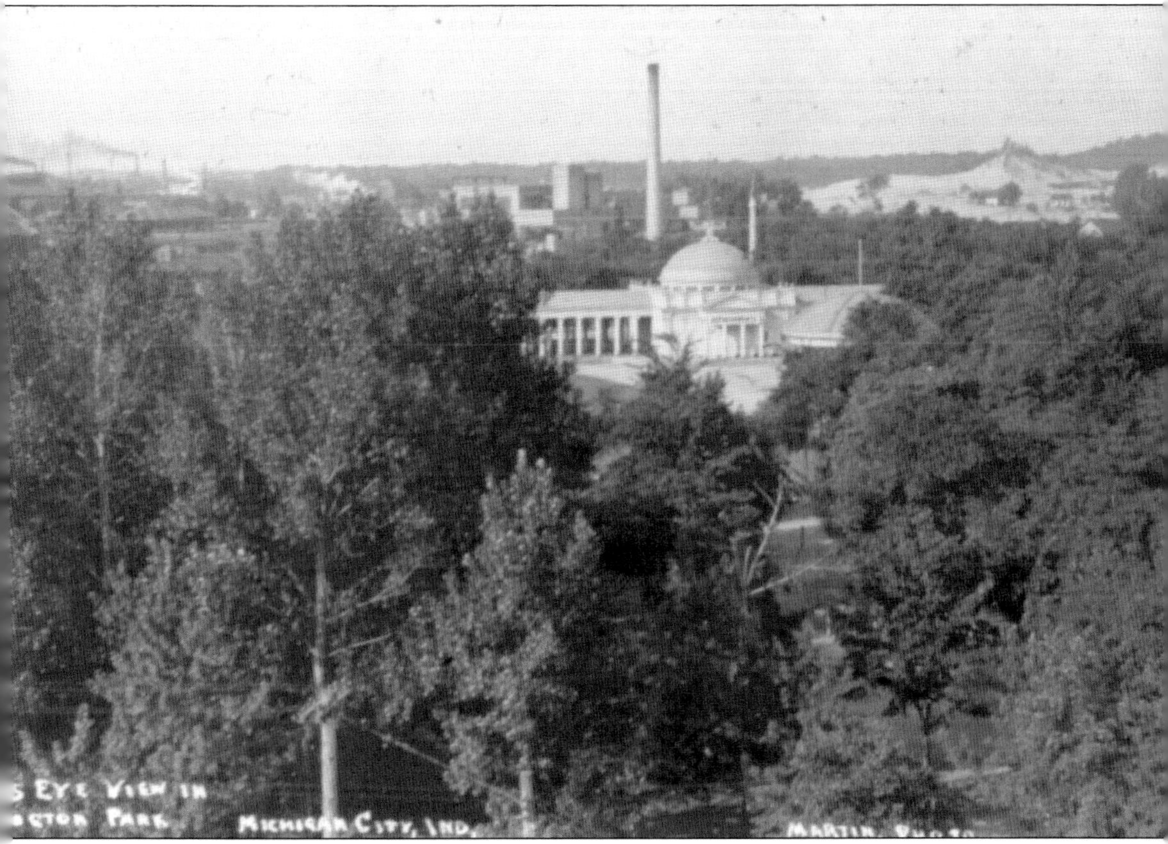

Open-air entertainment by a band was one of the cheapest forms of entertainment in the early 1900s, before the era of a television in every room. Homes were equipped with a radio if the family could afford one. There was always theater entertainment, but ticket prices were not something many families could afford on a regular basis. Bands at the time consisted of people known around town or out-of-town players. Out in the park, one could hear the music while entering. The melodies could even be heard while frolicking at the Lake Michigan beach.

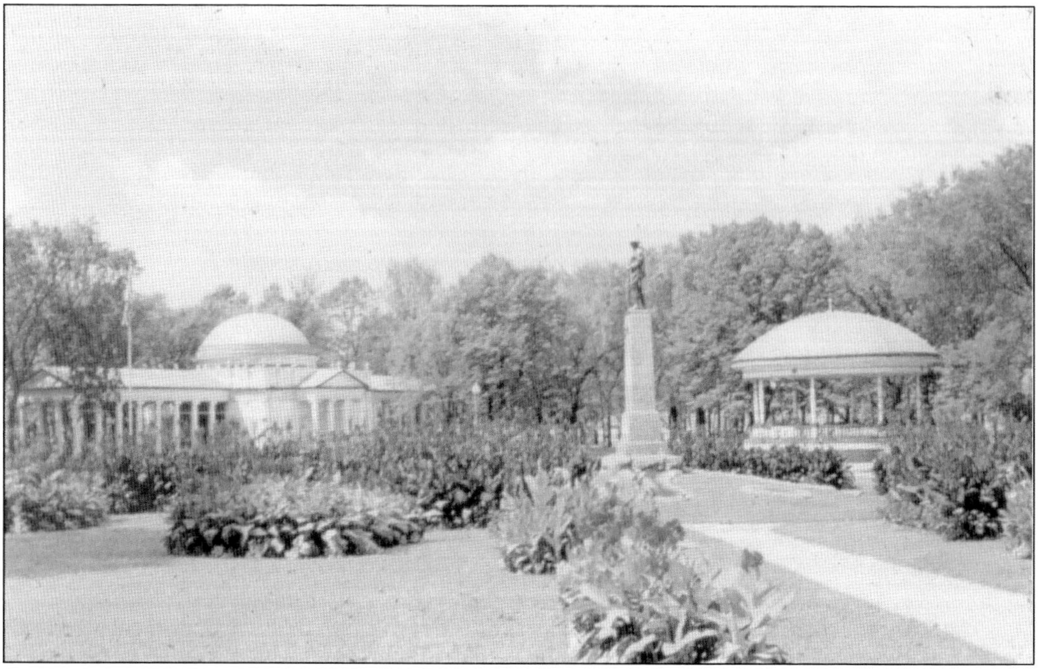

Barker's bandstand still stands today, positioned as seen here; however, the peristyle is no longer in the park. The park commissioners landscaped the area to emphasize the beauty of the structures. The image below looks out over the monuments from the west side of the park.

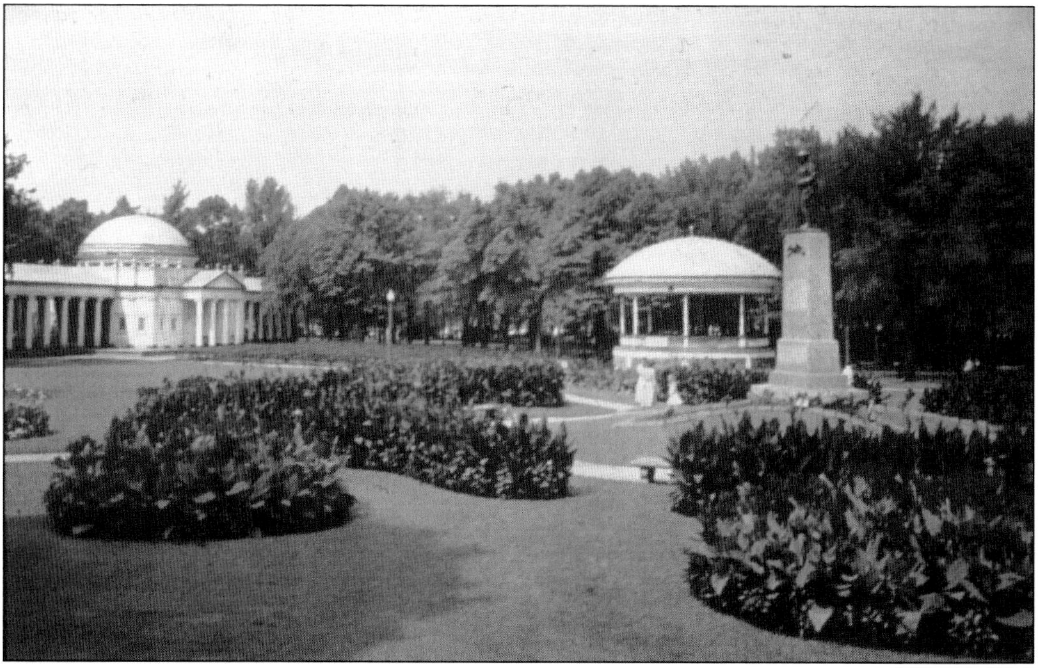

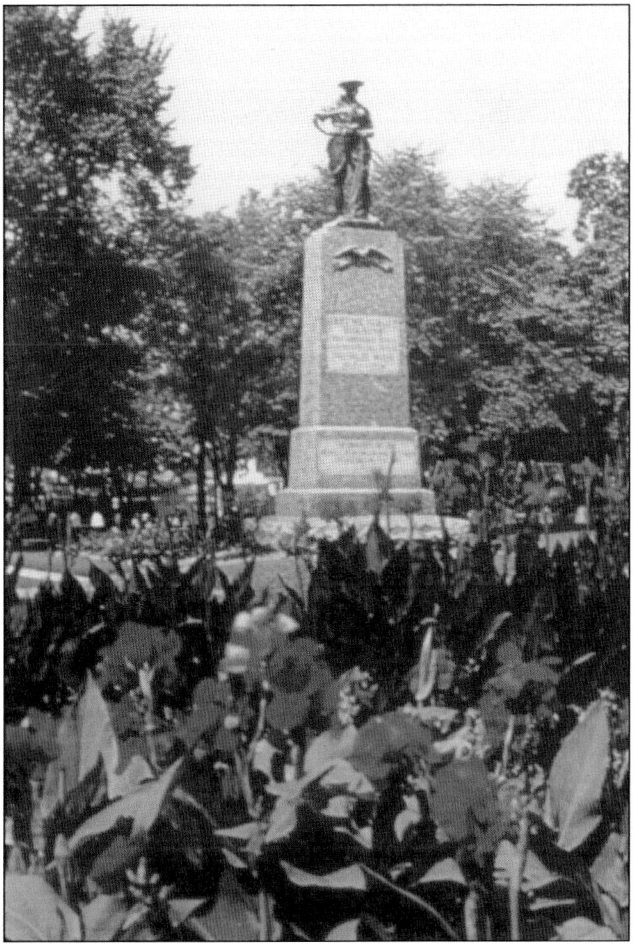

Donated by the American Gold Star Mothers of Michigan City, according to an edition of the *Evening News* from November 8, 1926, the memorial was a tribute to the soldiers who lost their lives during World War I from 1917 to 1918. The soldiers were represented by a figure known as a "doughboy," which was mounted on a granite pedestal.

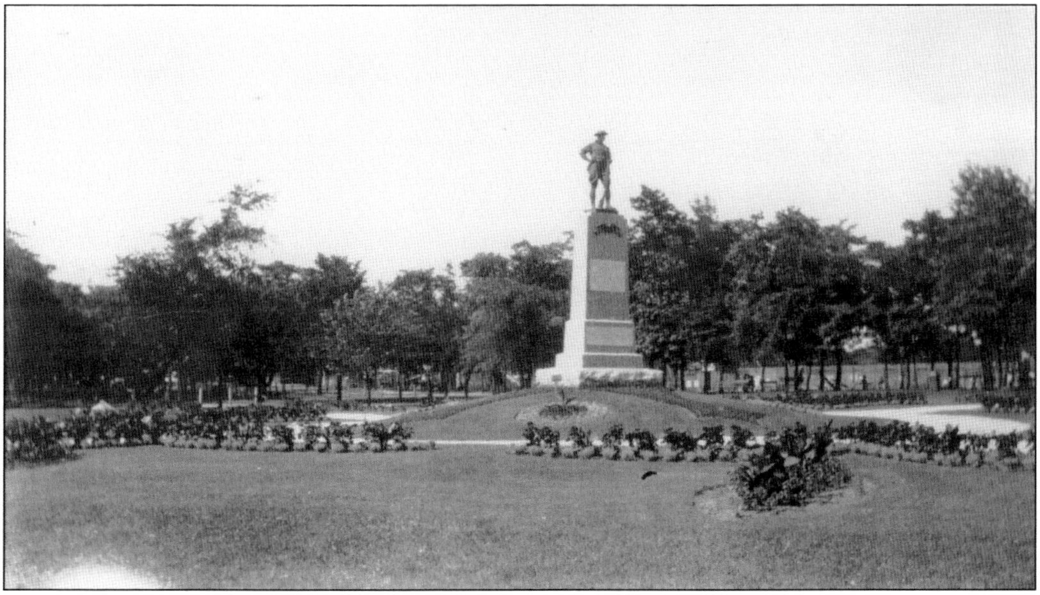

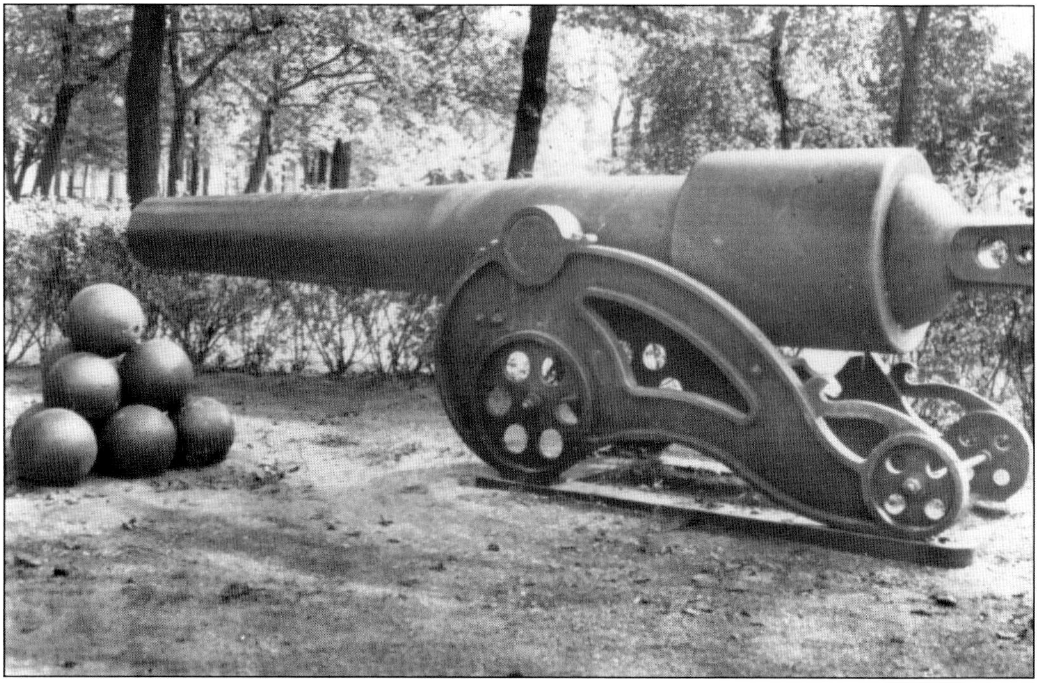

Other notable monuments decorating Washington Park in the early days were two cannons that were retired from the Civil War. On the park's eastern entrance was a gunner from the schooner USS *Orvetta*, a Union vessel. Before resting in Washington Park, the cannon had been used to bomb Vicksburg, Fort Jackson, Grant's Pass, Fort Powell, and other infamous locations.

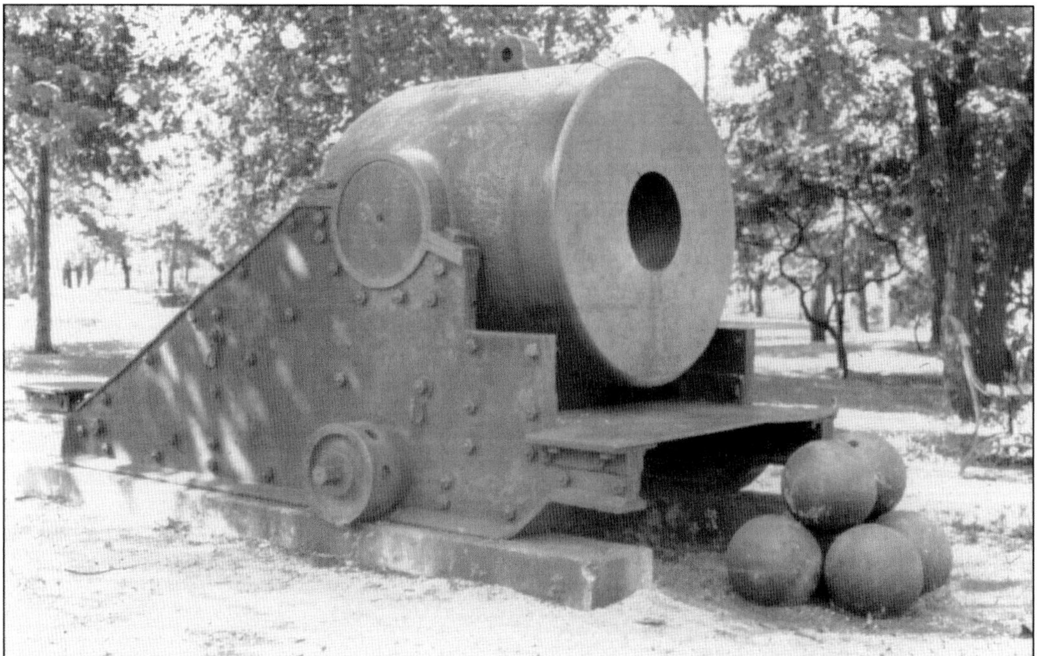

The gunner from the USS *Para* was placed at Washington Park's western entrance. It had seen action at locations such as Vicksburg, Fort McAllister, and Saint Phillip, among others.

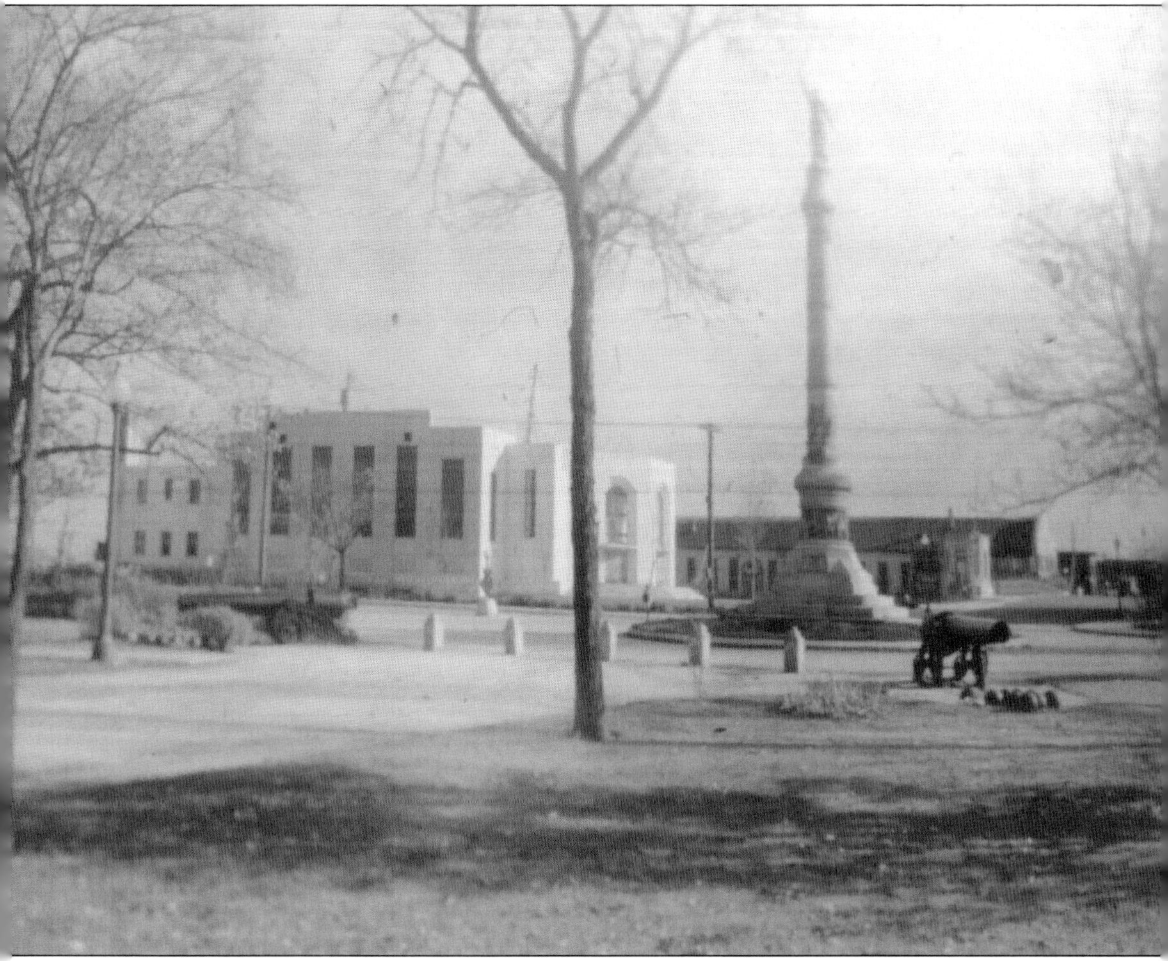

Both cannons stood at the entrances until 1942 when they were removed and melted down for the metal. While they stood, the cannons were thought of as sentries guarding the entrance to Washington Park.

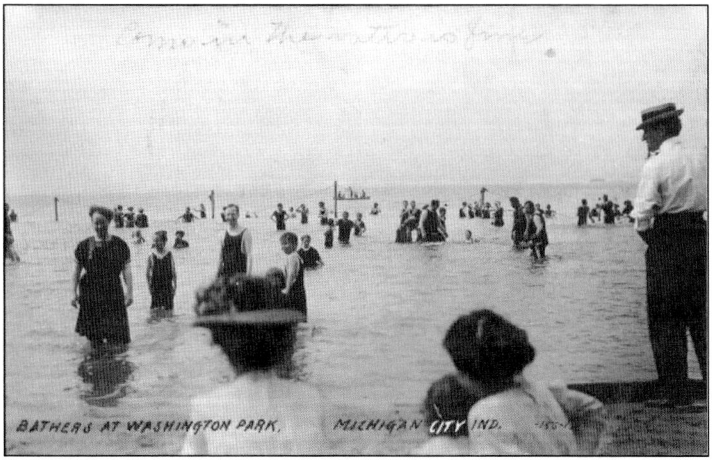

Krueger's plans, with the help of community groups and local philanthropists, opened not only the shores of Trail Creek, but also the white sandy beach of Lake Michigan to locals who never thought they would want to visit the area. Suddenly, the city had a bathing beach, as seen in this early-1900s photograph.

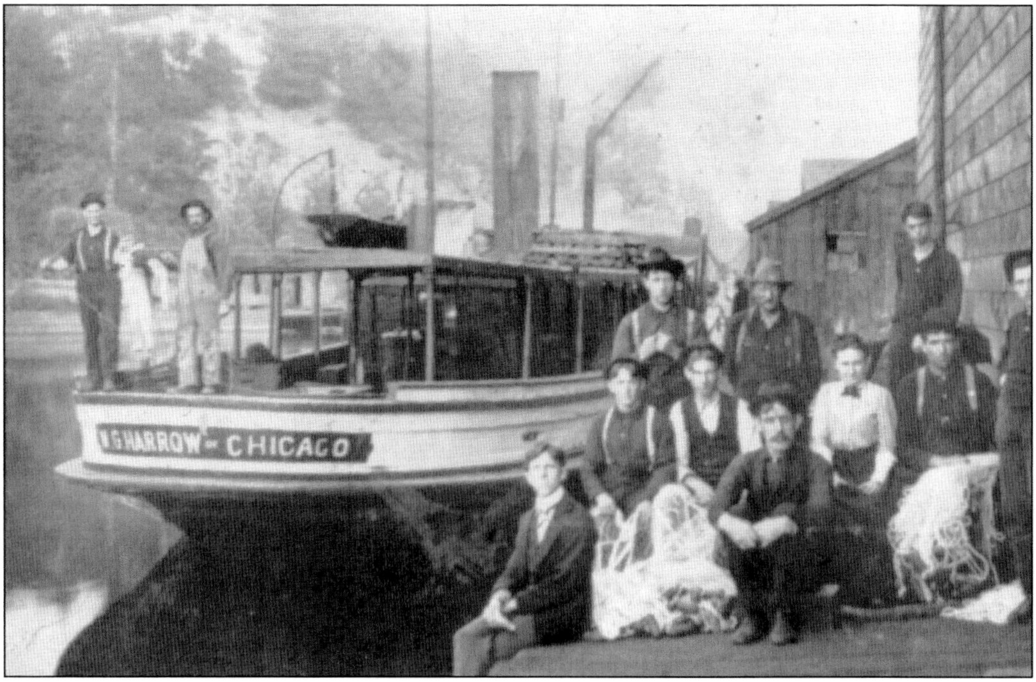

Washington Park quickly became much more than the park that Martin Krueger envisioned. Instead of lumber schooners and fishing vessels, ferries that were full of people looking for entertainment docked in Michigan City. These people soon found much more than the bathing beach and a few monuments.

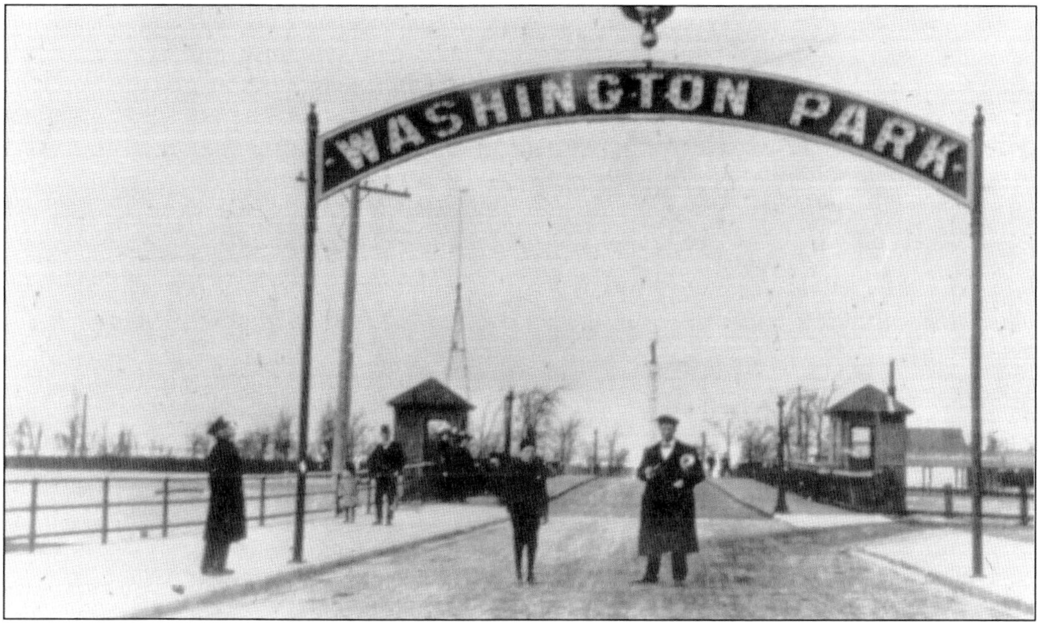

The Washington Park sign arched over the entrance during the first several decades of the park's existence. It could be seen as one crossed over the Franklin Street (or George Washington Memorial) Bridge. The sign arched over the south end of the bridge, greeting visitors before they crossed Trail Creek into the park.

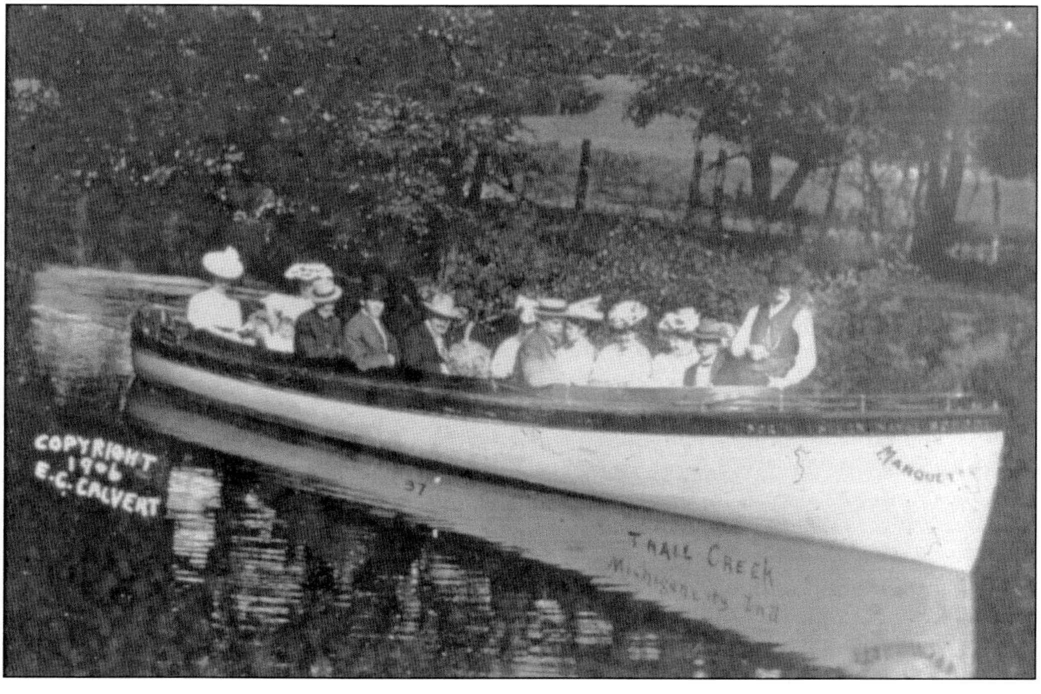

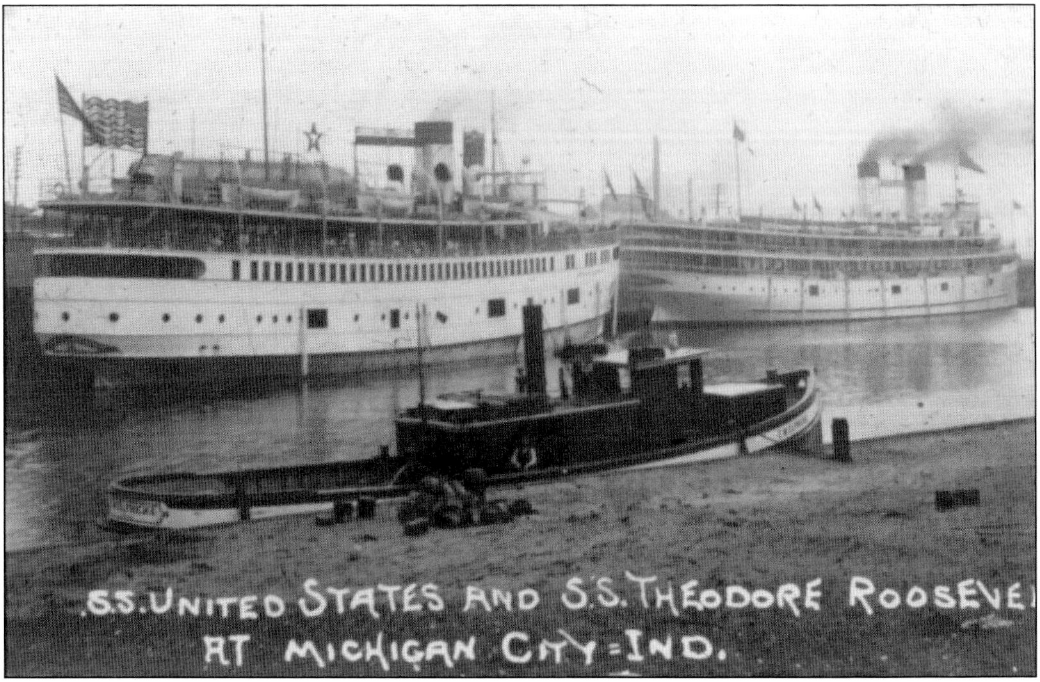

Soon there was no need for the sign's introduction. Every person who came into the city by boat (above), train (below), or carriage knew Washington from the wooden roller coaster that overshadowed the bathing beach.

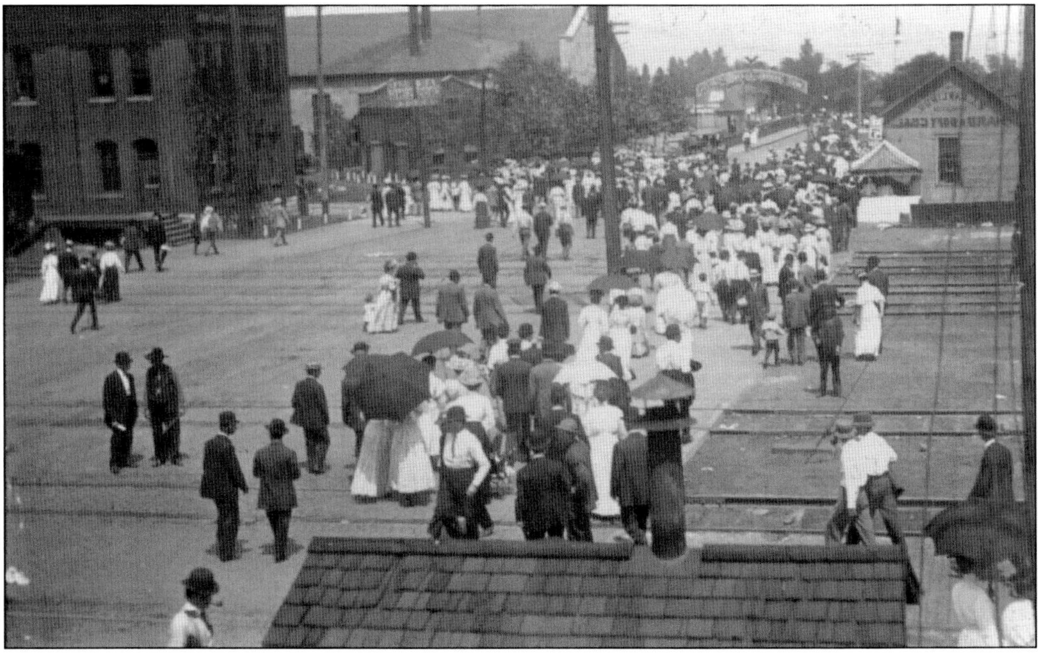

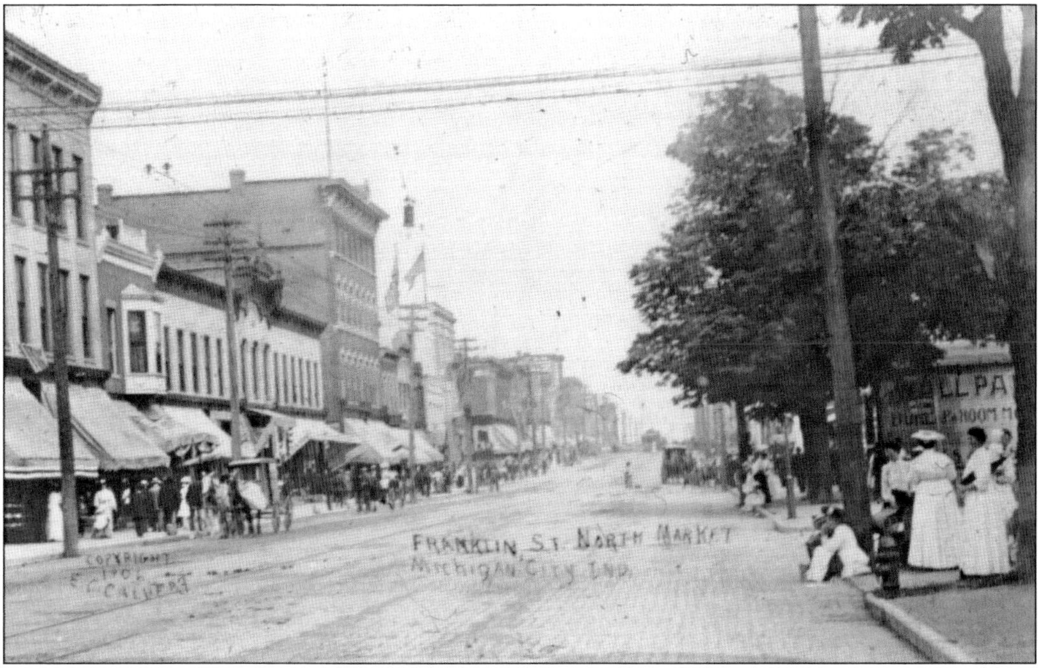

As seen in these photographs of Michigan City in the early 1900s, businesses sprang up along Franklin Street to accommodate and cash in on the new traffic. These images give a full picture of the activity in Michigan City during its growing role as a tourist destination.

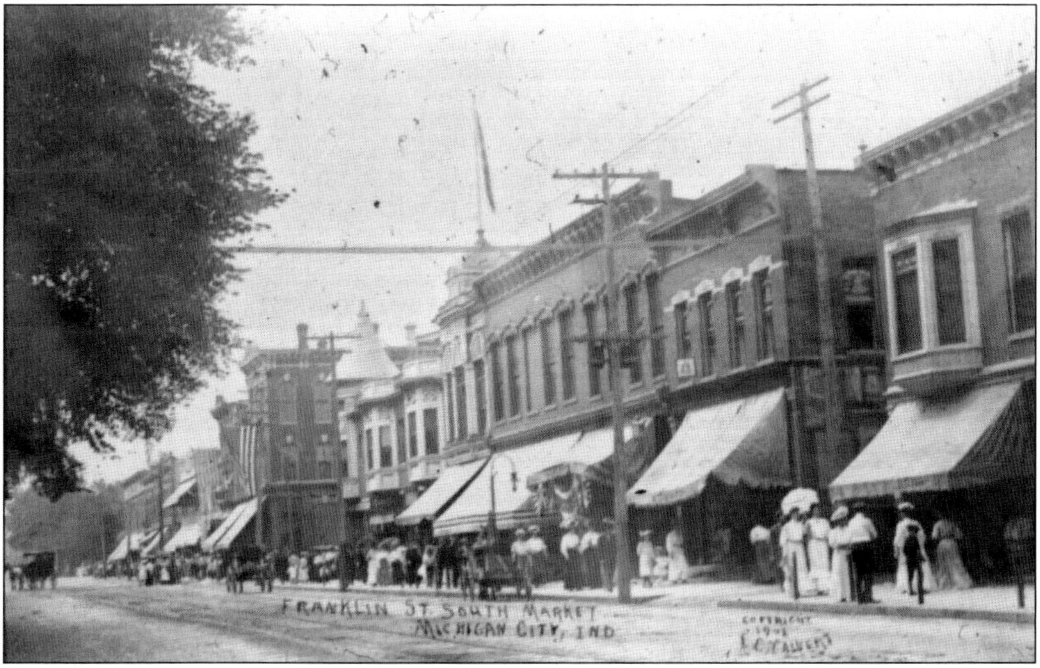

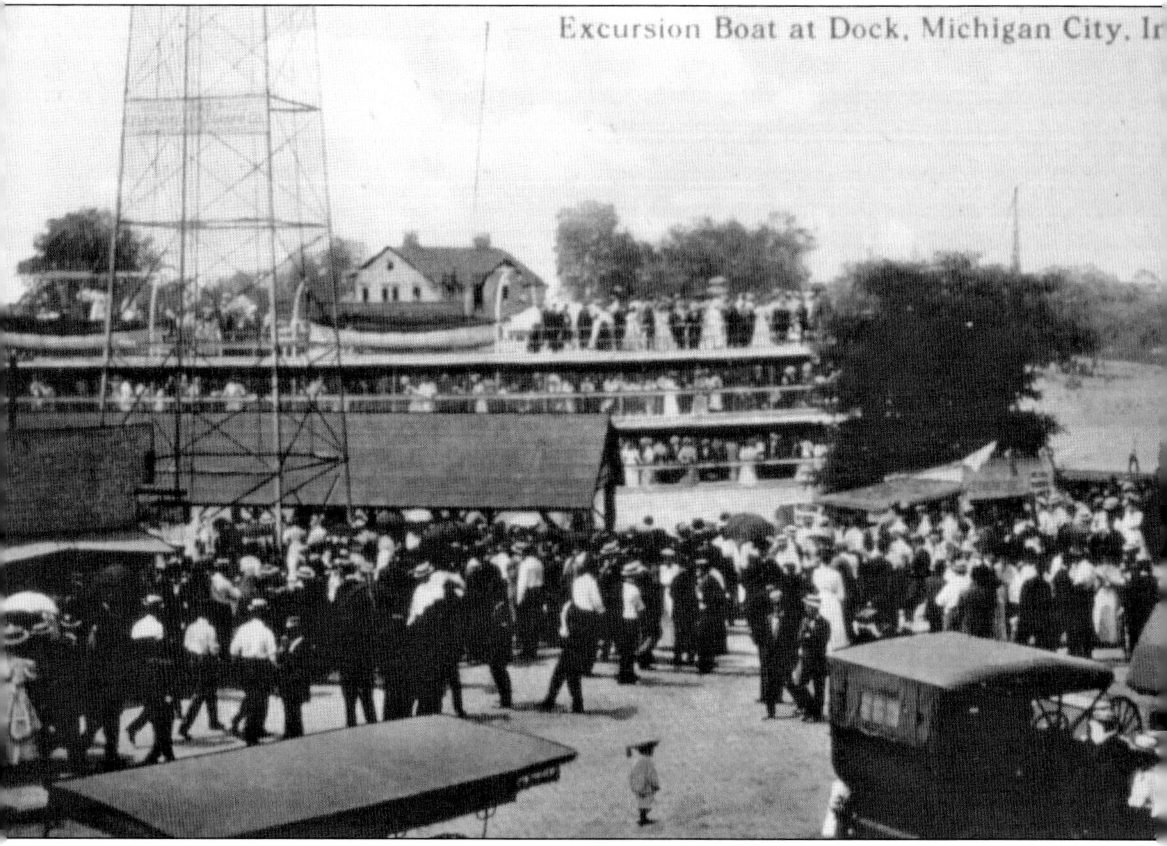

The unprecedented crowds at the docks were certainly a welcomed change to the lumber piles and shanties. For many city residents, a visit to Washington Park was an opportunity to explore not only Michigan City, but also Lake Michigan and Trail Creek. The accessible bathing beach also became an attraction for tourists and city residents alike.

Three

Amusements of Times Past

Washington Park was just the beginning of Michigan City's foray into the tourist trade. Once the park was cleaned up and landscaped, city residents looked for other ways to draw tourists. City residents saw even more potential for family entertainment. That potential was realized in before 1910, with the addition of an amusement area to the park. The large wooden roller coaster, carousel, waterslide, tennis courts, and later the Oasis Ballroom created an area that was much more than just a day at the park.

The era of the big amusement park in Washington Park is one that many people in Michigan City either never knew or have only heard stories of. The reason is that the period was so brief. By 1920, the major attractions of the park were gone, consumed by a fire that reportedly took place in 1915. Fortunately, the city forged ahead, rebuilding a few components and adding others that were not there before. One of those attractions was the Oasis Ballroom, built in 1922. A boardwalk, new carousel, waterslide, bowling alley, and roller rink were also added in the coming years.

While the city was struggling to keep its attractions rolling, tourism soared to astounding levels. According to the Michigan City Historical Society's *Little Bit of History* series, over 435,000 people visited Michigan City by ship and train in 1909. These numbers ebbed during World War I but were revived in the 1920s and 1930s. Unfortunately, economic conditions would not allow the success of the Washington Park amusement era to continue long after that.

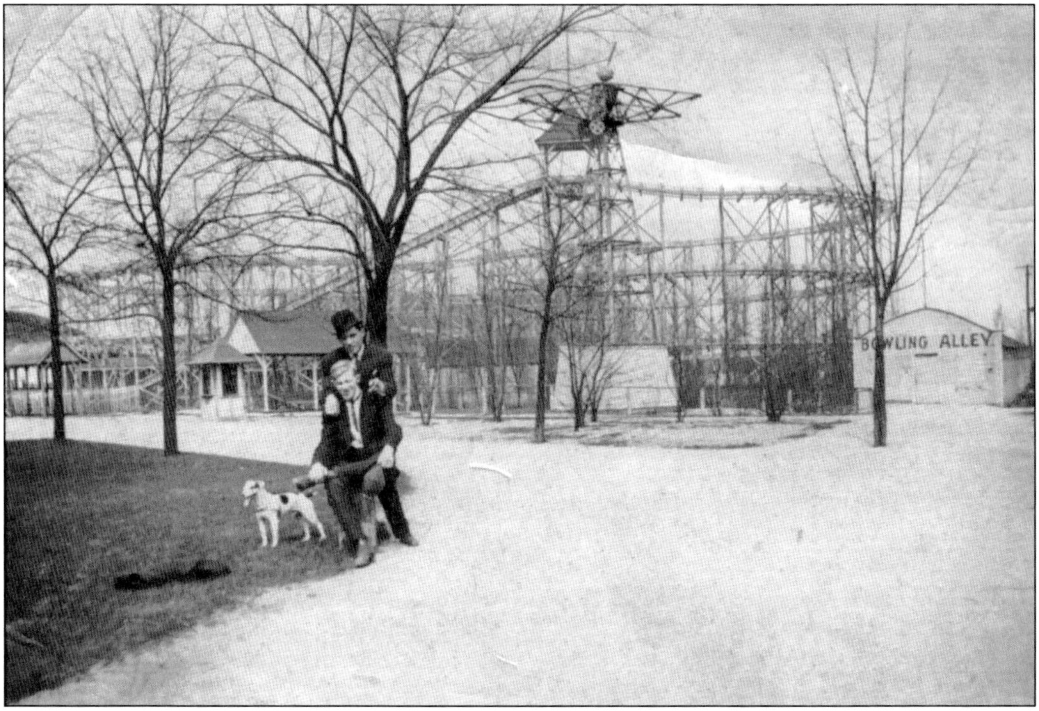

The most awe-inspiring pictures of the old Washington Park are those of the wooden roller coaster that stood in front of a bowling alley and overlooked the lakefront. The figure-eight structure is rare in the roller-coaster world of today. In fact, there is only one in existence in the United States.

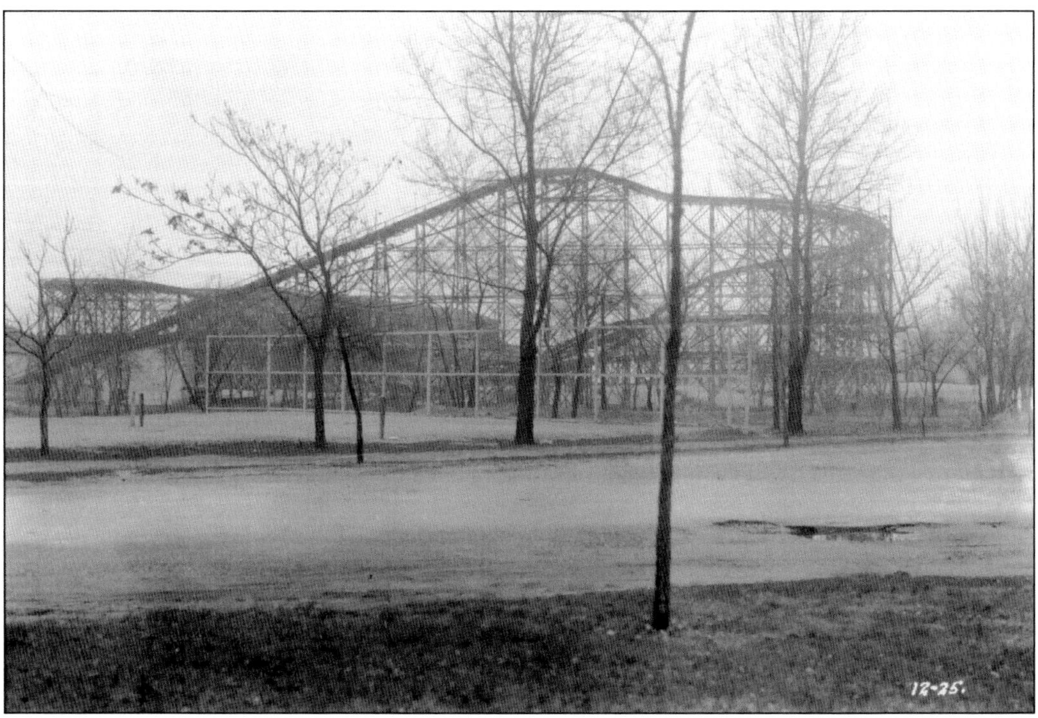

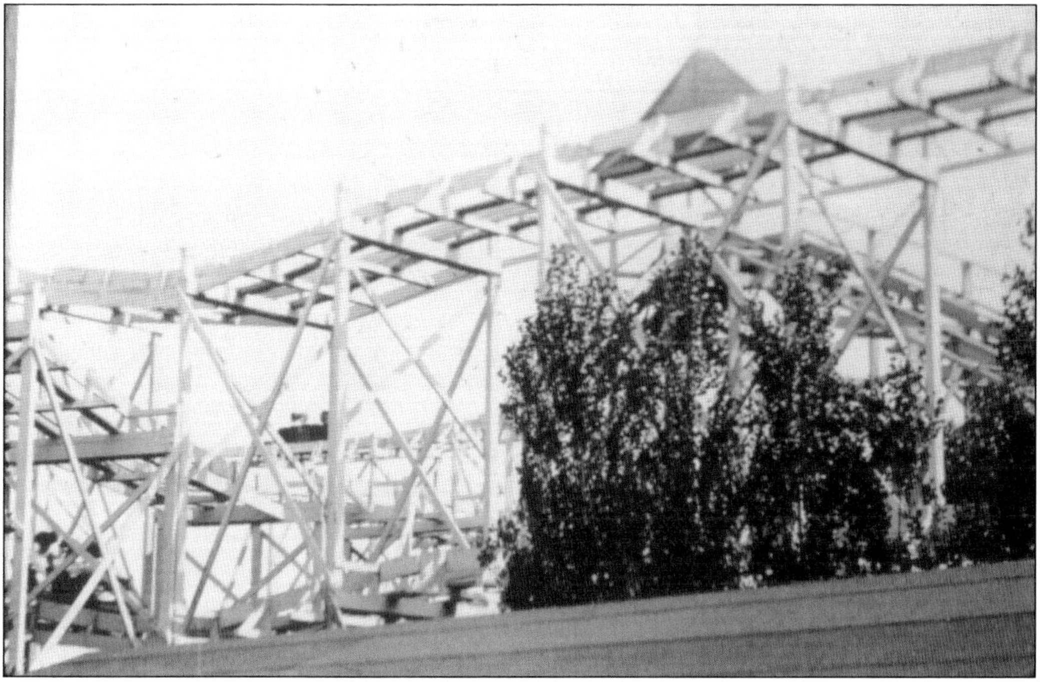

Riders were rewarded with a view of the lake and the city before plunging toward the ground at high speeds. Wooden roller coasters were the most popular style of its kind during the early 1900s. The image above is a closer look at a section of the roller coaster. The photograph below, taken in 1908, shows the beach in winter with the amusements in the background.

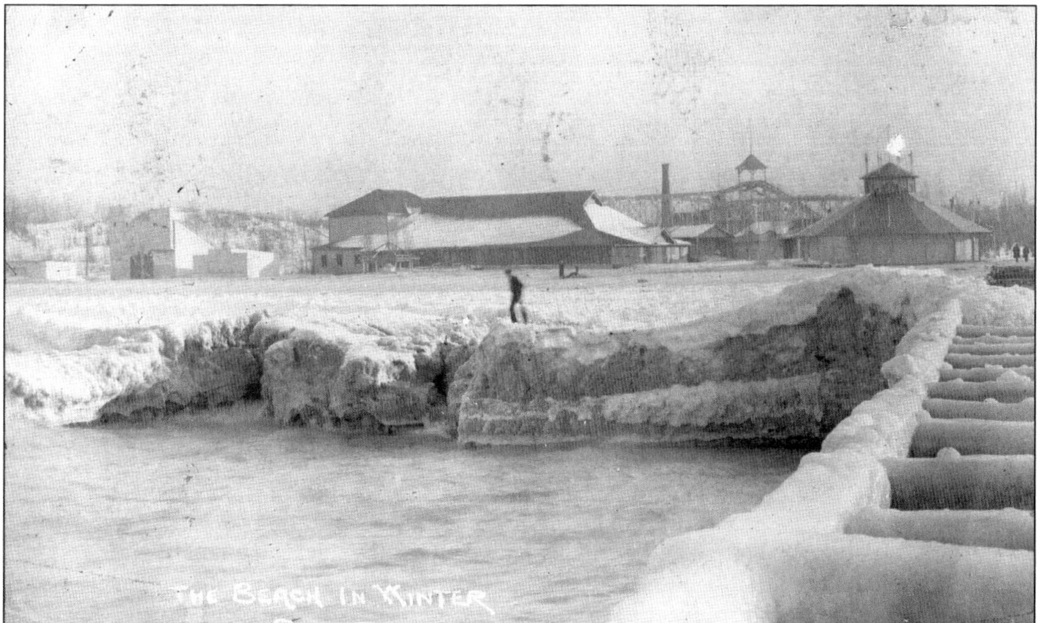

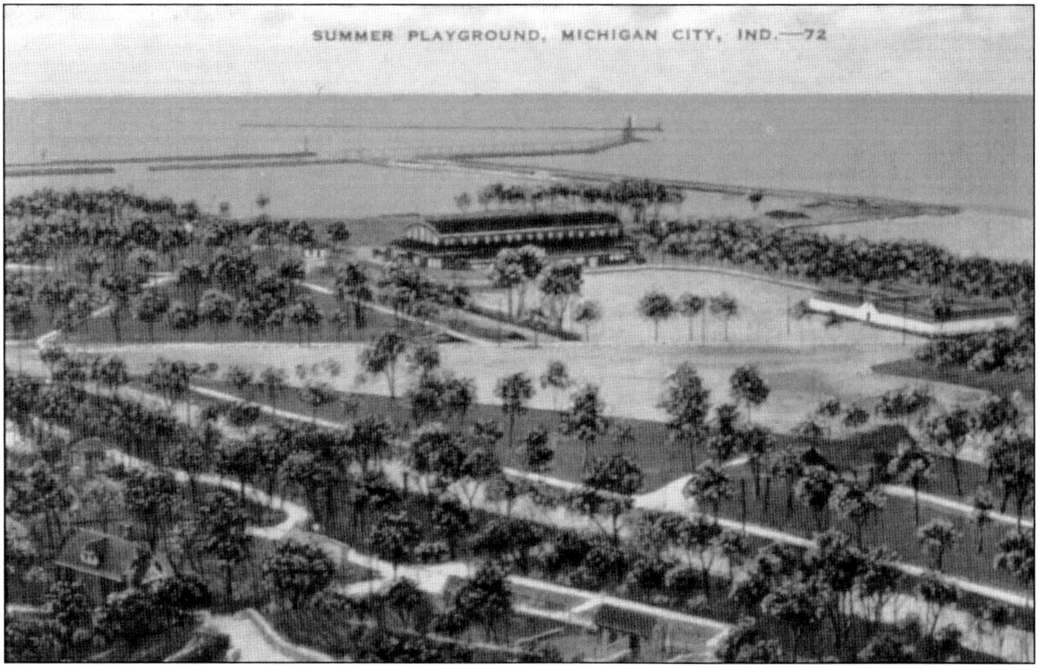

Photographs of the area at the time shows the wooden structure rising up over the trees at the lakefront, enticing travelers on their way to a day of fun the park. In this postcard image, the roller coaster is visible above the trees, giving one the idea of how spectacular the view must have been. The ride stood in front of a bowling alley, close to other amusements.

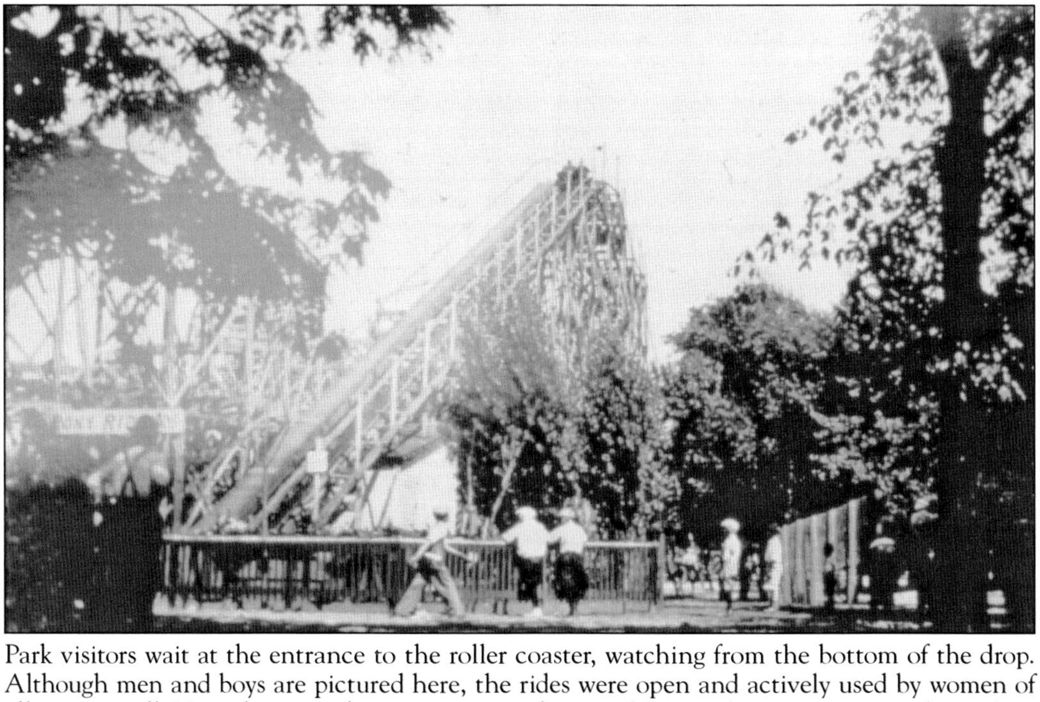

Park visitors wait at the entrance to the roller coaster, watching from the bottom of the drop. Although men and boys are pictured here, the rides were open and actively used by women of all ages as well. Note the sign advertising pony rides, another popular attraction, in the park to the bottom left.

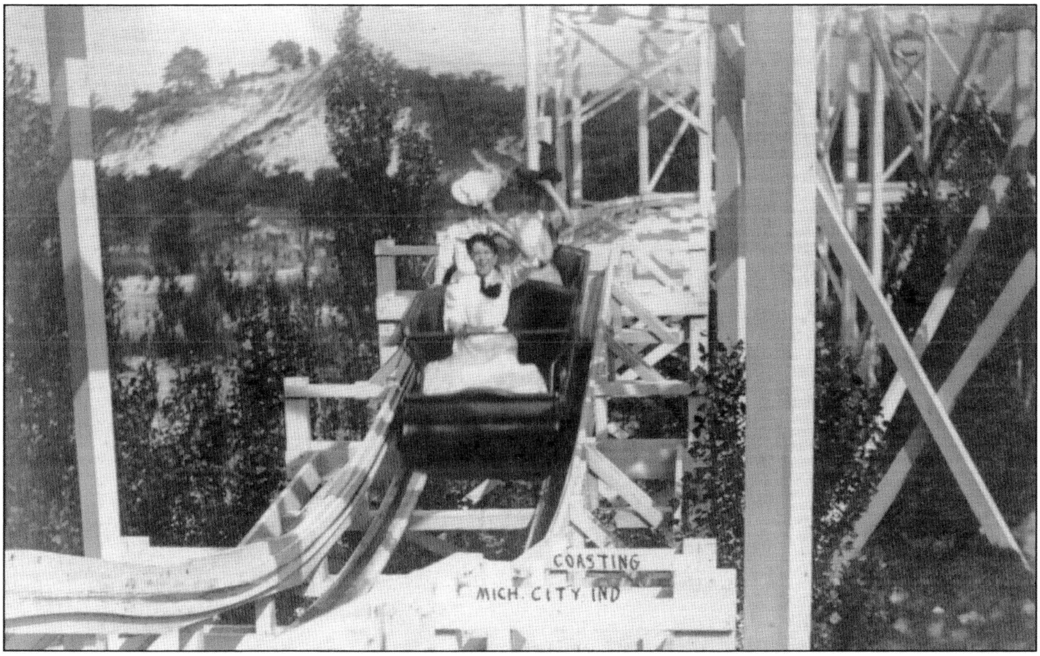

The women in the image above were captured at the top of the roller coaster, probably turning upward into a climb. The clothing and hats on the people in both photographs date them to the 1910s. In the image below, a man and woman are shown making their way on the ride. At the time, adults were drawn to the amusement park activities just as much as the children.

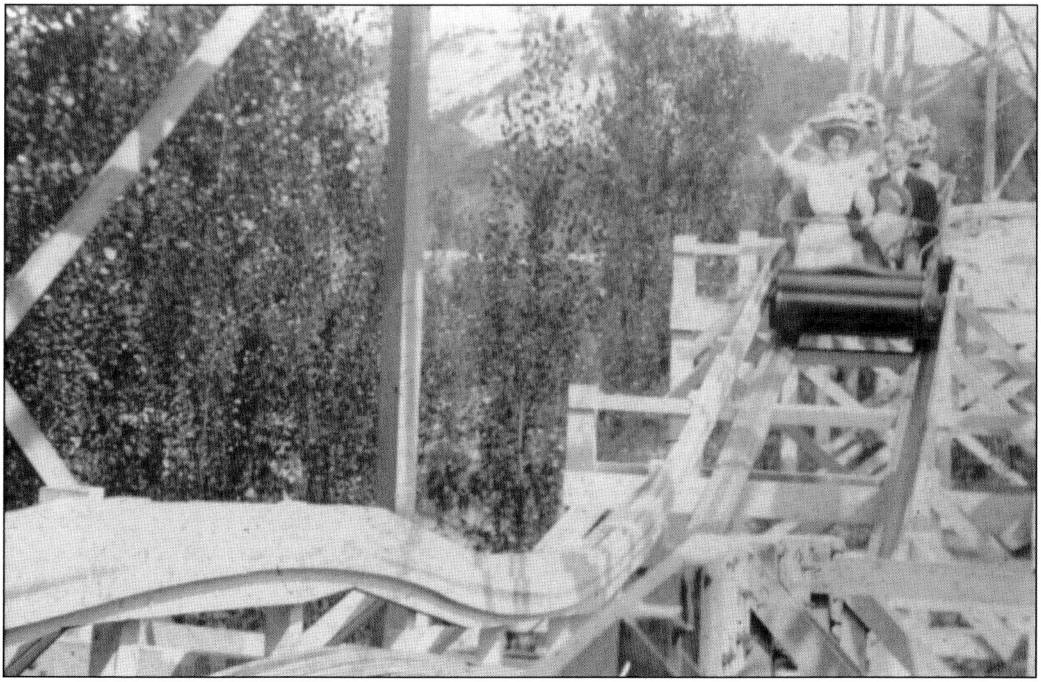

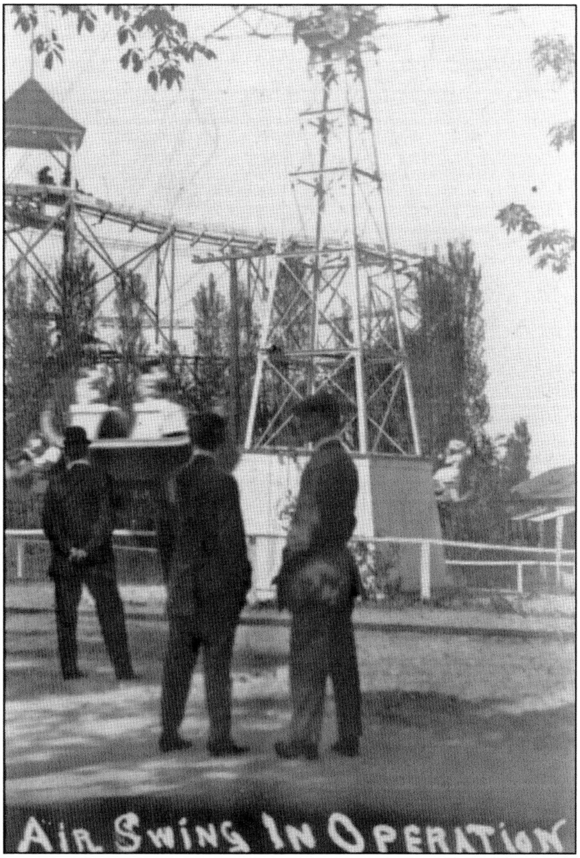

The Whirligig was also known as the Whirling Swing or Air Swing. The swing was another wooden structure that had seats attached to sled-like platforms secured to a cable. It swung around at high speeds, lifting the sled seats closer to a horizontal position as the speed increased.

The Whirligig, seen here at a wider angle, operates much like the modern-day Tilt-O-Whirl. Women and children often enjoyed the rides as the men looked on, though the entire family usually took part in the activities. Behind the Whirligig in this photograph, the roller coaster can be seen.

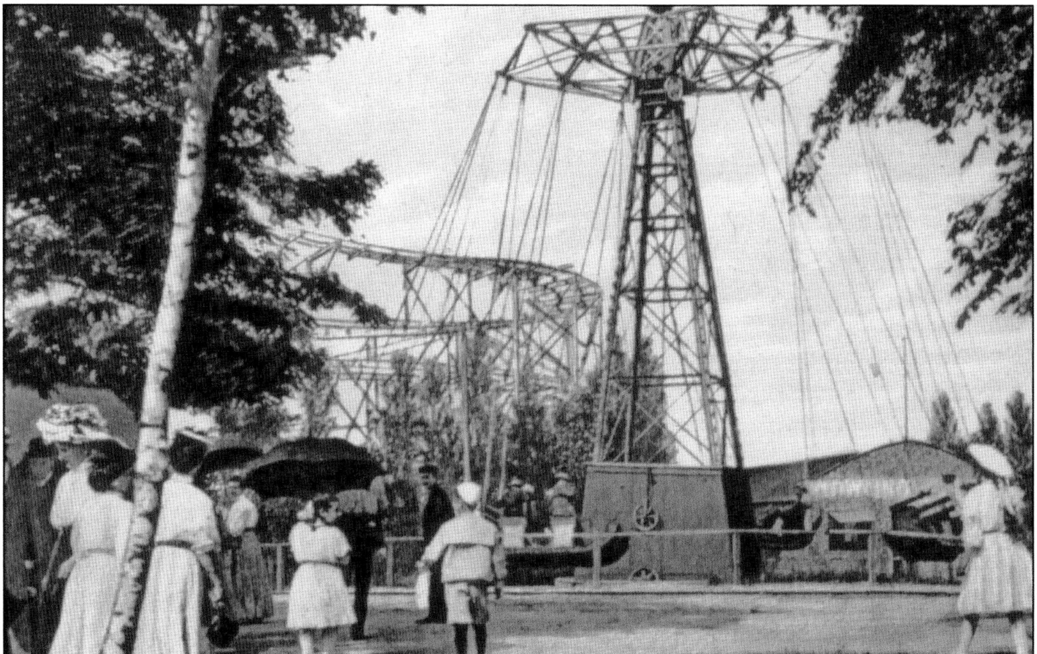

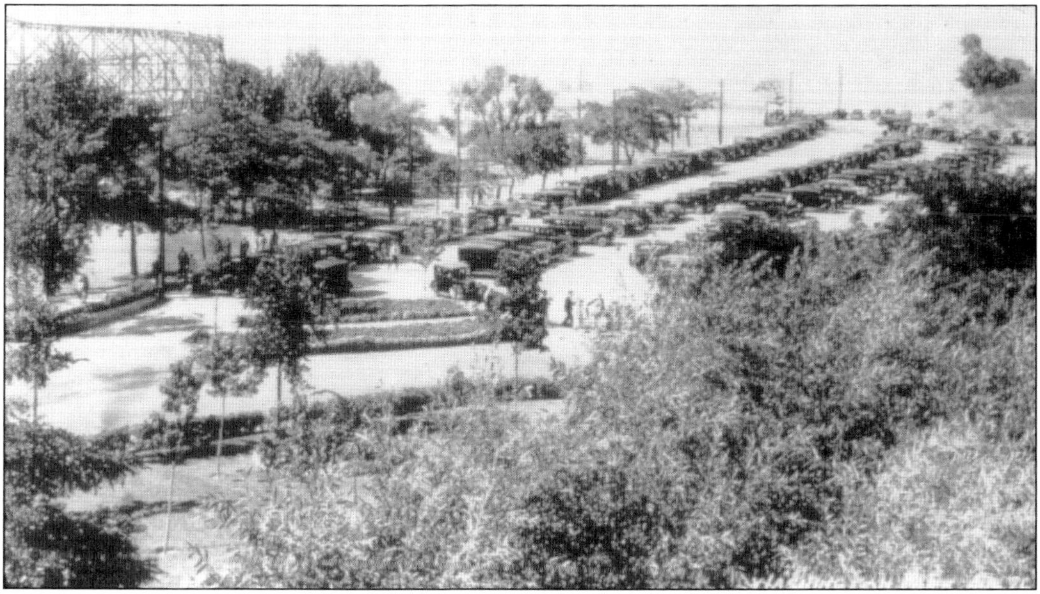

Parking was free at Washington Park, as was a visit to the beach and the park. The amusements did cost a small fee that many families were willing to pay. Here, the cars are lined up in the parking area outside the amusement park. Today, Washington Park's parking areas fill up in a similar fashion when the Michigan City Summer Festival Committee brings carnival rides to town. (The amusement area stopped being a permanent fixture in the park in the late 1960s).

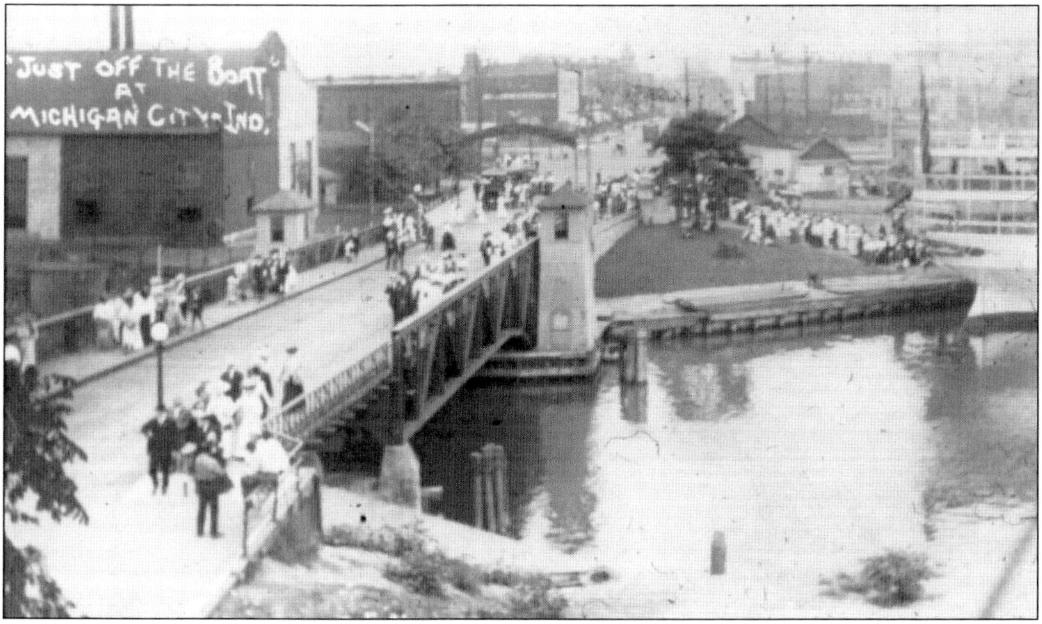

The hundreds of thousands of people who visited Michigan City during the early 1900s came for the park and later the zoo; the beach was also a draw. A person could spend one day and enjoy a full vacation without heading to a far-off place or remaining in the congestion that was Chicago. In fact, as many out-of-town visitors began their trek to Michigan City from the sister city across the lake. In this photograph, Chicagoans are arriving from an excursion boat and heading into the park.

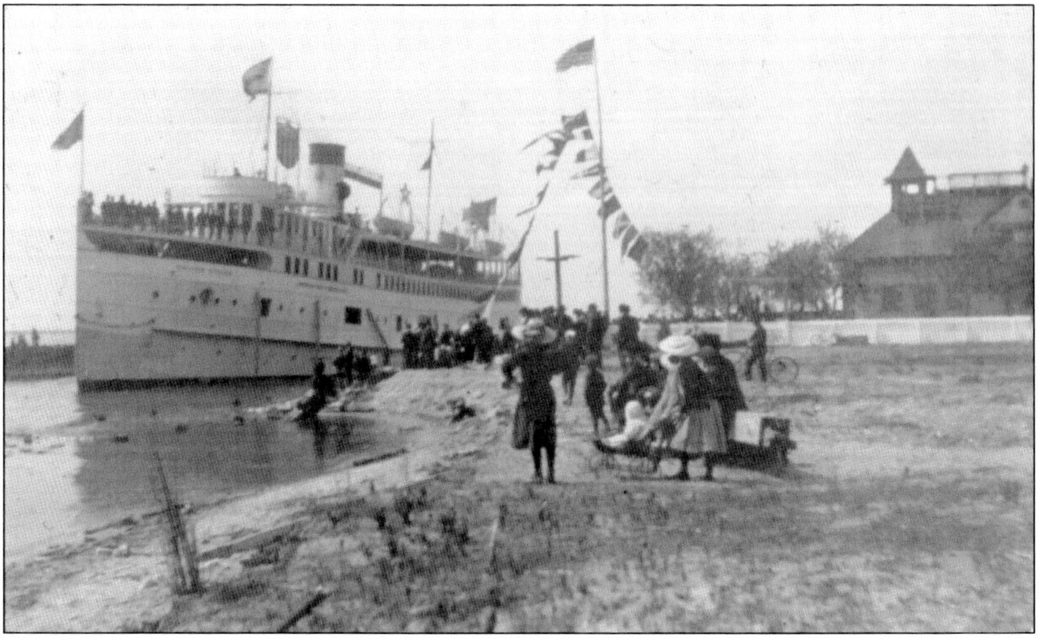

Large ferry ships like the *United States, Theodore Roosevelt*, and the *Eastland* ferried large groups of people from Chicago to Michigan City on a regular basis. In this photograph, the *United States* is unloading passengers along Trail Creek in Michigan City near the old lighthouse visible to the right. These large ships stopped making the trek to Michigan City in the 1950s after years of waning attendance.

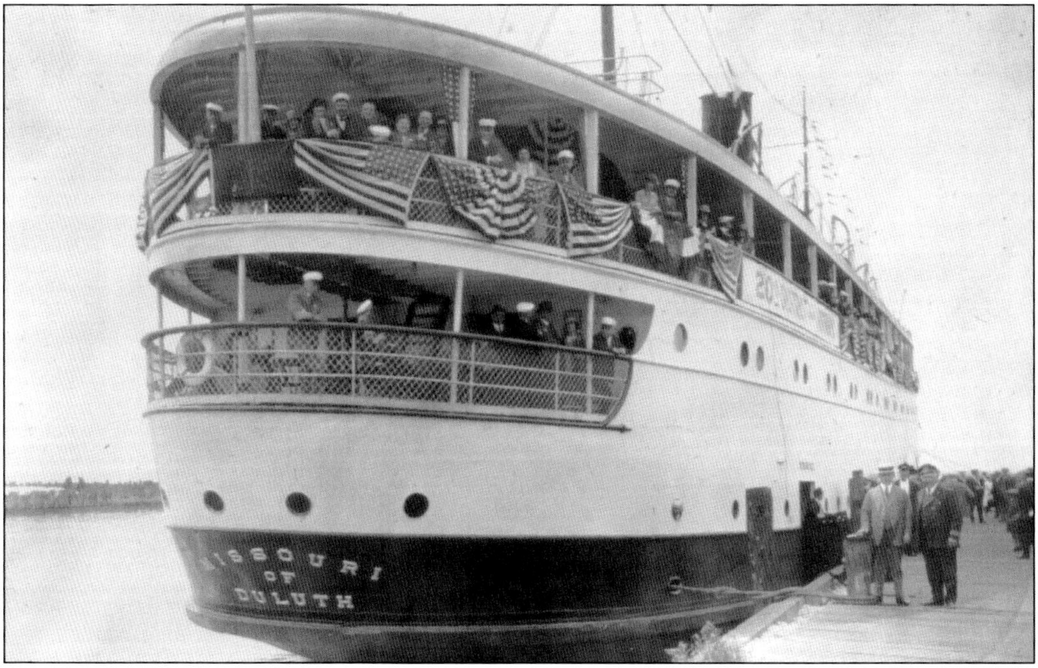

At the time, this was the quickest route to Michigan City. People took the ferry over early in the day, stayed until late afternoon, and rode it home at night. In this photograph is the *Missouri*, another popular steamer that brought visitors looking for an excursion for the day.

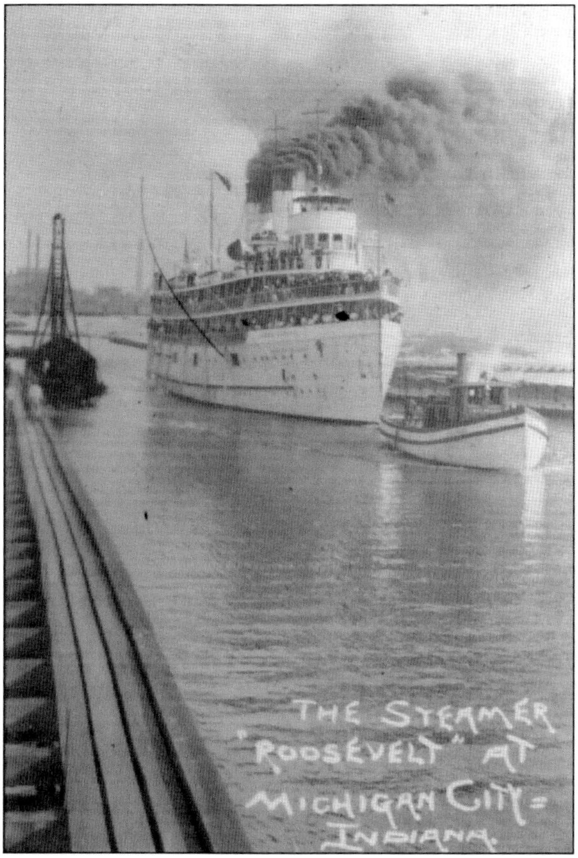

The *Roosevelt* is seen here, pulling into the harbor at Michigan City. A regular fixture on the lakefront, it actually became a symbol of tourism in Michigan City on postcards and other advertisements. The *United States* was like a constant companion. In the image below, the steamers are captured while full of passengers.

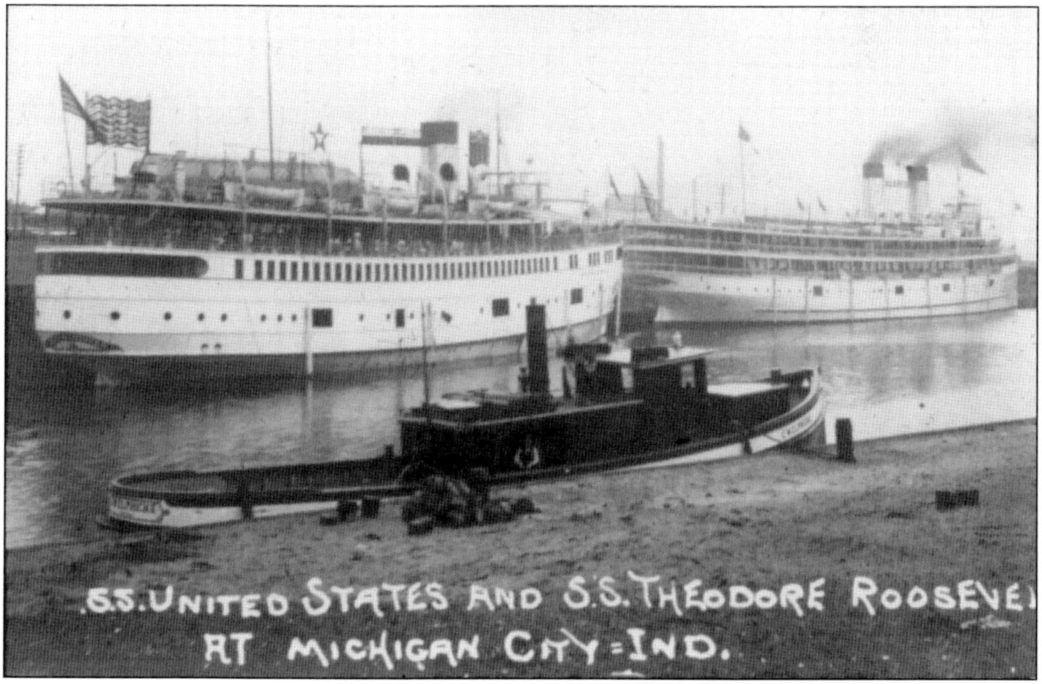

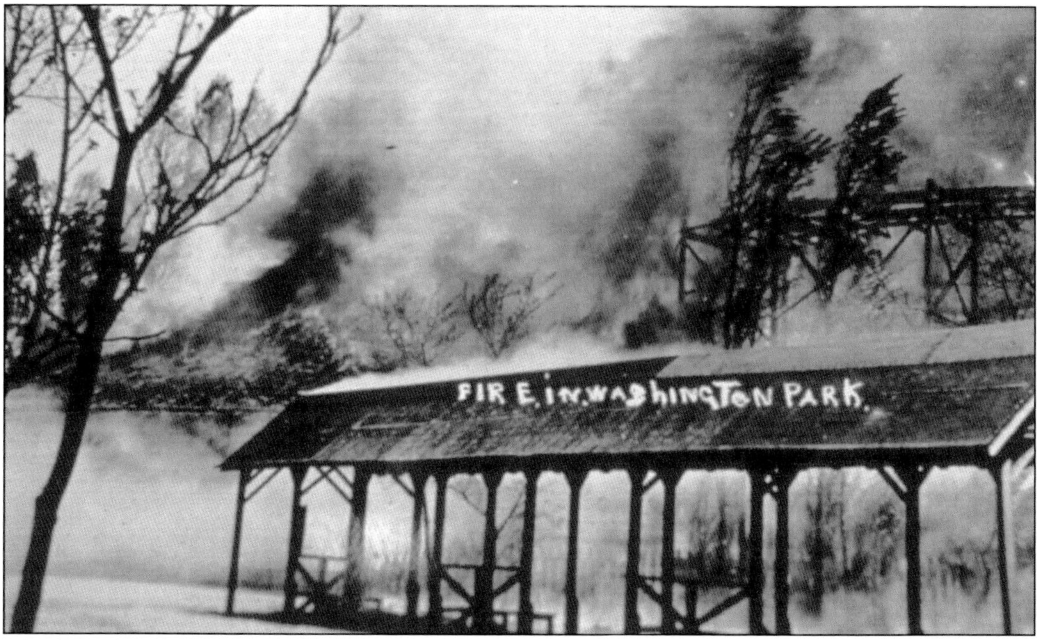

The fire that hampered the park's progress, which reportedly took place in 1915, was large enough to damage many of the structures. This is also where the history of Washington Park becomes murky, as records that were not destroyed were subsequently lost. The structures were rebuilt after the fire, but it is unclear when and how this was accomplished. Park department records indicate that the amusements located where the Oasis Ballroom would later stand were minimally damaged as they continued to operate while the park resurrected itself. (Courtesy of Mike and Kathy Fleming.)

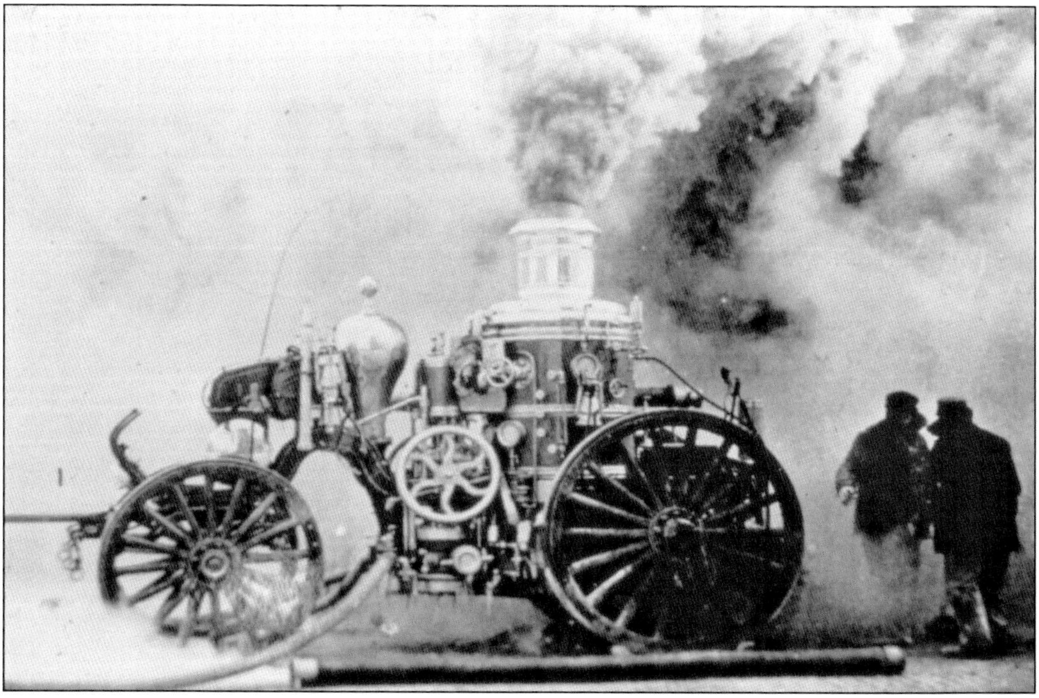

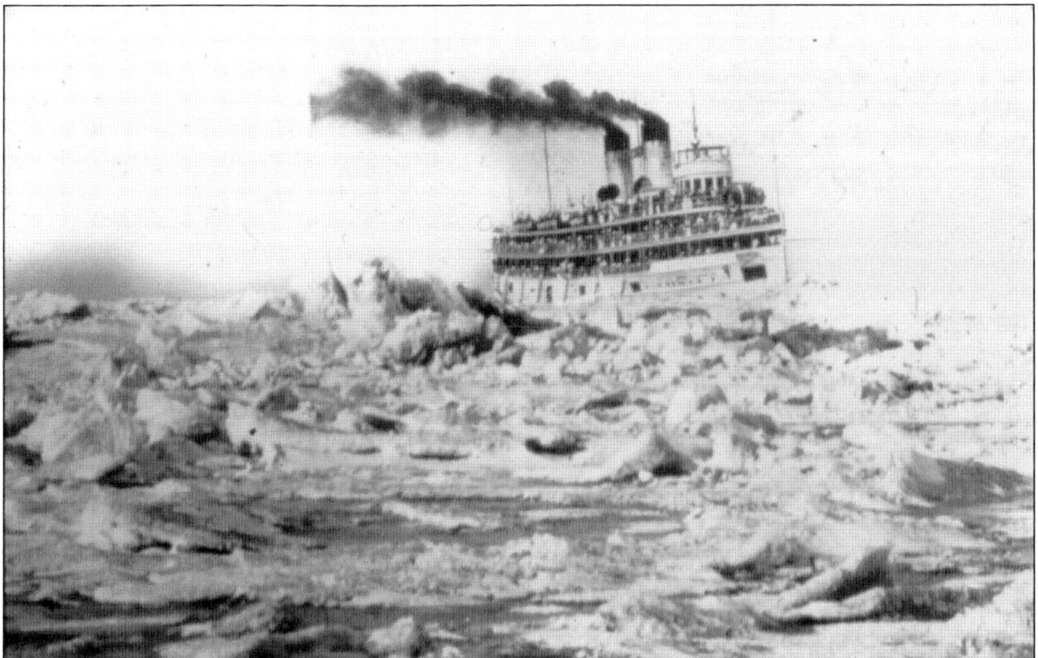

The fire, seen below engulfing the wooden roller coaster, occurred during the period when several ferry accidents were also taking place on the lake. The most notable was the *Eastland*, which went down on its way to Michigan City in 1915, the same year as the fire. Over 800 people drowned when the ship sank. These accidents did hamper visitor numbers a bit, but the park experienced a surge in the 1920s that helped pick up business. However, the numbers brought in via ferry never did fully recover. (Courtesy of Mike and Kathy Fleming.)

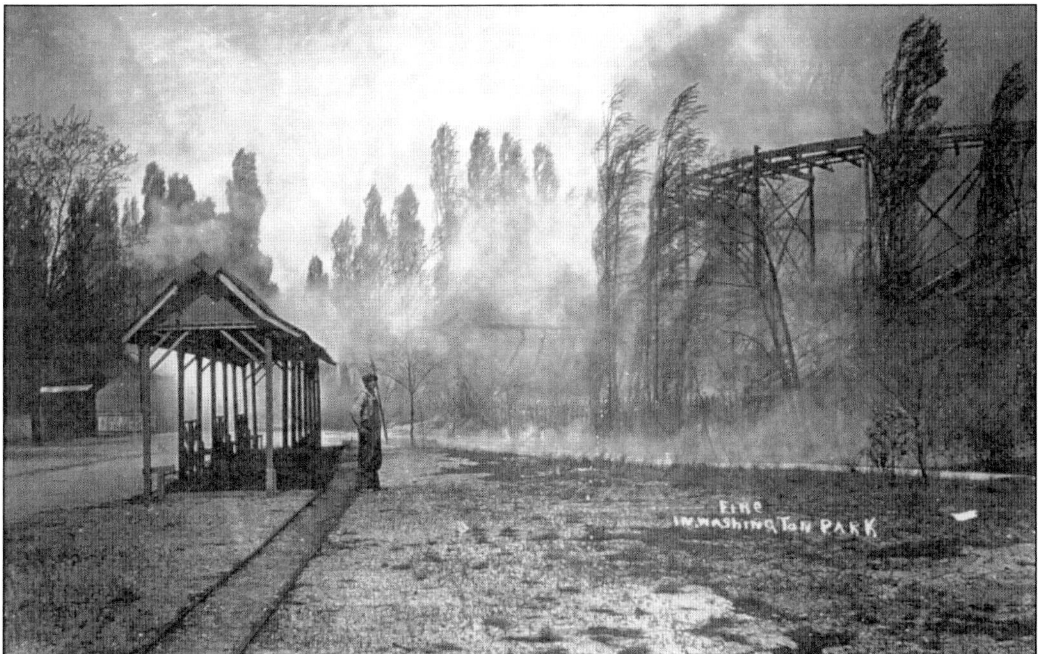

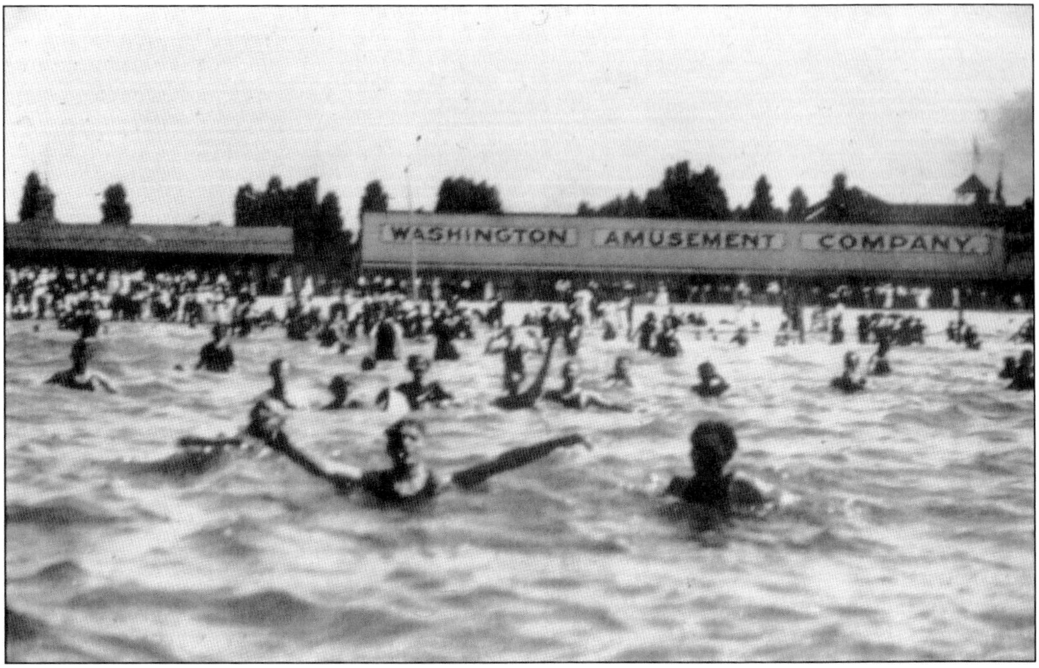

The recovery was also helped by a change in focus from big amusement rides to a more diverse type of entertainment. Tennis, swimming, the boardwalk, and games began stealing the spotlight in the 1920s and for the next 30 years. Golf courses would become a part of the recreational offerings as well. And then there was always the beach, seen in the image above. The photograph below shows the tennis courts at Washington Park in 1934, yet another amusement for families. The tennis courts would survive Washington Park's remodel toward a more natural aesthetic, but the courts are not a part of the park landscape today.

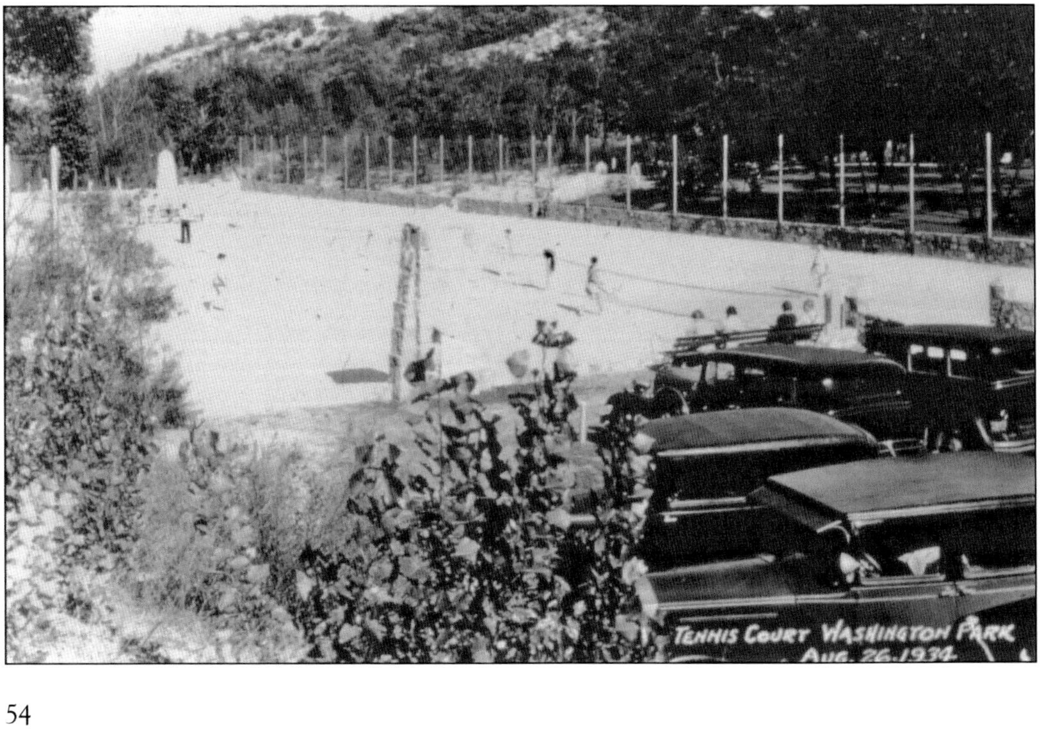

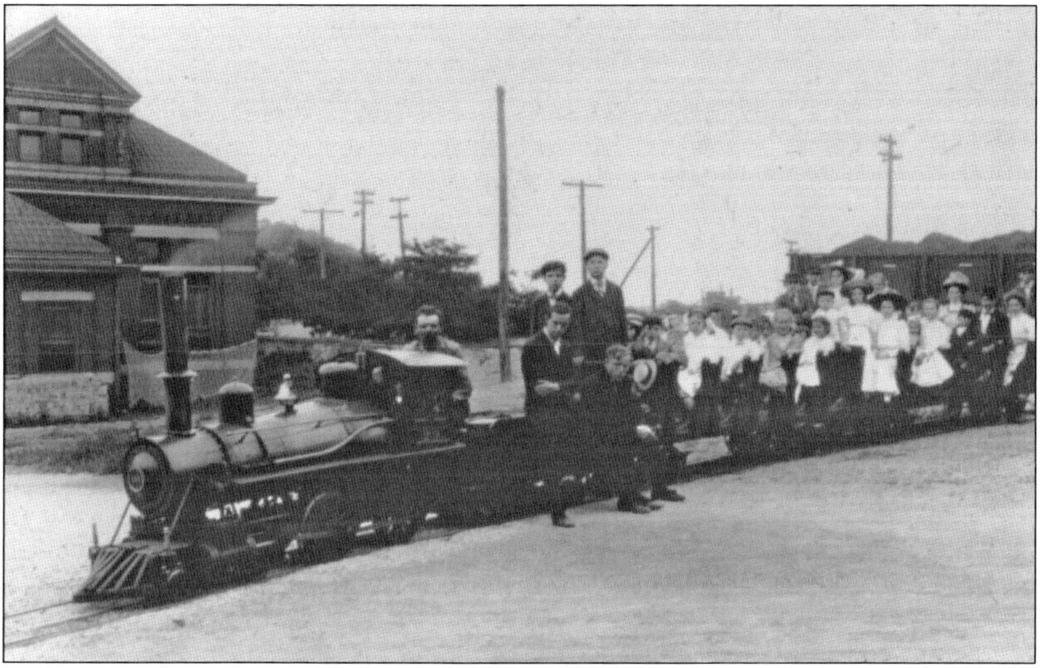

A train, known as the Kiddieland Limited Train, accommodated both adults and children as it took visitors for a ride throughout the park. The date of its operation is unclear, but photographs that seem to date as early as the 1910s display a locomotive that also pulled visitors with rides. Other pictures taken in the 1930s through the 1950s also show what appears to be the ride. Park records are scarce on the topic of this little locomotive, as they are on several aspects of the park during the amusement period. The image below shows the slightly altered train in the 1950s. The Kiddieland is said to be on display at the Hesston Steam Museum.

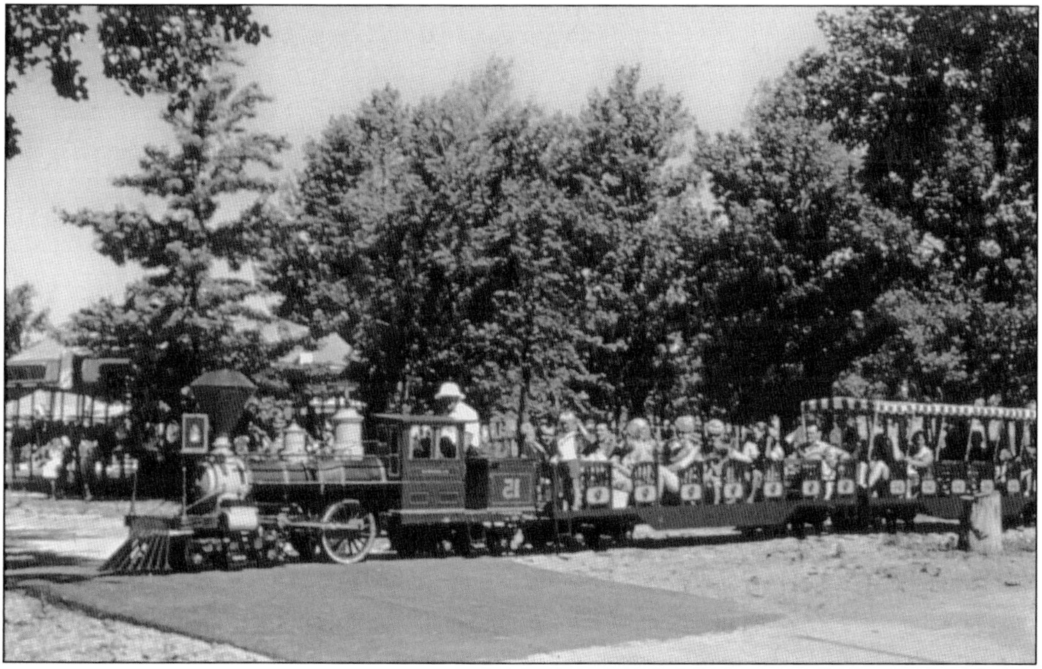

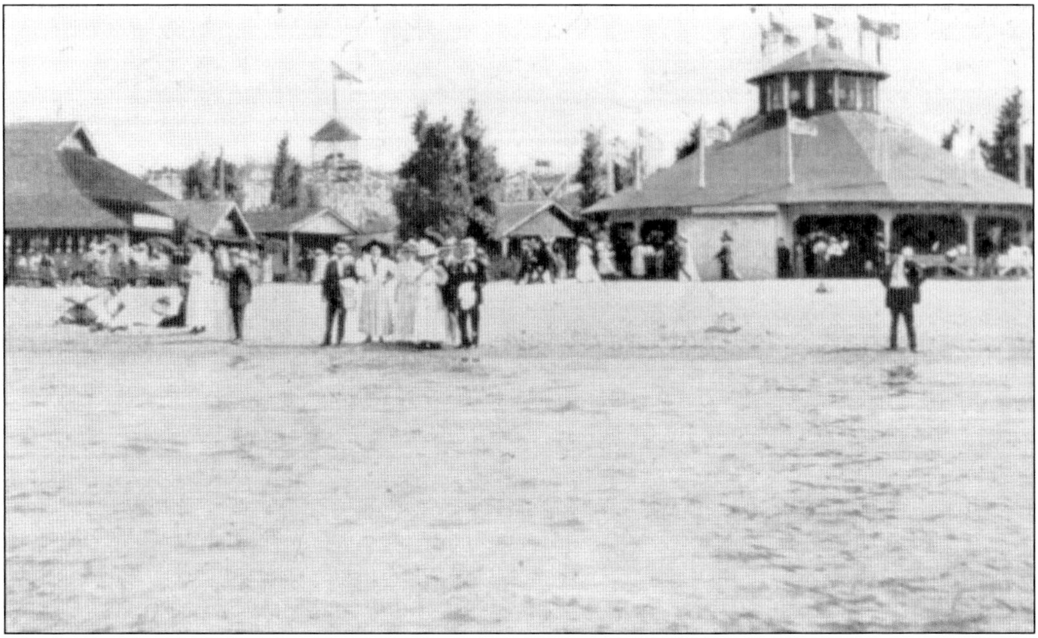

From the mid-1920s to 1962, Harold Barr worked with Lakeview Amusement Park in Washington Park. He oversaw the day-to-day operations in the park alongside his partner, Vic Sturken. The amusements sat on land Barr and Sturken leased from the city. The operation was managed by Lakeview Amusement and later Washington Park Amusement. Barr also supervised the park during the era of the merry-go-round (on the right) and the wooden coaster.

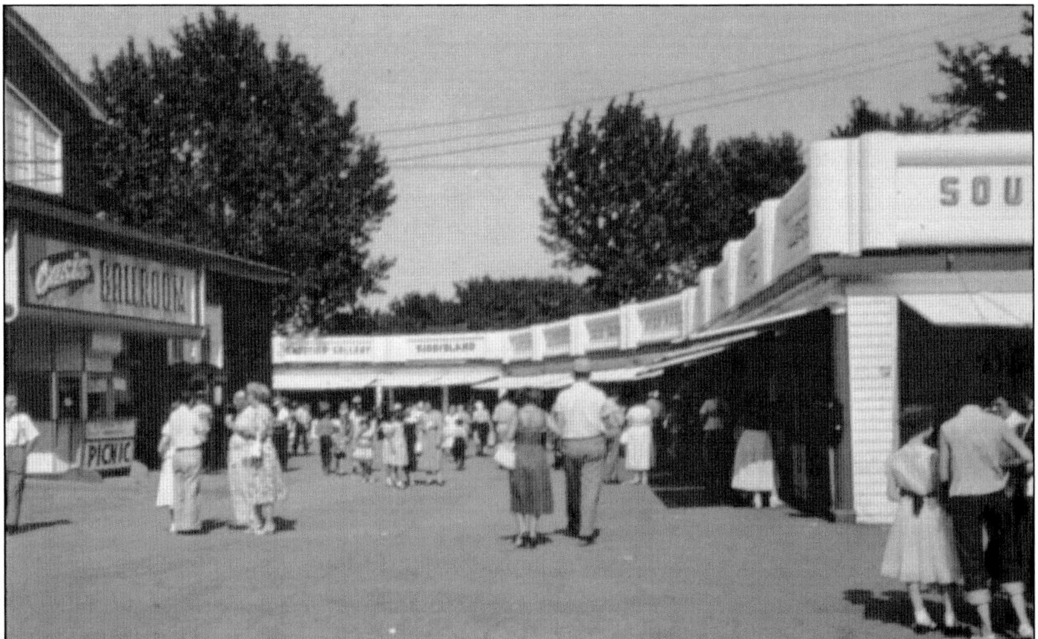

Rides were added and rotated in the popular Midway section of the park, which was the biggest draw from 1940 to 1962. The area consisted games and concessions, as can be seen here.

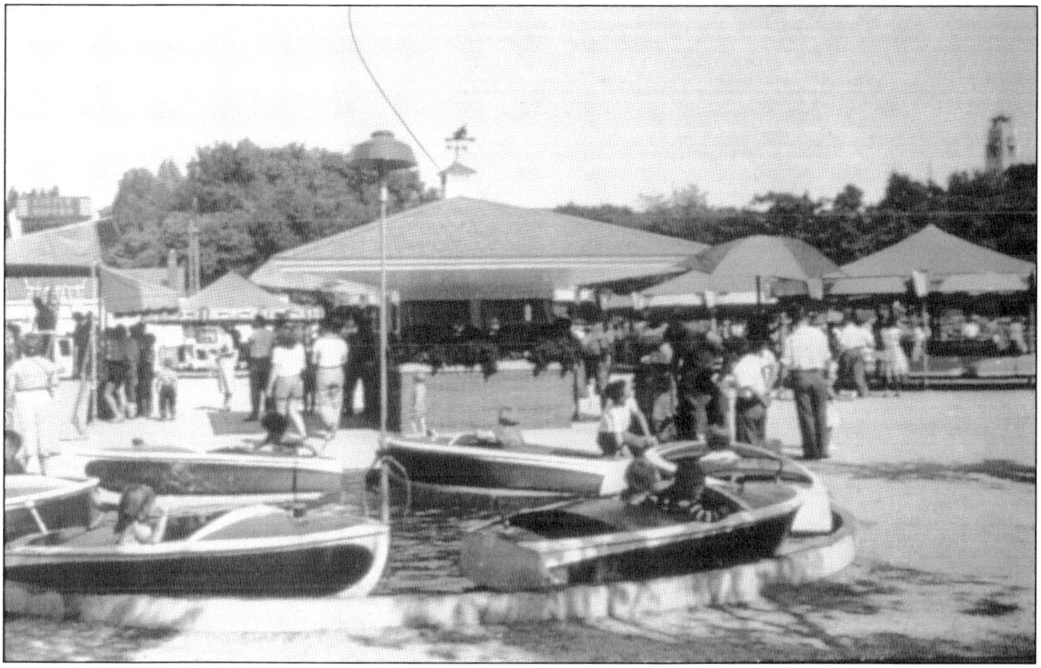

Other rides found in the Washington Park's amusement area included the boats, pictured here in 1954. The image below illustrates the sheer size of the carousel in the early 1900s before it was revived for Washington Park Amusements decades after the Washington Park fire.

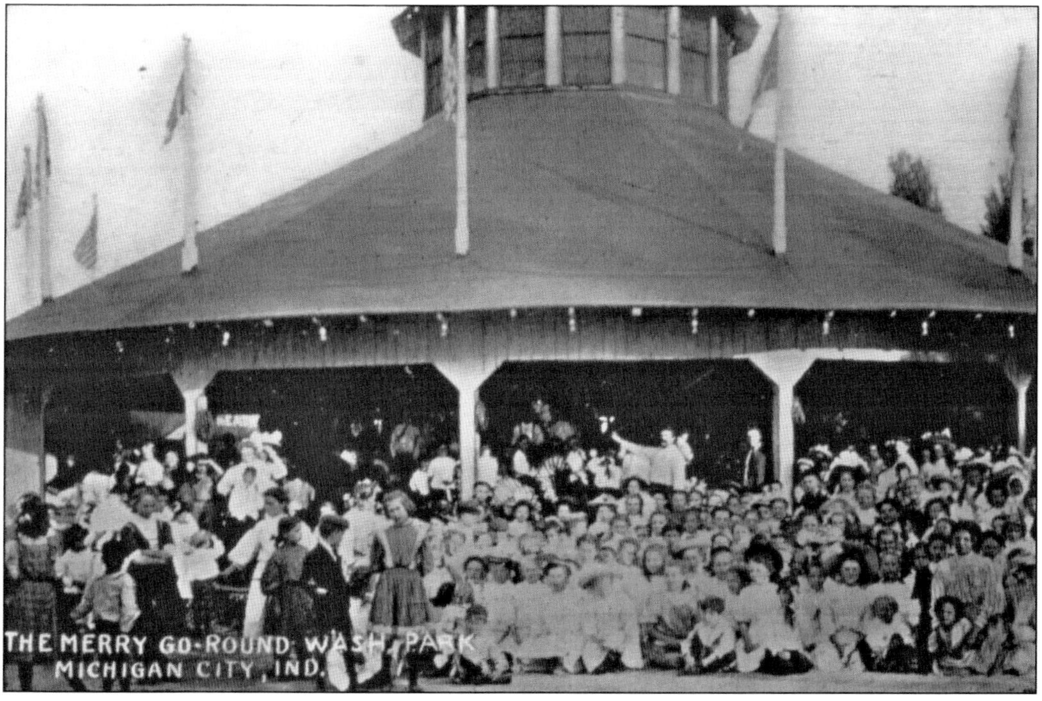

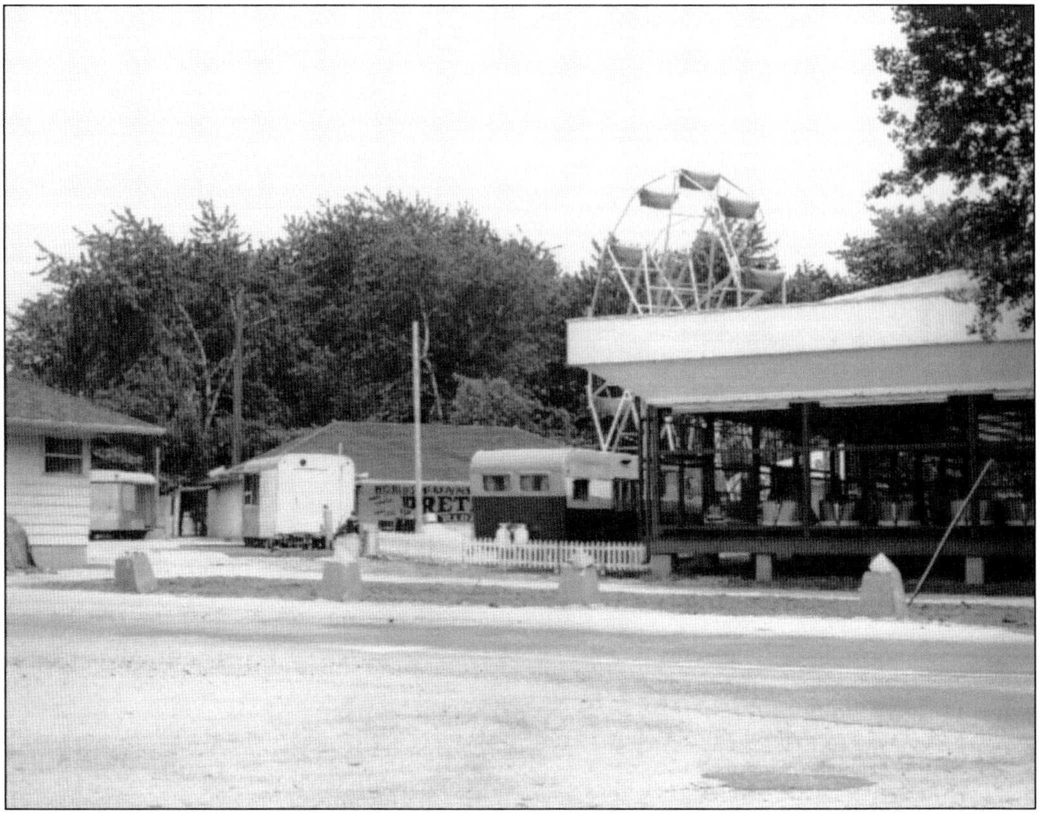

The Ferris wheel, pictured here in the background, and waterslide were a part of the amusements long after the days of the wooden roller coasters.

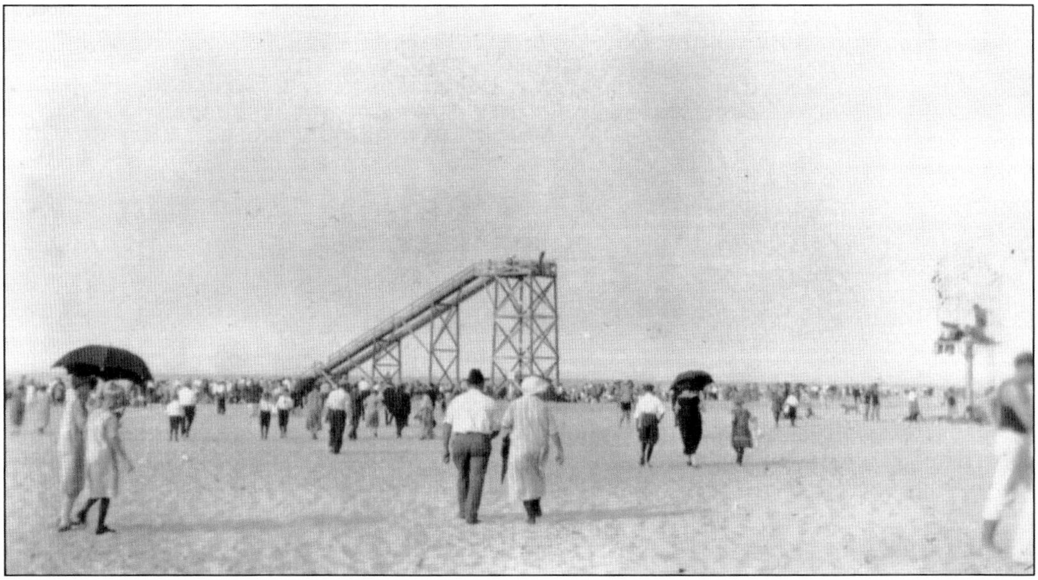

The waterslide leading into the lake was an attraction devised by Barr and Sturken. At this time, the Michigan City Zoo was also gaining popularity. Washington Park's attractions coupled with the zoo animals compensated for the loss of the large rides.

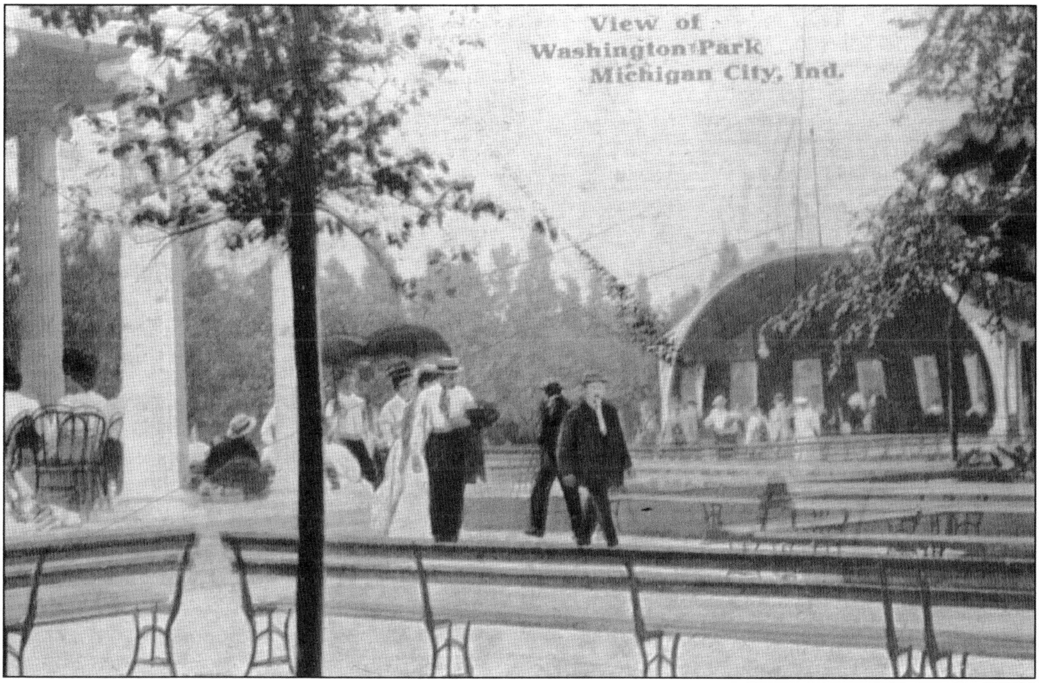

The Bicentennial Amphitheater, later known as the Guy Foreman Amphitheater, was constructed in 1978. The structure was built in honor of the 200th anniversary of the United States. The amphitheater was constructed entirely from donated funds raised by the Michigan City Bicentennial Commission and contributions from a federal revenue sharing fund.

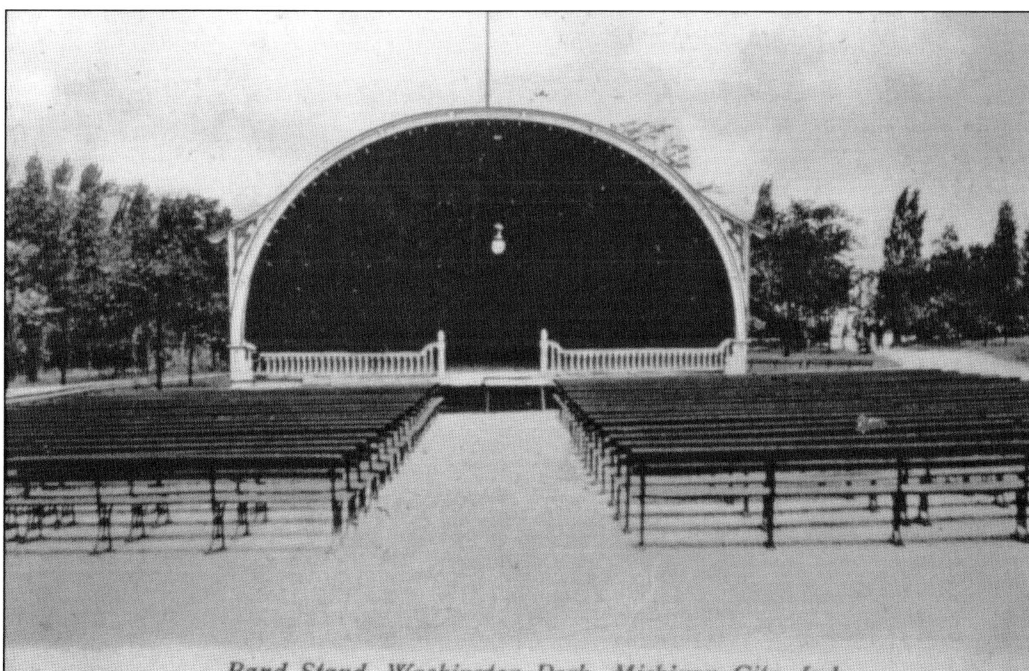

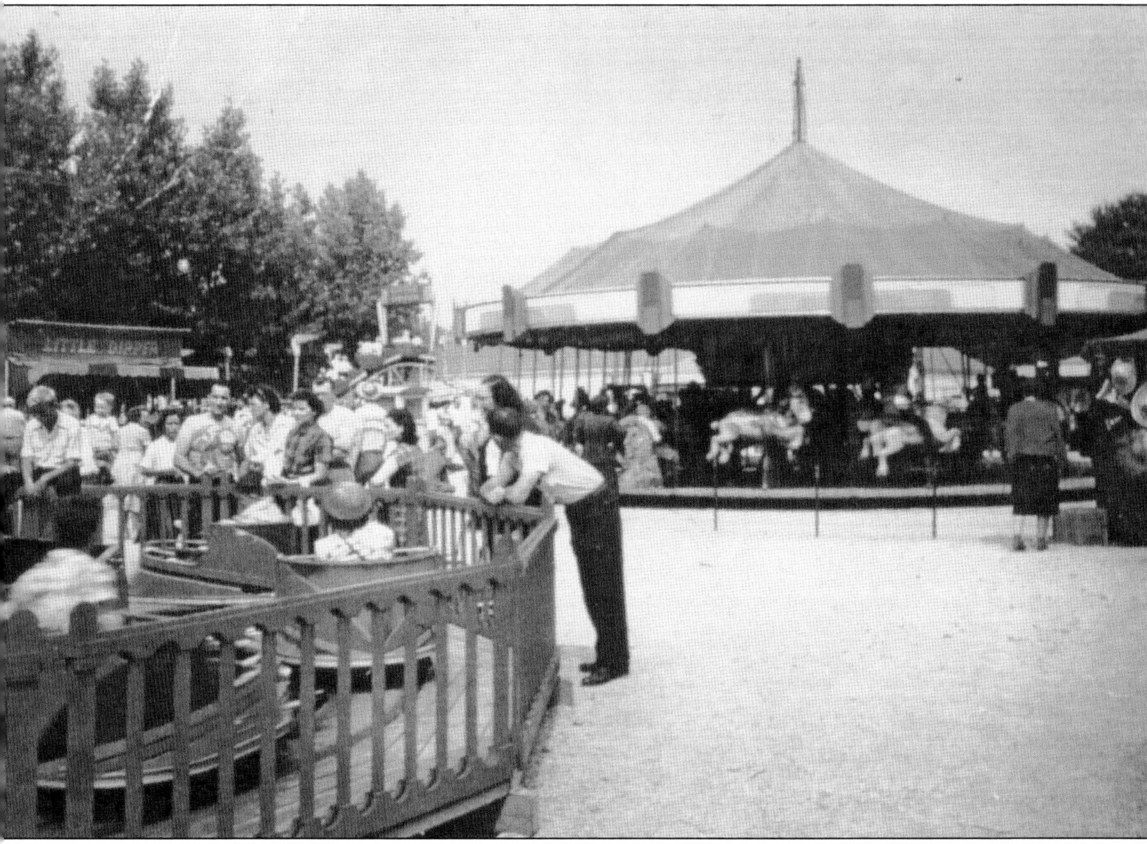

The amusement area contained six or more rides at a time, with the carousel being one of the permanent fixtures. Harold Barr also ran specials to boost crowd numbers, especially after the park department started charging fees for parking. One such promotion was 3¢ rides on Fridays. This photograph was taken in the 1950s, when the Midway and the park were still experiencing peak crowds in spite of parking fees.

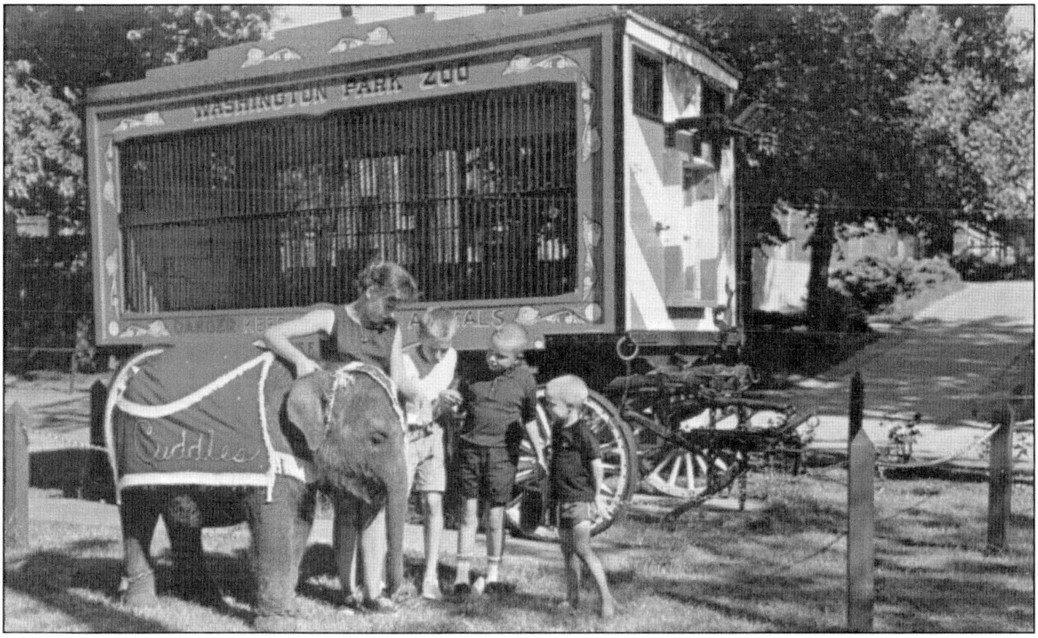

The zoo was a main attraction, with animals from all over the world. Pictured above is the popular baby elephant Cuddles. Miniature golf was another pastime, seen below in this 1960s family photograph. (Courtesy of Mike and Kathy Fleming.)

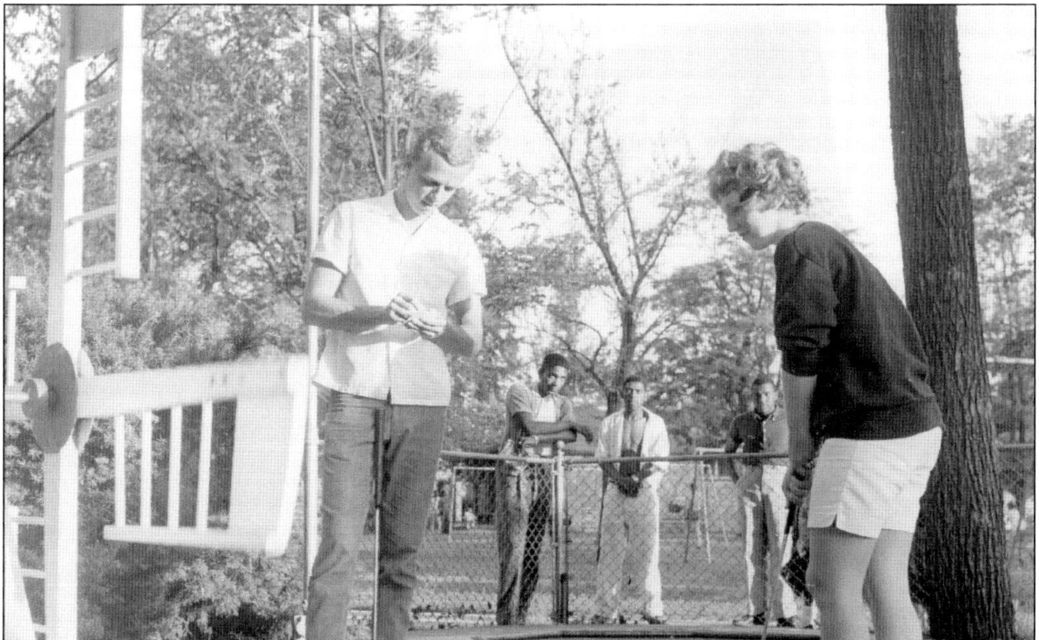

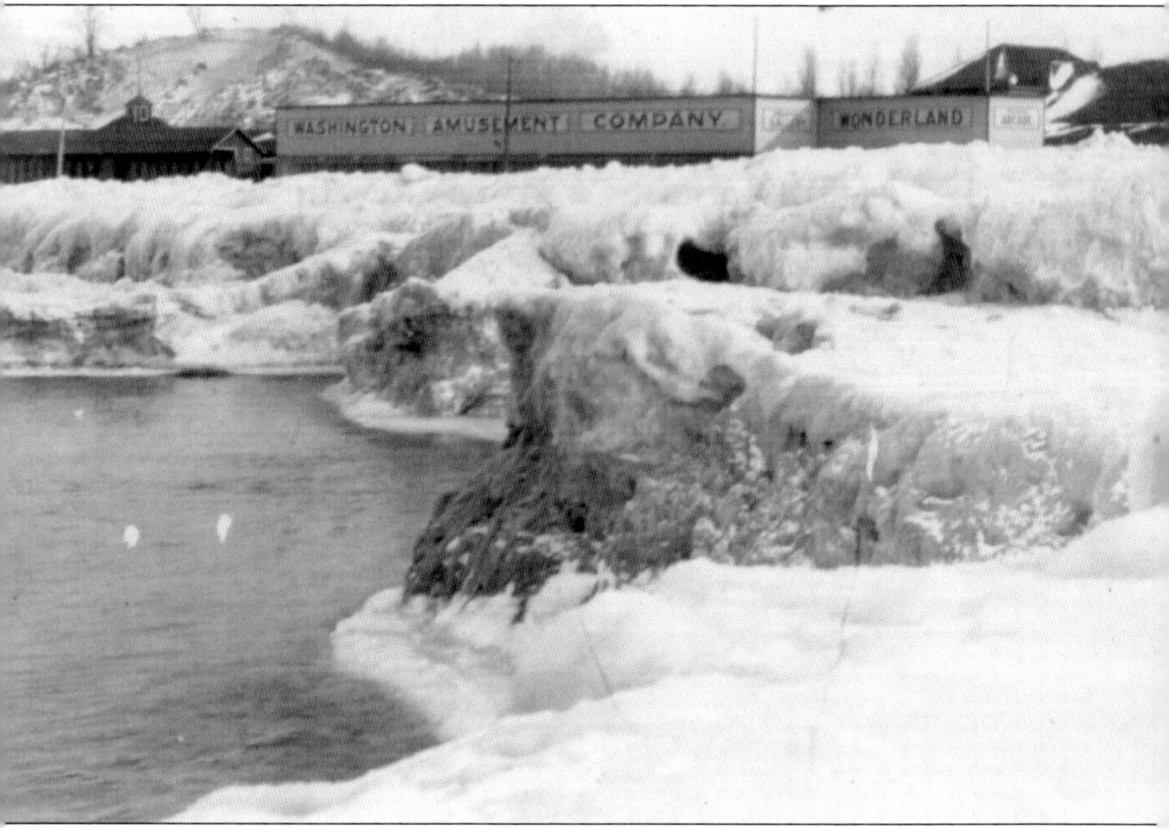

The arrangement between Harold Barr, Vic Sturken, and the park department worked well until it was time to renew the lease in 1960. Until then, Michigan City had become the most popular amusement spot on Lake Michigan, second only to Chicago (and even that was questionable). Parking fees were only the beginning of the trouble that Washington Park would face.

Four

Works and Progress

Before moving on in Washington Park history, one must explore the importance and impact of the Great Depression in the park's development. The Great Depression devastated Michigan City and the rest of the nation, and the city had no funds for public entities like Washington Park. By the time the economic hardship set in, the park's facilities were already nearing 10 years in age, including the peristyle, monuments, and park structures like the roads, benches, and some of the landscaping features. A reincarnation of the wooden roller coaster and other structures damaged in the 1915 fire were also aging and in need of repair.

The Civilian Conservation Corps (CCC), Federal Emergency Relief Administration (FERA), and Works Progress Administration (WPA) were the solutions to the city's needs. These programs were designed by President Roosevelt to employ millions of unemployed Americans across the country. Michigan City alone employed 2,000 people, mostly local workers, utilizing $660,000 in aid between 1929 and 1939. The materials for the park's restoration were donated or scavenged. According to *Lakefront Legacy*, the wooden roller coaster was torn down and used to create picnic tables and shelters to place throughout the park. Other structures met their demise in the same manner.

The areas in the city that benefited most were the park and the zoo. Washington Park saw the addition of rock structures that still stand today. Cages and housing throughout the zoo exhibit the work of the WPA, CCC, and FERA workers. In addition to structures in park, the workers implemented gardens, new tennis courts, parking lots, and an administration building for the park department. According to *Lakefront Legacy*, 400 concrete picnic tables and 700 benches were placed in the park. A water wheel and other structures were created during this period, including a sewage plant, naval armory, and a symbol that Michigan City has become proud of—the observation tower.

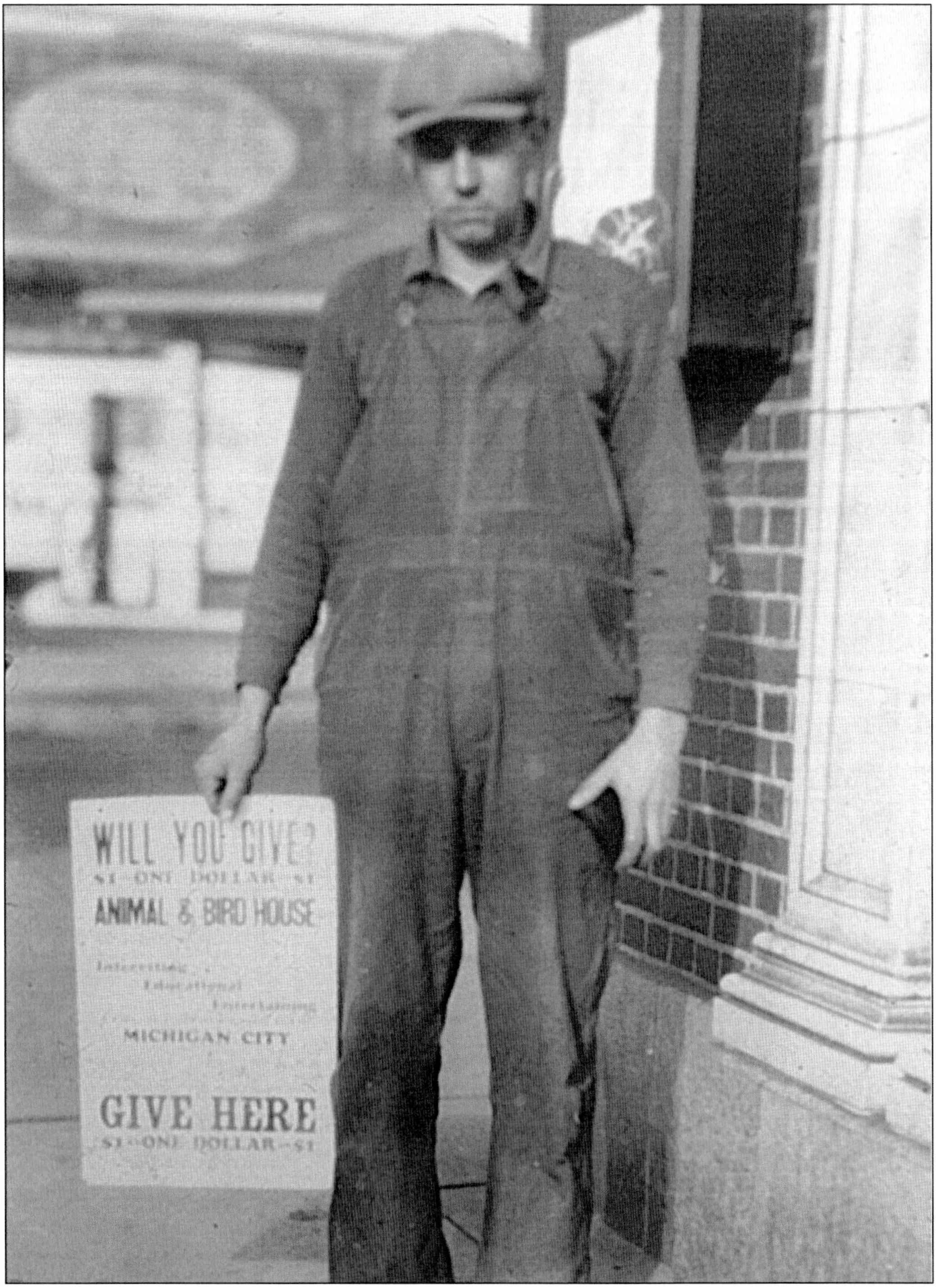

Donations provided financial support for the construction of a large part of the zoo and park during the Depression. The federal programs paid for the labor, but cities like Michigan City had to supply their own materials. This became a citywide effort. The man in the photograph holds a sign soliciting funding with the suggested donation of $1.

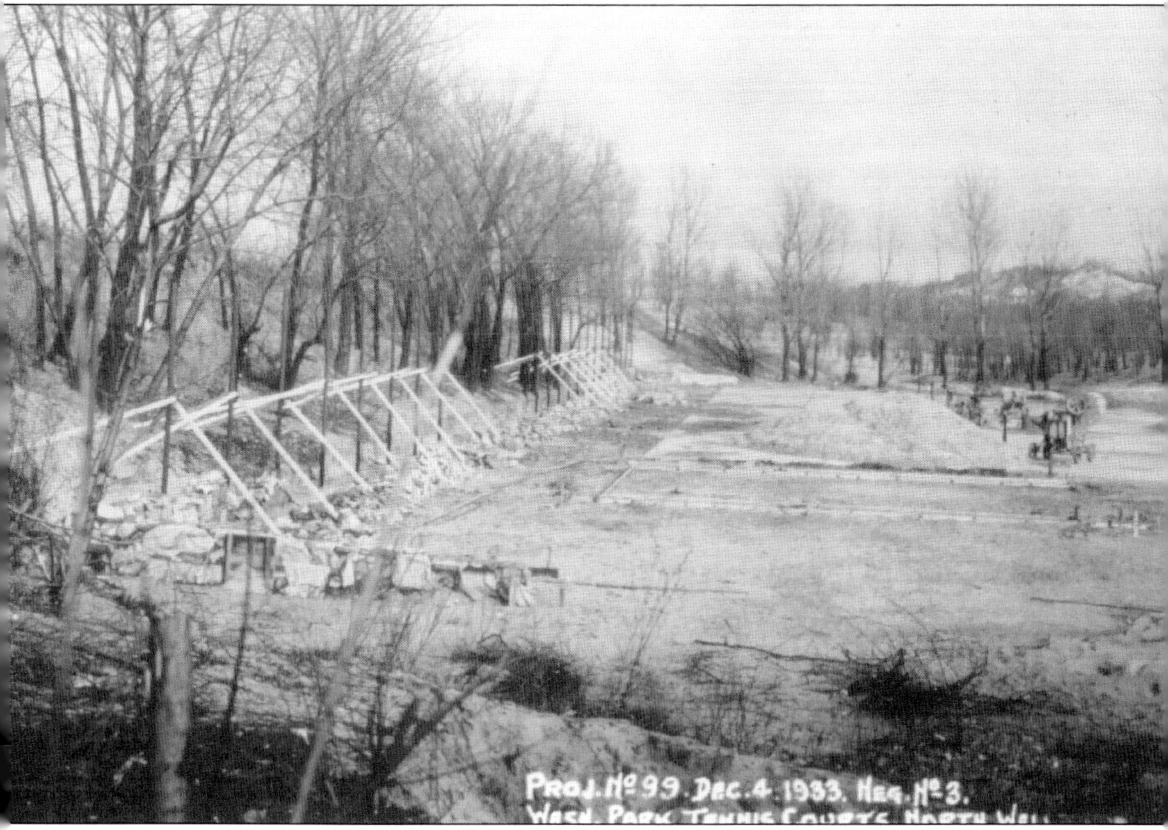

City residents worked shoulder to shoulder in building the modern version of the park and the zoo. Construction during the Depression created a park that varied greatly from the one that Michigan City saw through the park's beginnings in the late 1800s and early 1900s. Although the amusements would return, they were never as grand. Instead, the city opted for a more scenic, aesthetically pleasing park. This new concept would overtake the Washington Park landscape once the amusements left decades later.

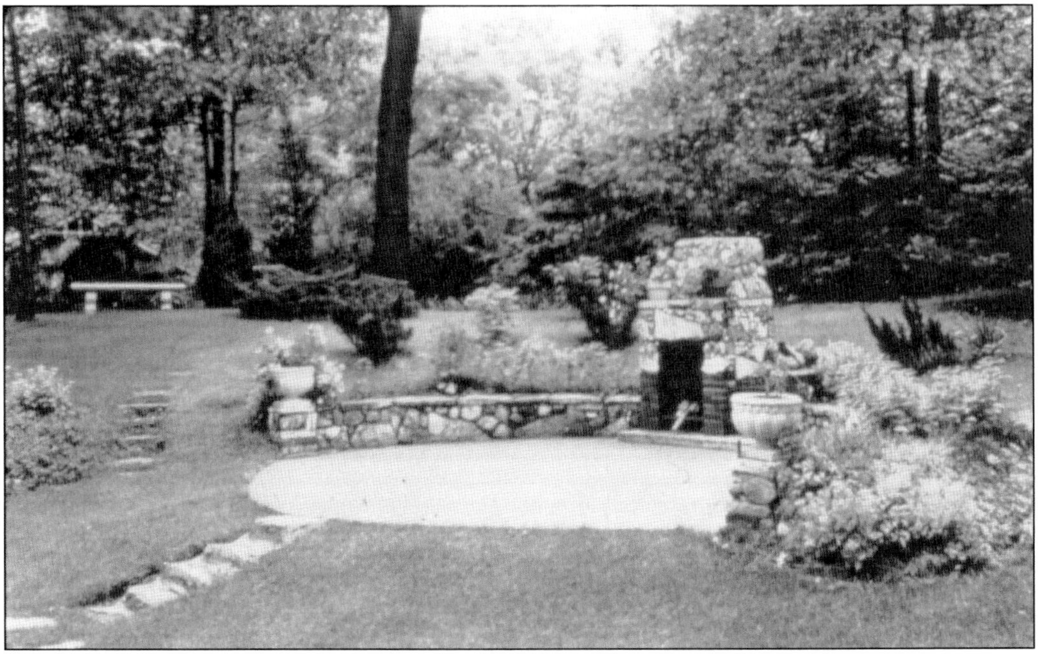

The stone and concrete structures like the one in this photograph have become familiar in Washington Park. The workers who built the structures in the 1930s did so in order to feed their families and were unconcerned with the legacy that was being left behind in the process.

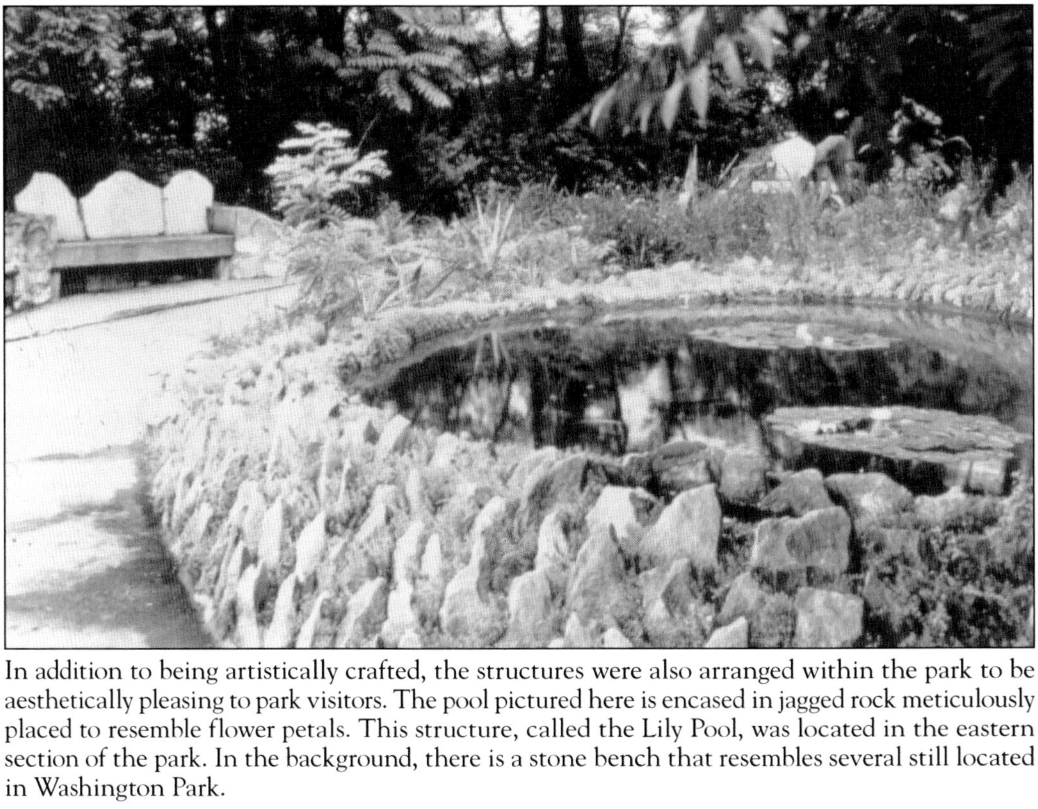

In addition to being artistically crafted, the structures were also arranged within the park to be aesthetically pleasing to park visitors. The pool pictured here is encased in jagged rock meticulously placed to resemble flower petals. This structure, called the Lily Pool, was located in the eastern section of the park. In the background, there is a stone bench that resembles several still located in Washington Park.

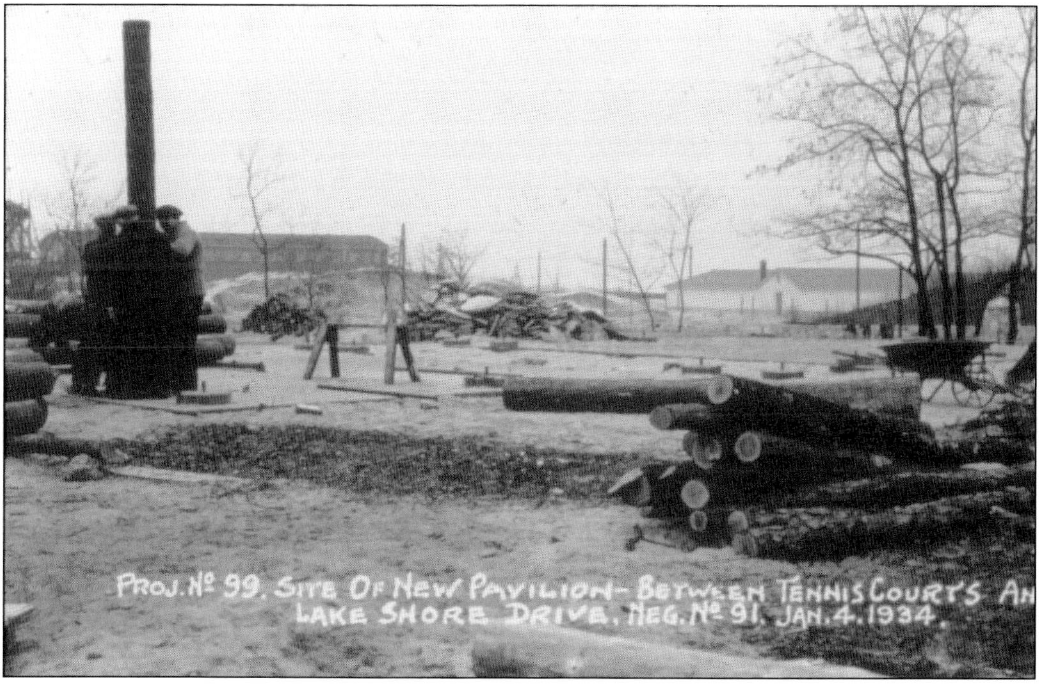

The above image captures work on a pavilion or shelter in Washington Park. Notice the project number, site description, and location; this photograph was probably taken as part of the project report on the federally funded work. The position of the work site between the tennis courts and Lakeshore Drive (the road running along the south side of Washington Park) indicates that this is the construction of one of the large pavilions in the park (below) that very well may still exist.

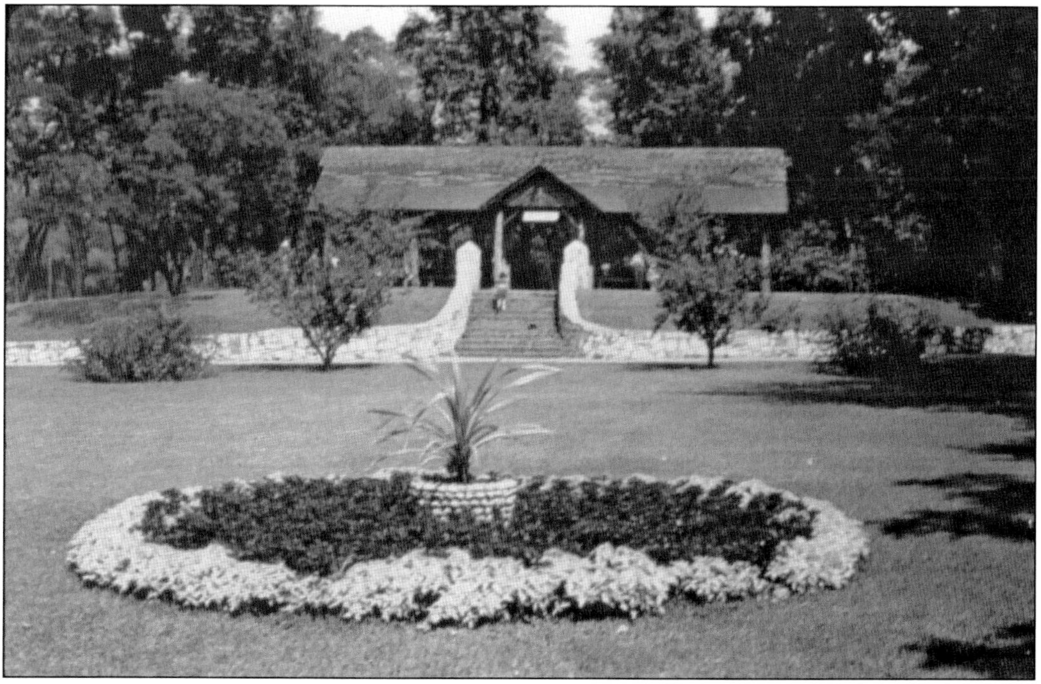

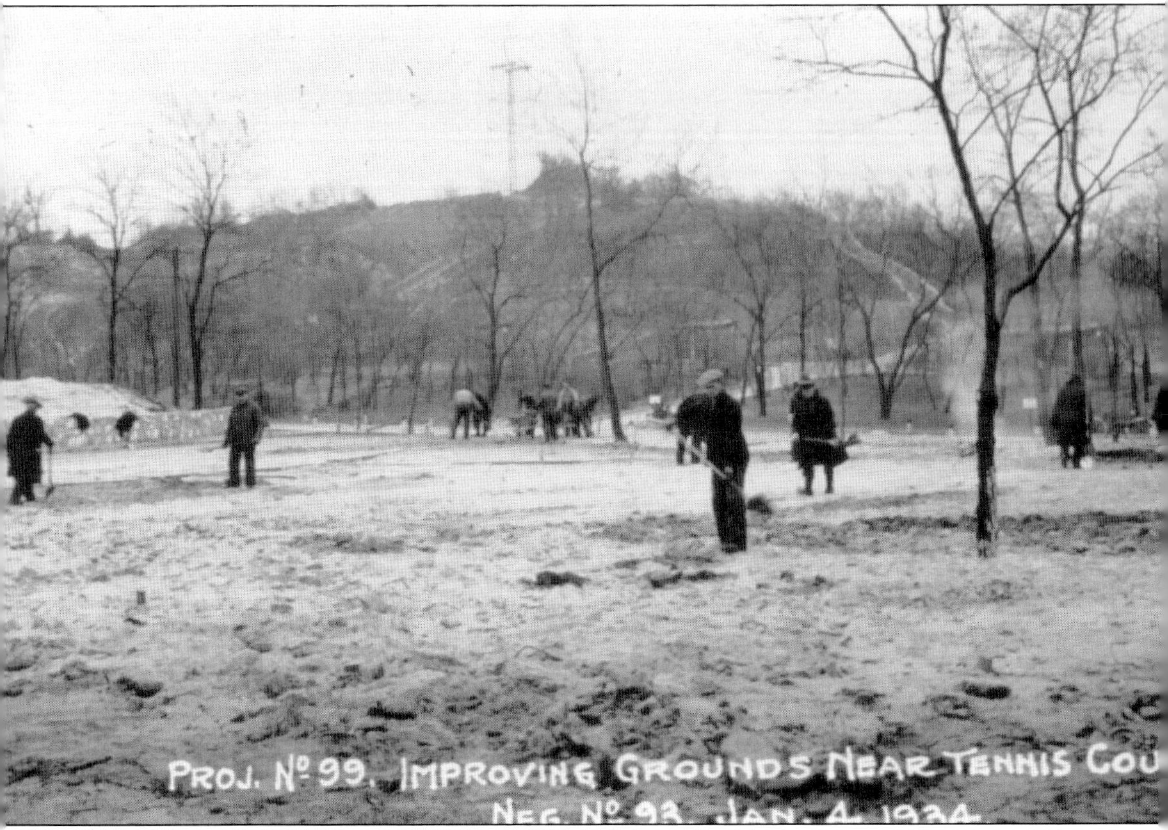

The famous Washington Park tennis courts were improved using shovels and manpower. The structure at the top of the hill is the observation tower in progress; the stone-lined roads running up to the tower can be seen. These were built by WPA, CCC, and FERA workers as well. To the back left stands a new stone wall that is still in the park today.

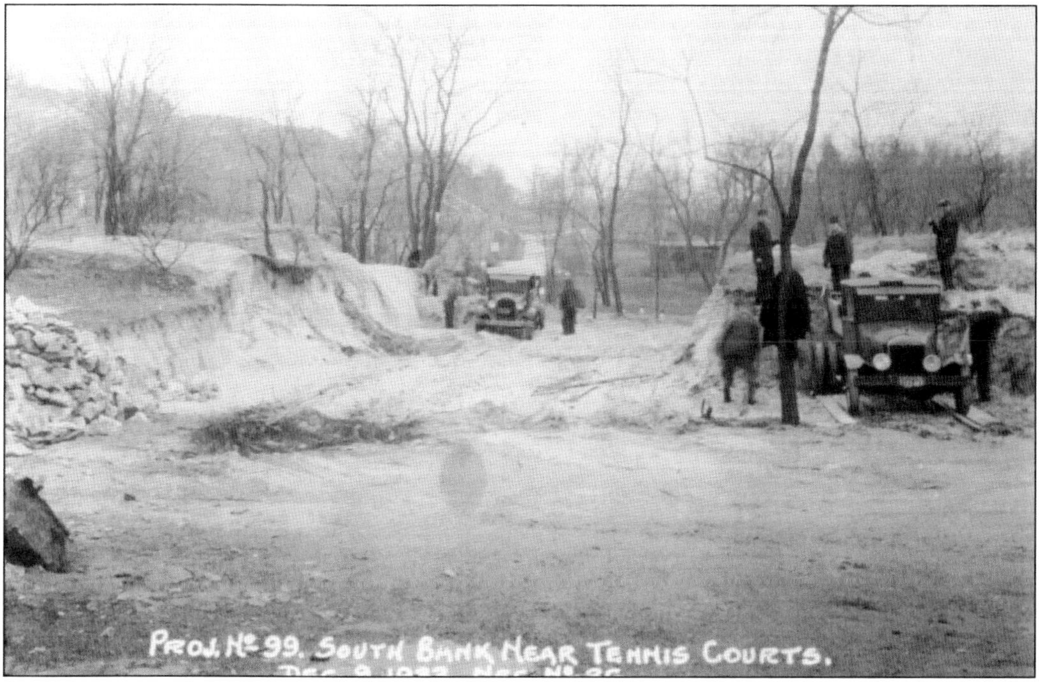

Cutting into the sand dune that part of the park was built on was necessary in order to aesthetically improve it. Again, manpower and shovels were the tools used to do the job in many cases.

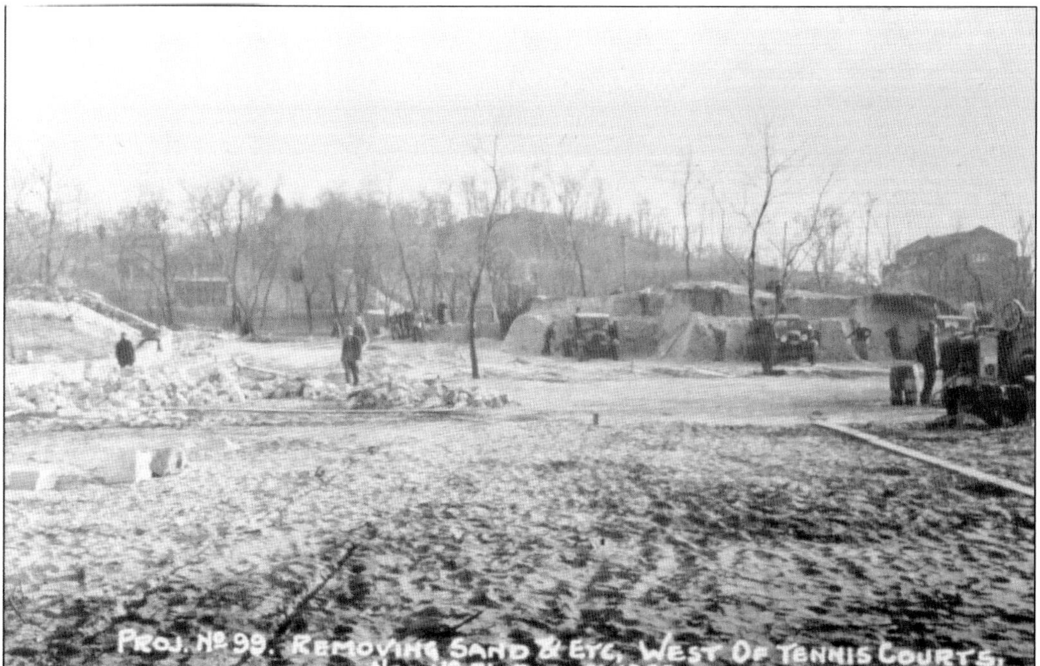

Work on the tennis courts did require filling the space with sand in order to raise it. The bleak look of the park at that time was a far cry from the finished product.

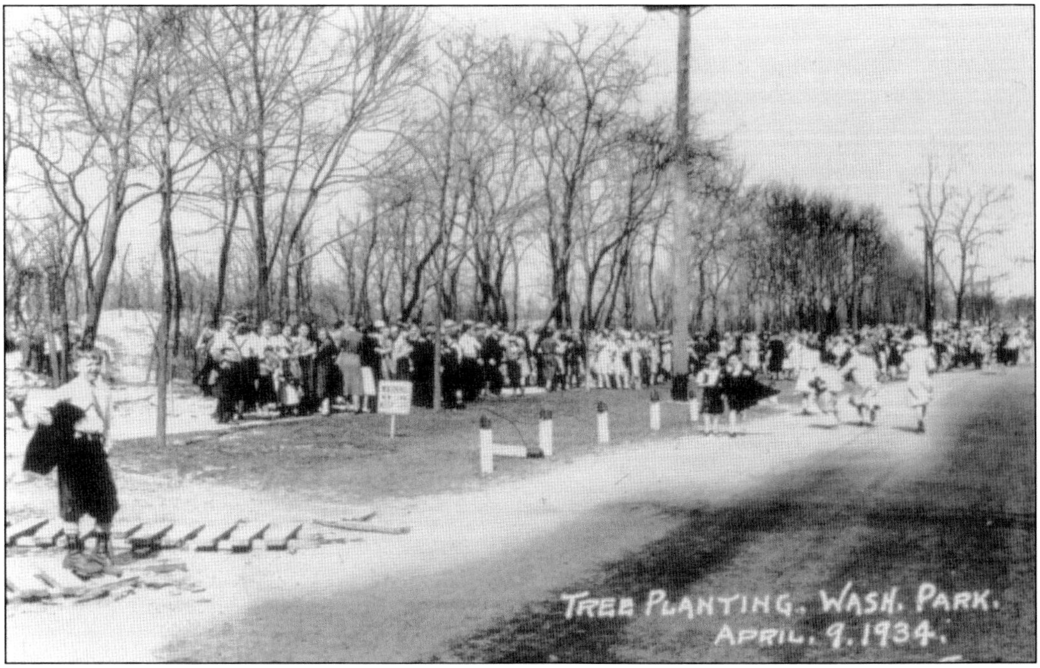

On Arbor Day in 1934, several businesspeople in town donated trees to the park. Children from the Michigan City schools were brought out to Washington Park to plant them. As the workers finished projects throughout the area, the ravaged land looked barren. The tree planting was a way to fill in these spaces, as well as plant a forest for future park visitors to enjoy. The planting is very similar to that performed by the townspeople after Washington Park was cleaned, cleared, and graded in the 1890s, and the trees were planted for similar reasons in both instances. The saplings became the towering arboreal beauties that shade the park today.

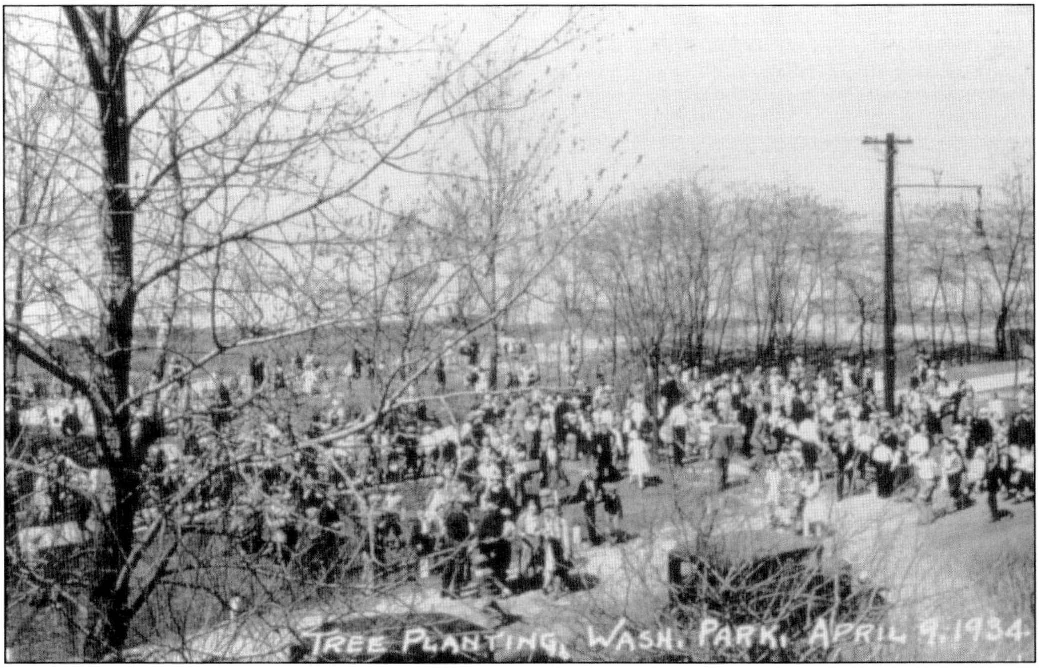

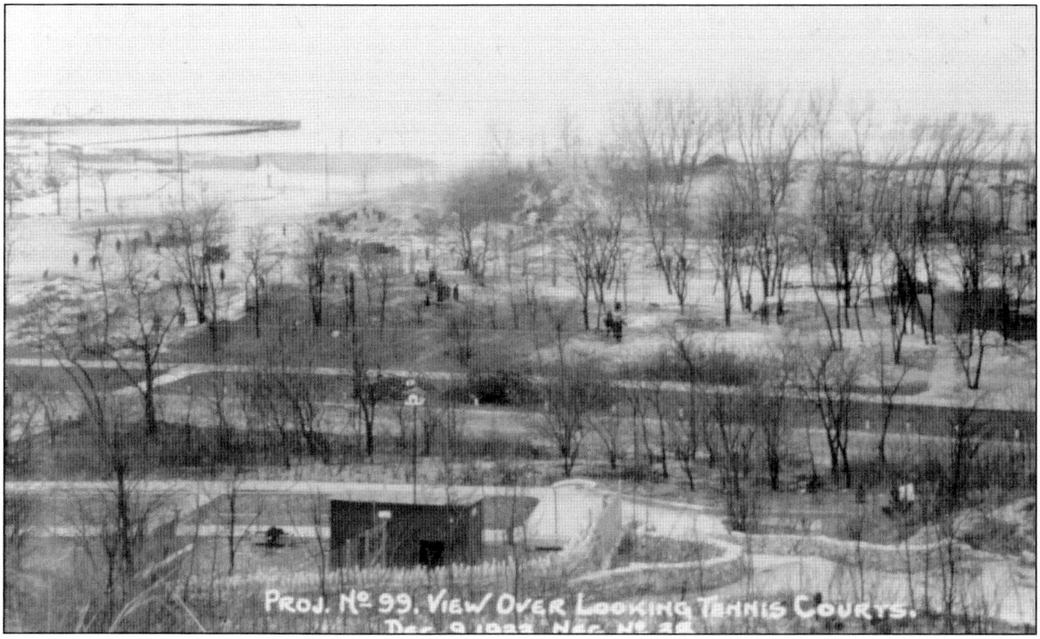

This image was taken from the top of Yankee Slide, Hoosier Slide's sister hill that went untouched during the sand harvesting. The view of the park illustrates the extent of the reconstruction. Gone are the large amusement structures that dotted that lakefront. Fortunately, the Oasis is still there. When it was completed, Washington Park's landscape included pavilions, gardens, trails, benches, and stone walls. The tennis pavilion is still adorned with the stone walls created during the Depression.

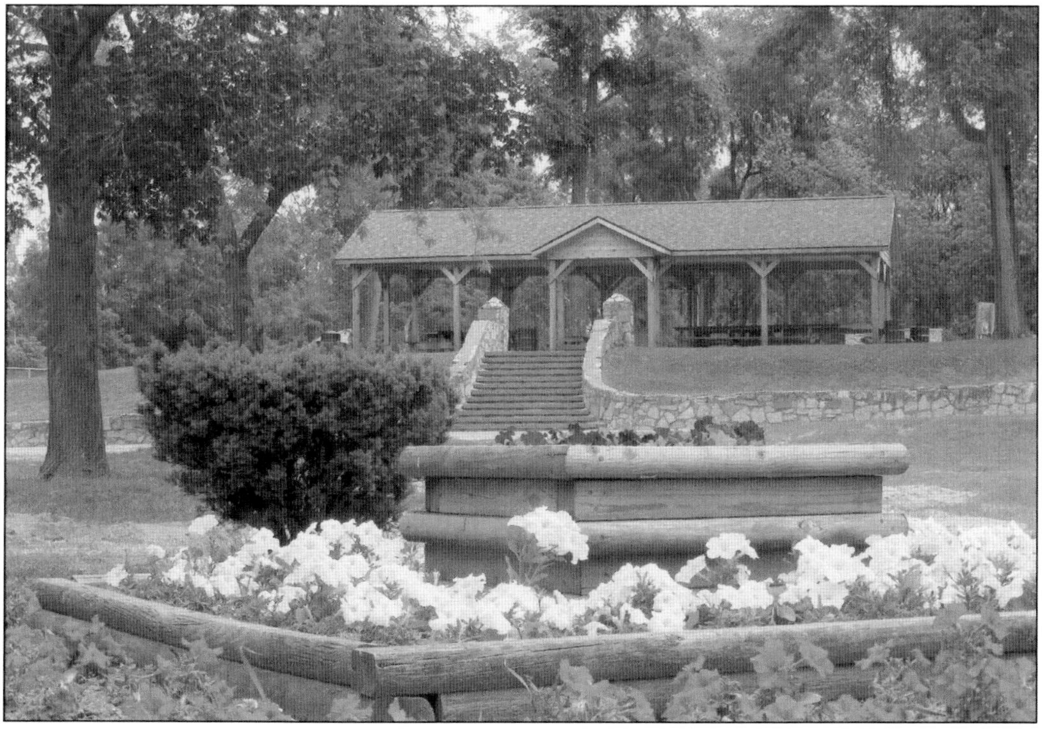

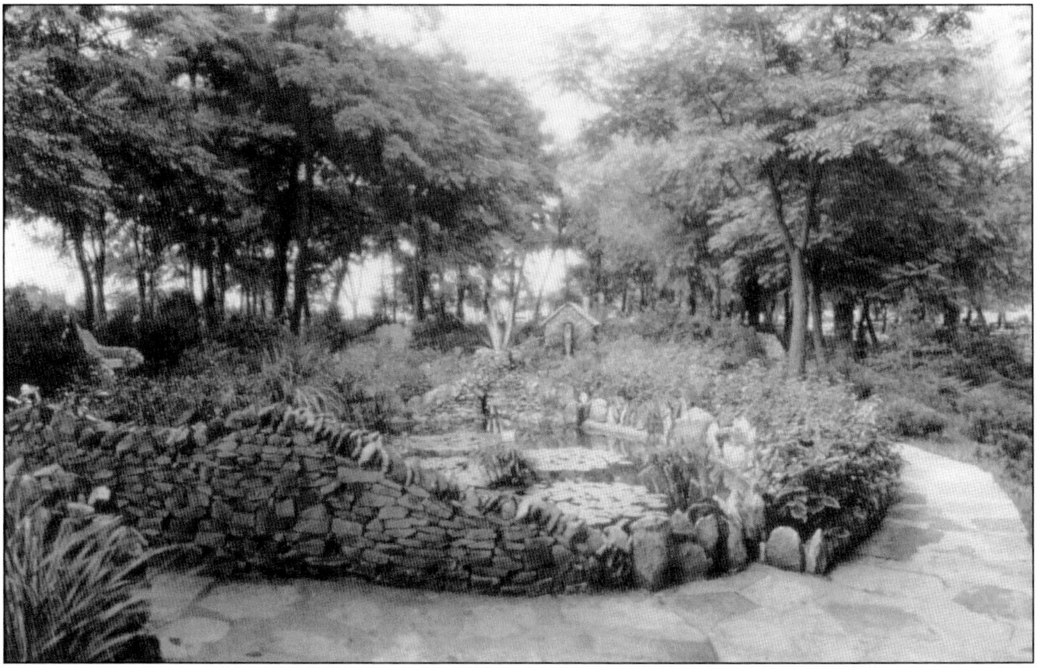

Found in Washington Park, this pond and fountain display more of the artistry that went into the work performed by participants in the WPA, CCC, and FERA projects. Over the years, the park department worked hard to protect and preserve these pieces. In the image above, the stonework pathways that were placed throughout the park can be seen. In the photograph below, the stone benches are shown in Washington Park today. They are still utilized by the public and maintained by the park department.

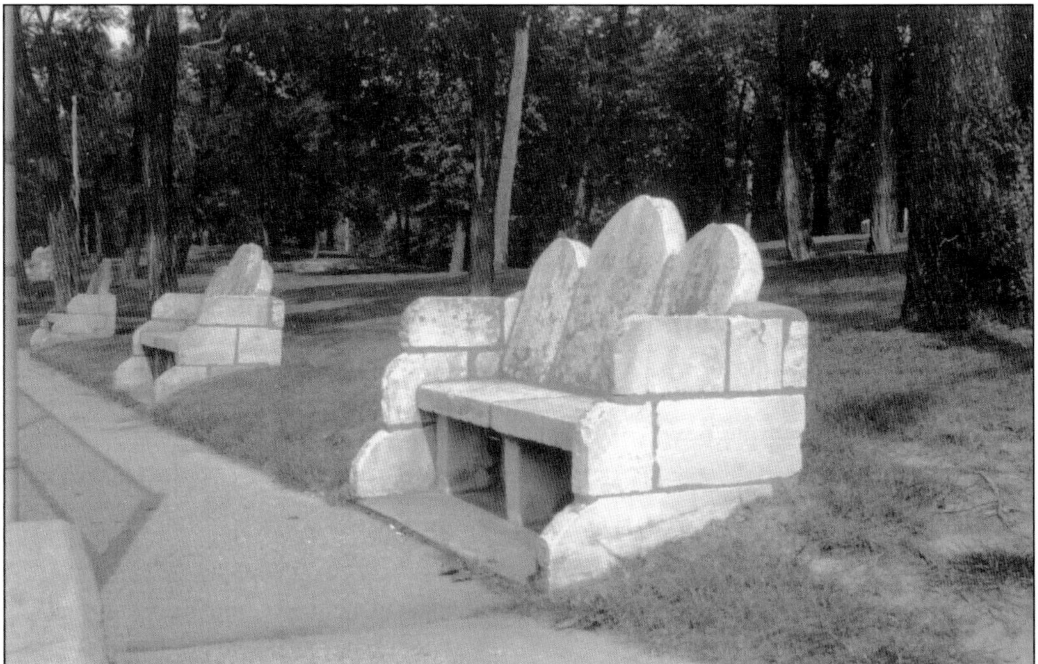

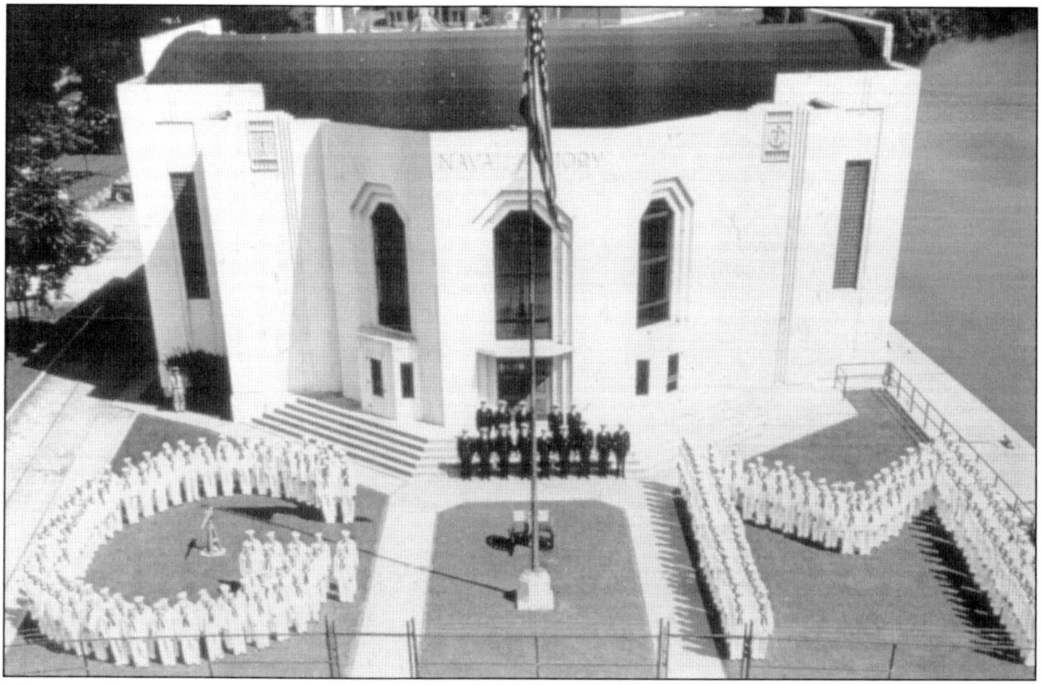

The naval armory was resurrected during this period. It stands on the shore of Trail Creek, immediately to the east of the Franklin Street Bridge and across Lakeshore Drive from Washington Park. The design is considered art deco, constructed of white stucco, and very modern for the times. The naval armory has stood overlooking the park since its construction in 1939.

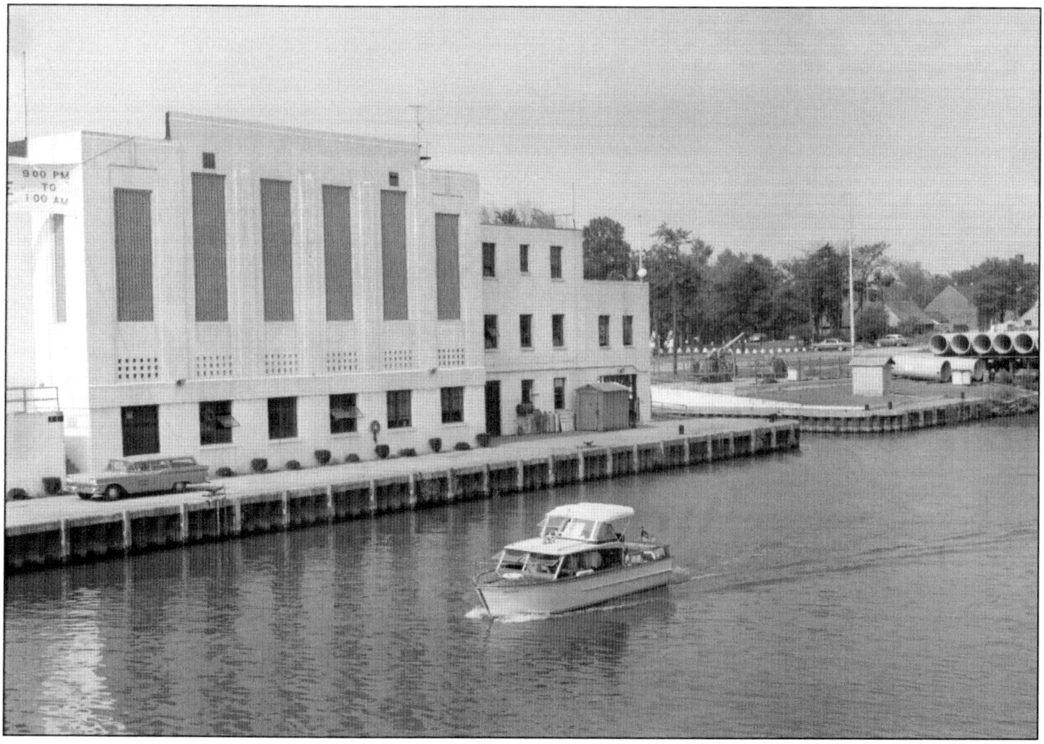

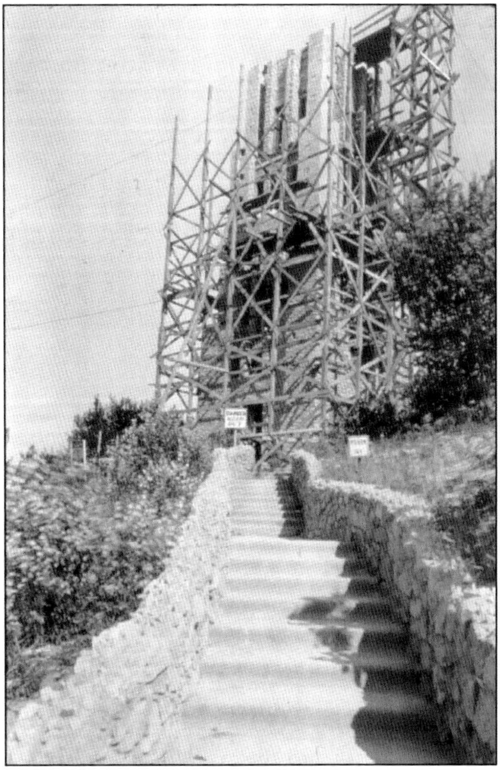

The observation tower was reportedly the first project application that Michigan City submitted to the federal government for funding. Established in 1935, the tower was built from steel donated by the South Shore Railroad. Michigan City residents working under the WPA at the time constructed the stone steps and walls seen in both images. They put considerable amounts of labor into the building of the tower.

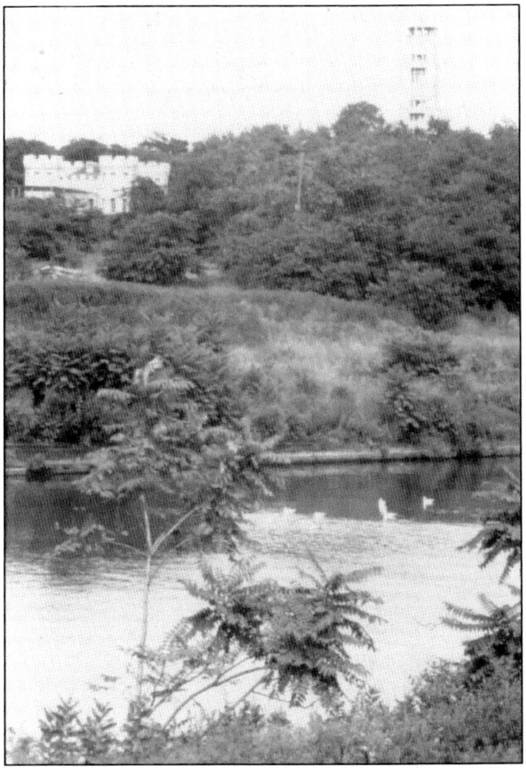

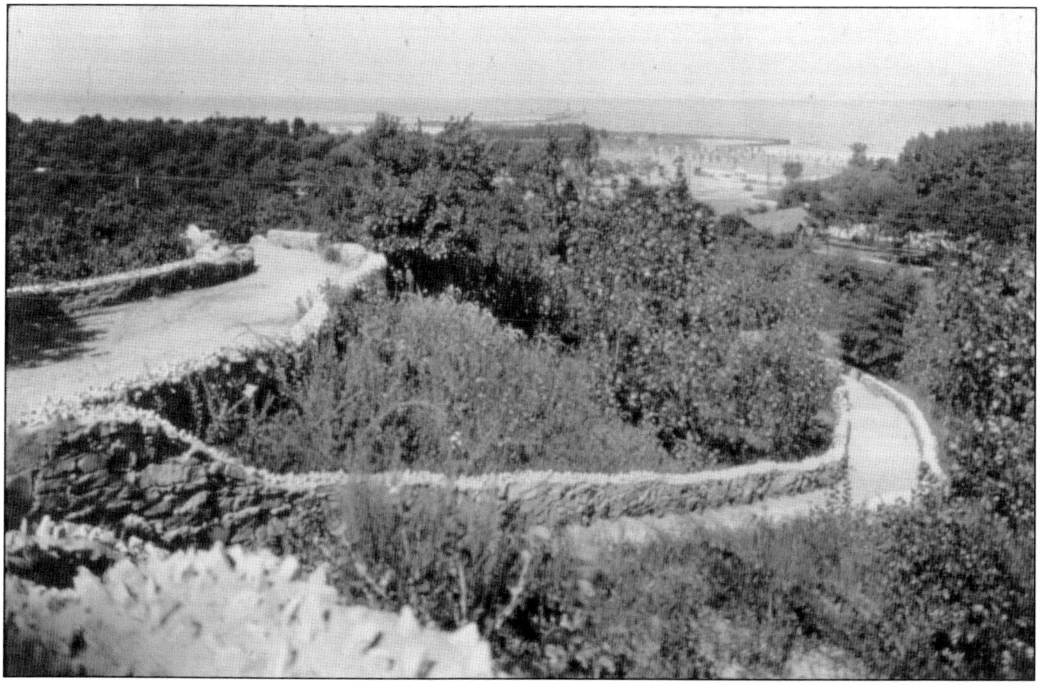

In constructing the observation tower, the city chose a place that would give the viewer an unimpaired view of the city and the lakefront. Even pathways leading to the tower on the north of Yankee Slide provide visitors a panoramic view of the park and beach. Although trees have filled in the dune since the tower was constructed in 1937, the effect is still the same.

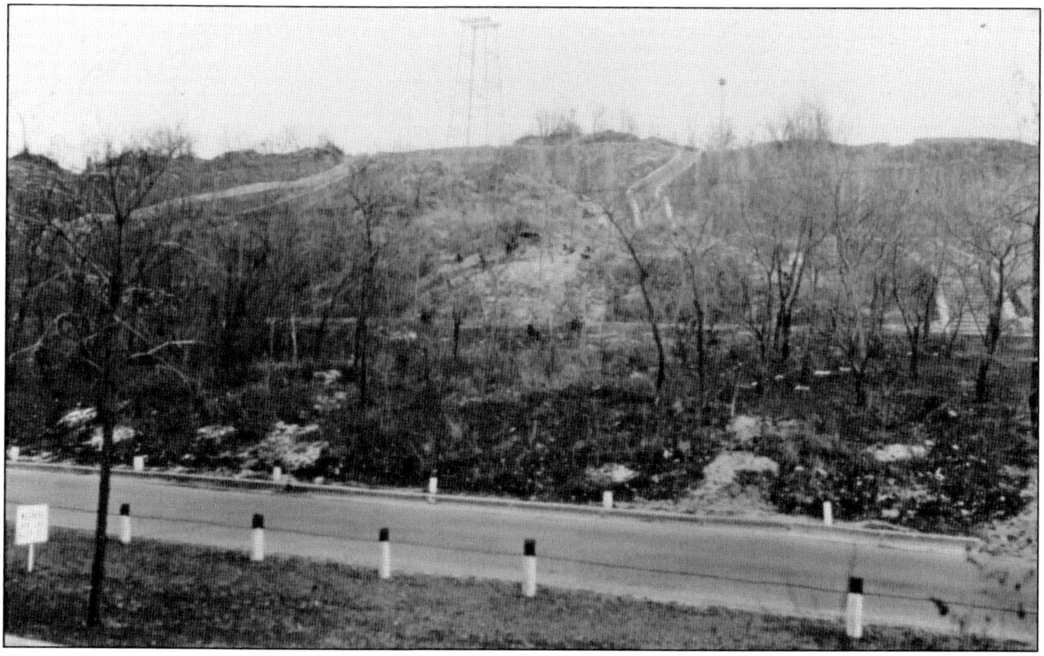

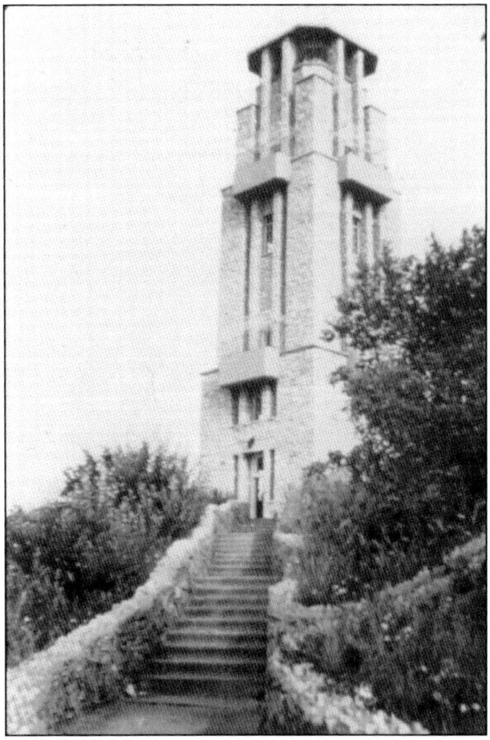

The observation tower was dedicated on May 5, 1937. Among the many points of interest in the building was the chrome top of the tower. It is a compression chamber that came from the very first fire engine Michigan City owned. Park department officials experimented with lighting to make the tower more visible and attractive in the night sky. (Courtesy of Mike and Kathy Fleming.)

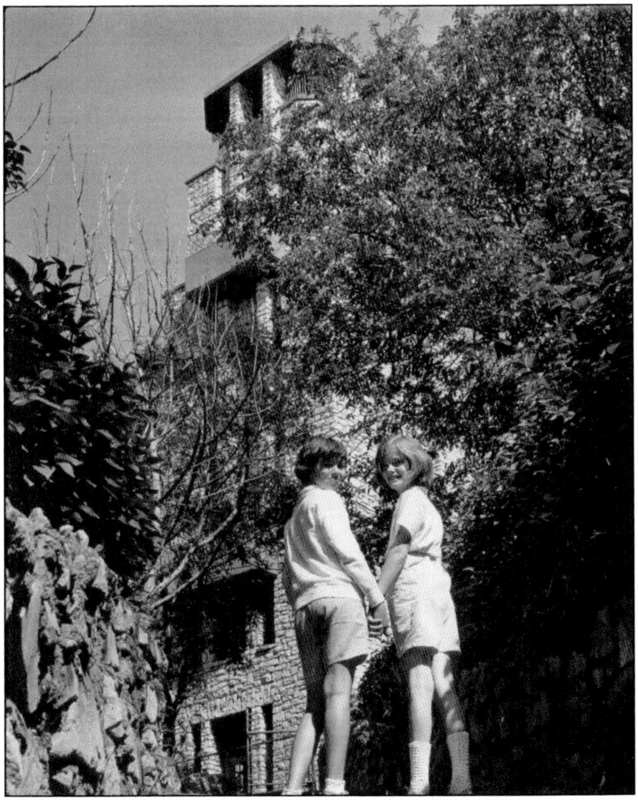

Five

Oasis in the Sand

In the 1920s, Michigan City already had a dance hall. This was not the initial purpose of the Oasis, and, in fact, that was not even the building's original name. Gambling was a craze, making its way through the nation, and many visitor hot spots like Michigan City sought to cash in on it with its own casino with a lake view. In 1922, the Lakeview Casino opened next to the amusement park, offering adults the opportunity to gamble away their hard-earned dollars that were not spent by the kids on rides and concessions. The casino was similar to those found in Atlantic City at the time, featuring slot machines, food, a hall for entertainment, and table gambling.

The casino did not take hold in such a family-friendly atmosphere. The desert oasis theme used to decorate the place became the new name after the slot machines were removed and a dance floor was installed. In 1927, the Oasis was born. According to the memories of those who once frequented the ballroom, the dance hall was the best in Indiana. It was also said to be the largest, capable of holding 2,400 people comfortably.

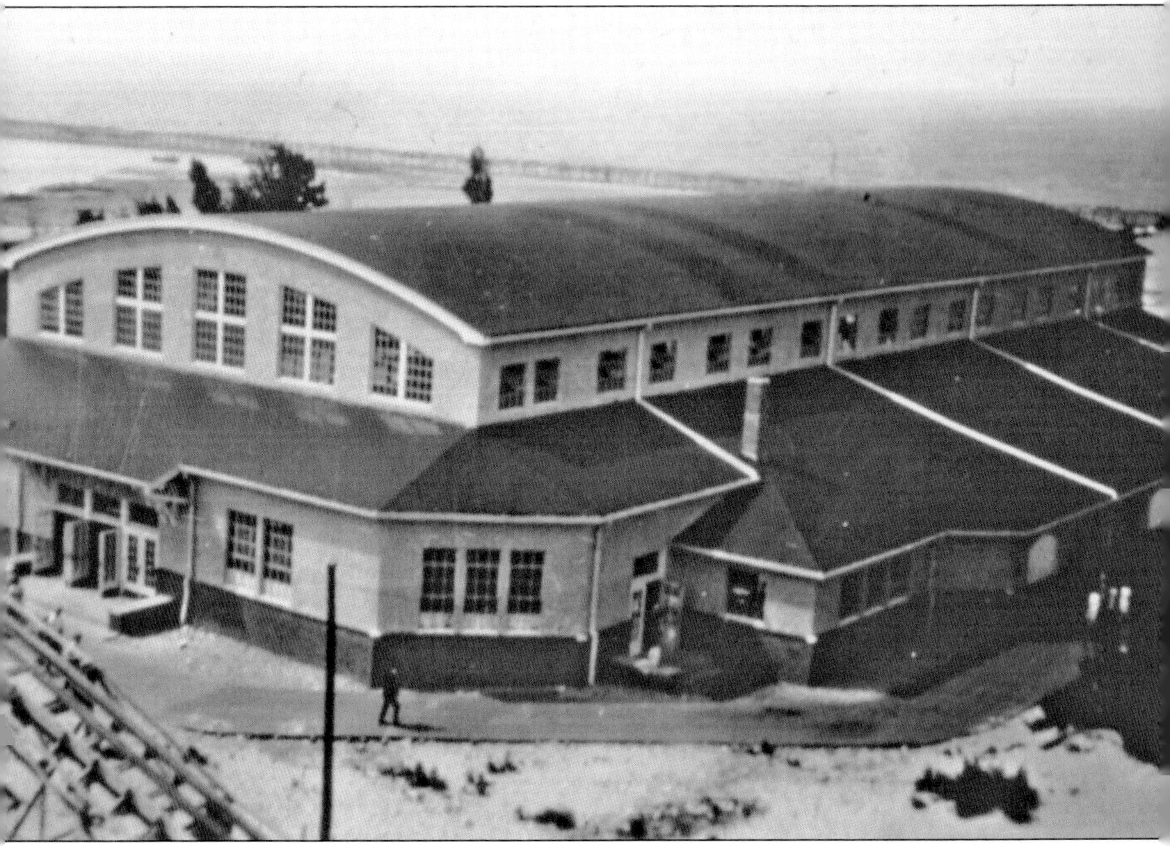

The building was not air-conditioned, but it was cooled with night breezes off Lake Michigan. The large building accommodated multiple events with room to contain food services as well. There was a café to feed hungry dancers before or after a spin on the dance floor. According to the *News Dispatch* article "Michigan City's Oasis by the Lake," written by Fern Eddy Schultz, the cafe served a common menu of fried chicken sandwiches, steaks, pork chops, and various snacks. Schultz remembers a soda fountain service at the cafe as well.

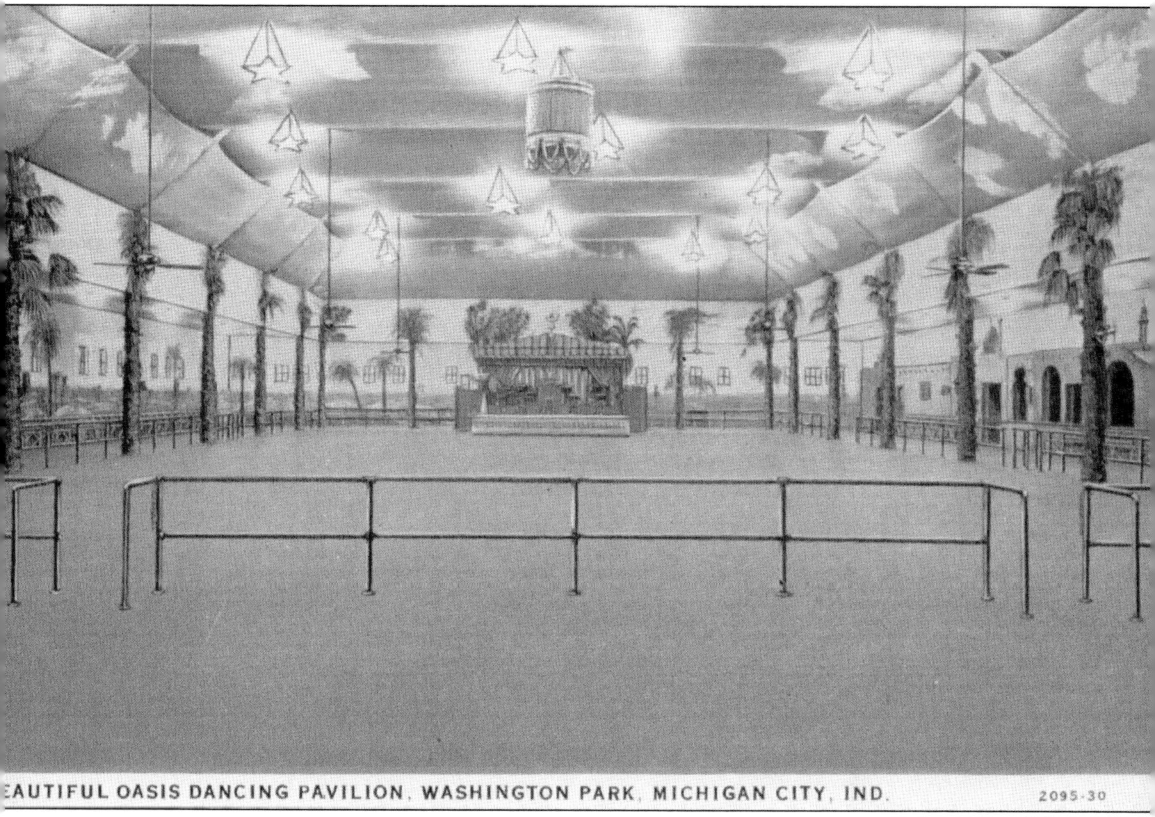

Inside, tropical-themed walls lined the dance hall. The theme was left over from the days of the Lakeview Casino. The Oasis decor became well known throughout the region, and bands regularly played on the stage seen in this photograph.

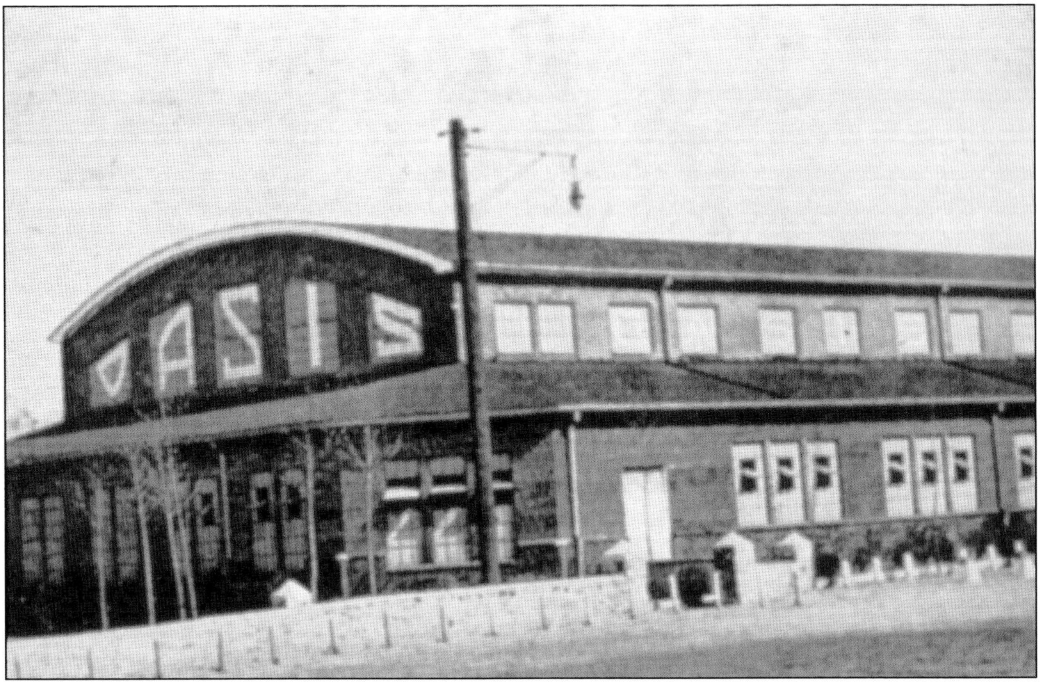

The Oasis sat on the property now occupied by the public beach parking lot. The immense space surrounding the building was to accommodate parking at the time as well. Patrons could come and go at the Oasis without paying a new fee each time, because the hands of each paying customer were stamped. Upon reentering the dance hall, a special light (not unlike those used in clubs today) highlighted the stamp. Outside, there was plenty more to see and do.

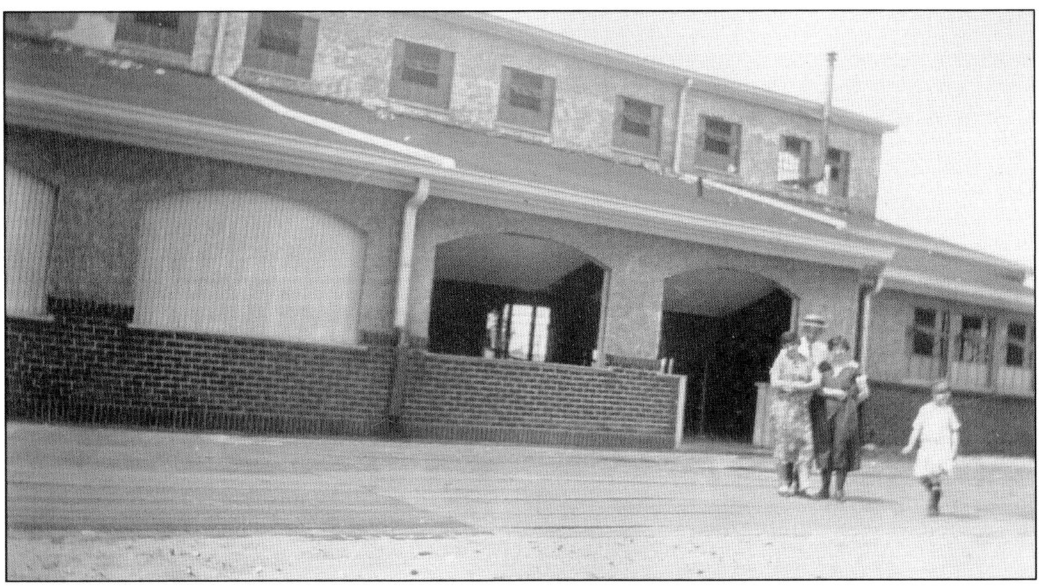

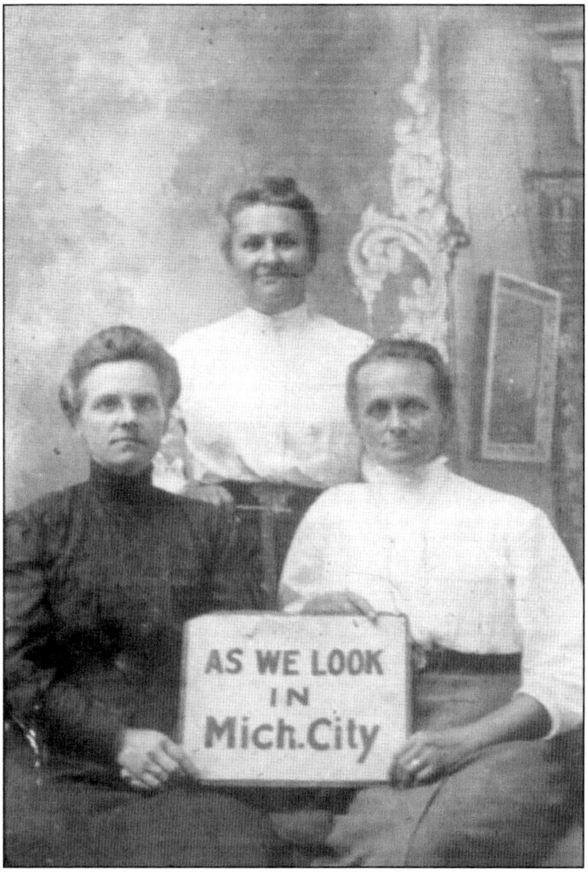

The Oasis was a part of the boardwalk connected to the amusement sector of the park, where visitors could ride the rides (the roller coaster and Air Swing were still in operation during these early years). Some city residents recall nickelodeons and a particular machine that told fortunes, while others remember posing for souvenir photographs to take back home.

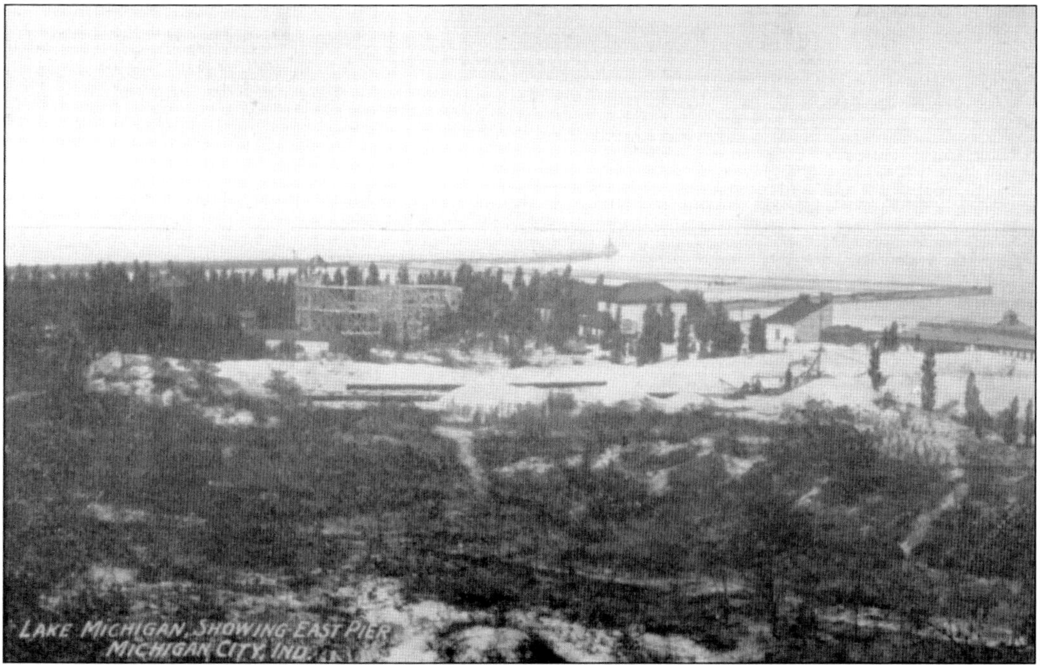

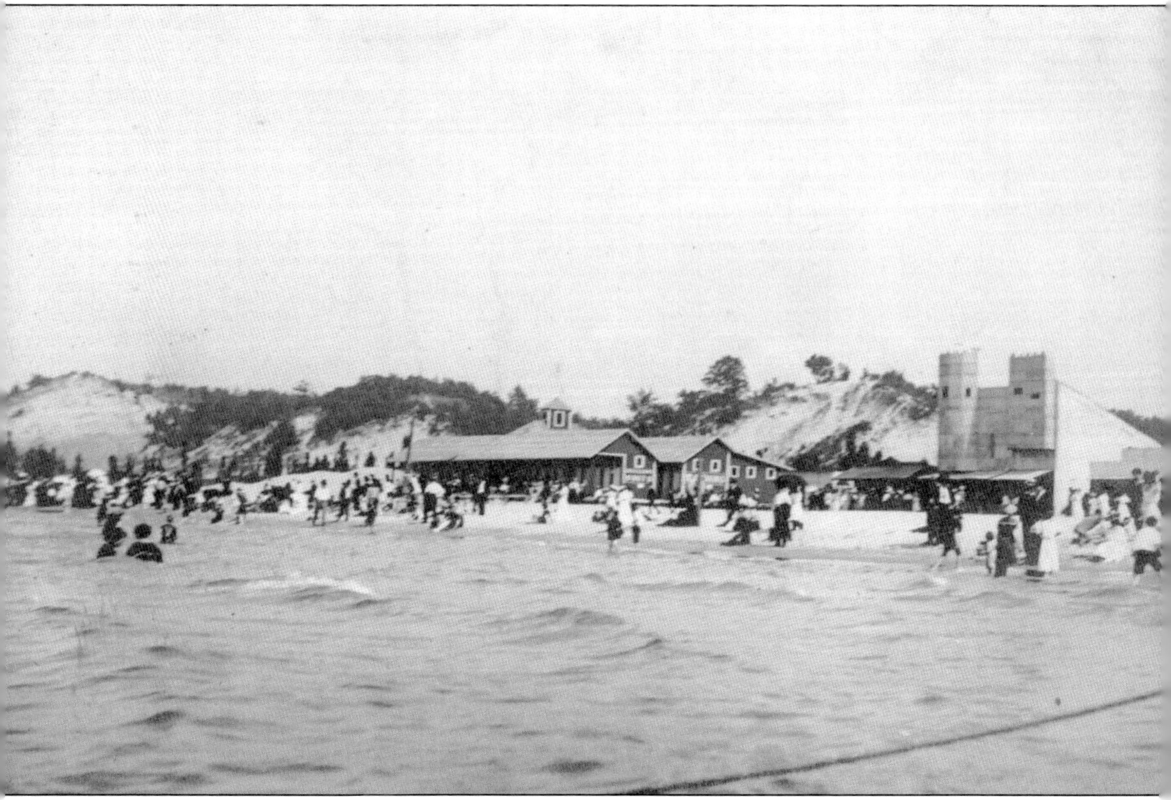

Dancers could play a game and try to win a souvenir or run out to the beach for a splash in the water. The latter was only for those who dared, as the water and dancing attire was not a good match. Many couples opted for a stroll in the cool summer night, taking in the scenery before heading home or returning to the party.

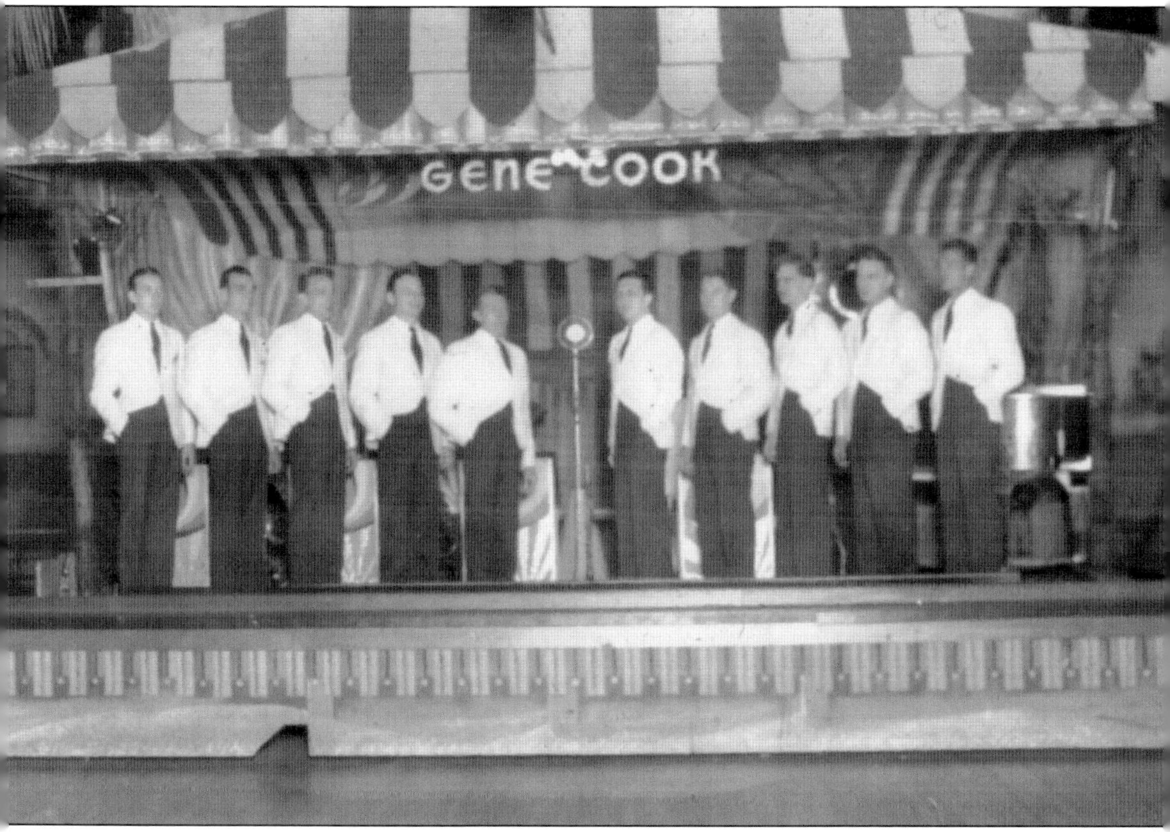

There was always a party at the Oasis. Created during the age of the big band era, the dance hall was a popular tour spot for the most popular big band names at the time. Gene Cook was one who frequented Michigan City to play with his band, Gene Cook and the Cookies, at the Oasis. Their presence was a big boost to business for the dance hall. The group is pictured here, performing onstage at the Oasis.

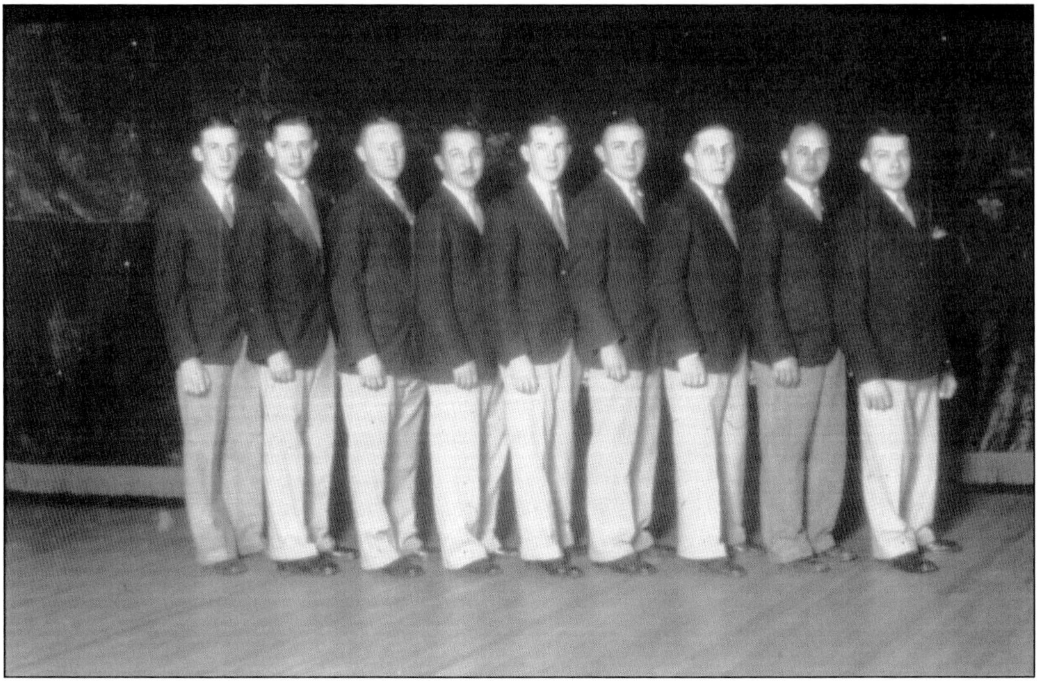

Instead of dancing along to the bands playing on a radio, one could go to the beach to hear, see, and mingle with them live. Other big acts to perform at the Oasis included Count Basie, Duke Ellington, Lawrence Welk, Tommy Dorsey, Jan Gerber, Clyde McCoy, Cab Calloway, and others. Sammy Kaye filmed his popular show, *So You Want to Lead a Big Band*, at the Oasis too. Local bands like Dick Cook and his Footwarmers, seen above, were also featured amongst the big names. Gene Cook and the Cookies are preparing to perform in the image below.

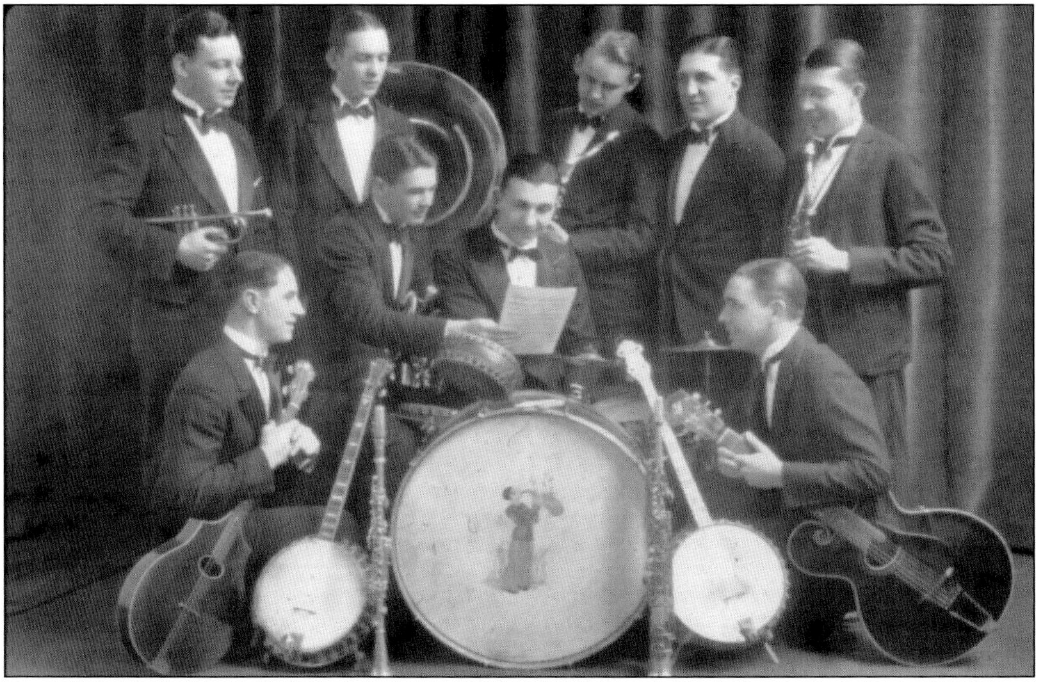

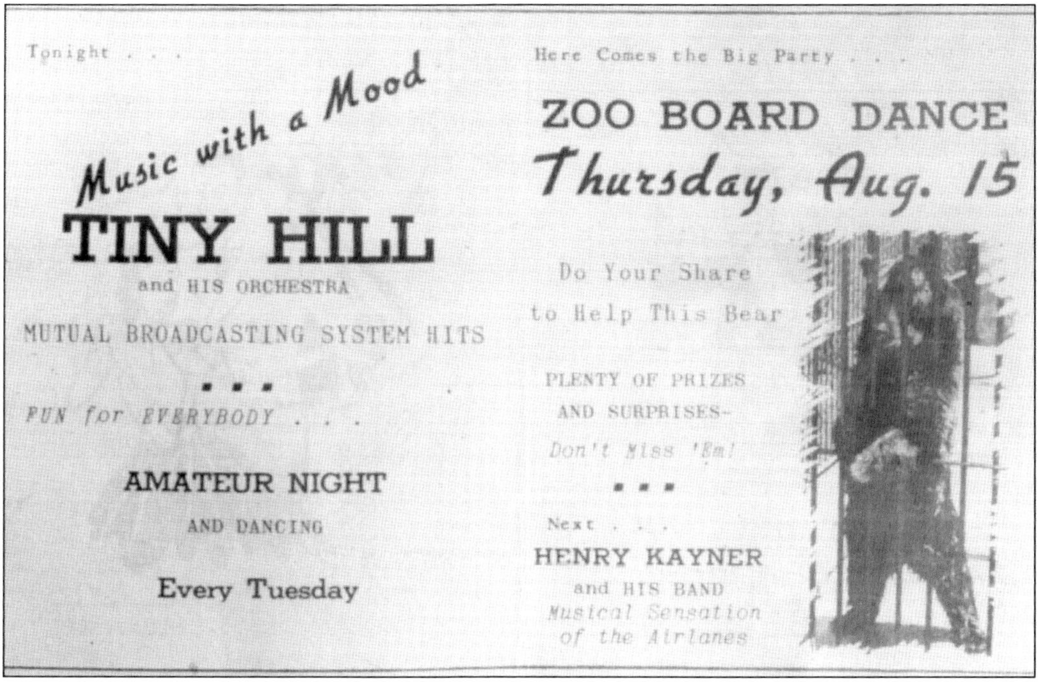

The Oasis had programs that encouraged visitors to dance the night away. They also admonished the holders not to throw the programs away, as there was a space for autographs on the back. The program seen above introduces Jerry Livingston and Martha Wayne, along with a night of swing music courtesy of Horace Henderson. The program below touts the Tiny Hill Orchestra and amateur night. Local agencies such as the Washington Park Zoo used the Oasis for fundraising.

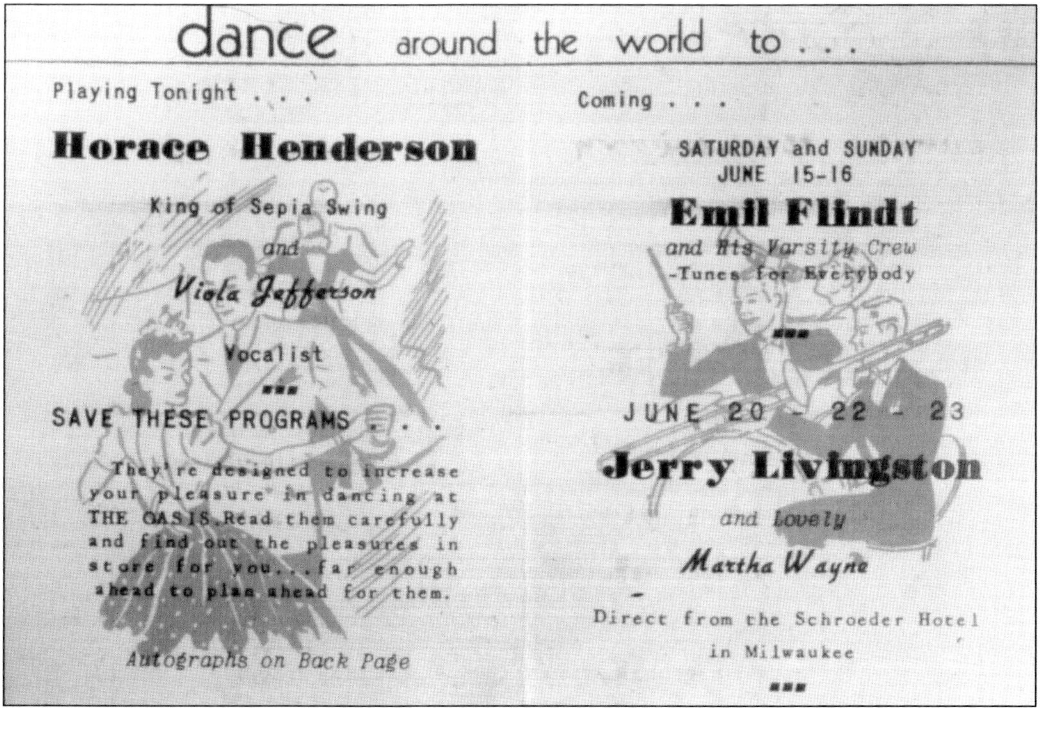

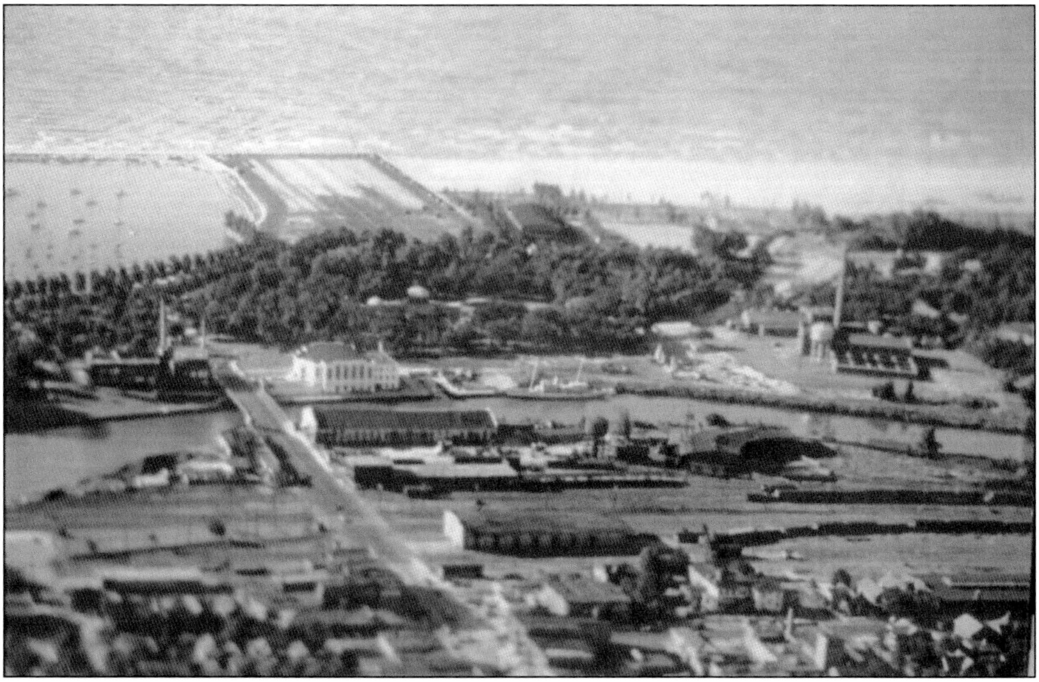

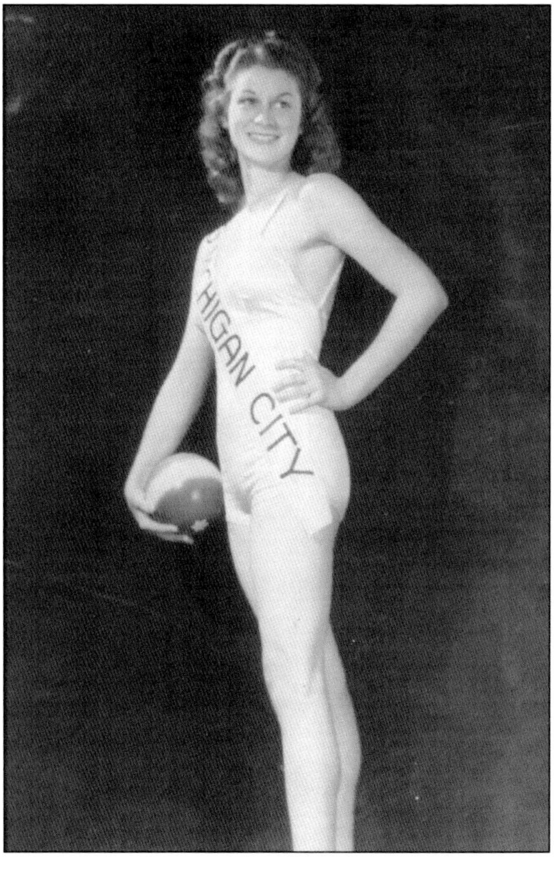

When not in use as a nightclub or dance hall, the Oasis was the perfect size for pageants and large shows. The annual auto show, Town and Country Fair, and home show were all staged in the building. It was only open for dances Thursday through Sunday nights, so weddings and gatherings were also possible if the parties were flexible. The park department did create a large parking lot between the Oasis and the marina to accommodate the increase in activity. The Oasis's rounded roof is visible in the aerial view above.

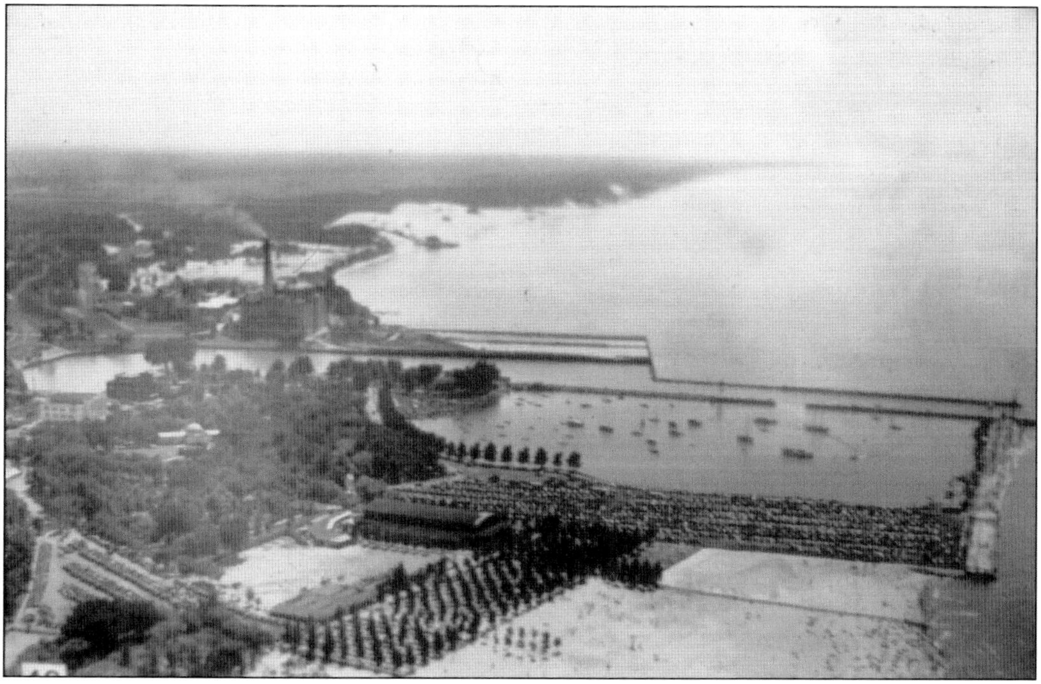

Another view of the Oasis from the air captures it on busy day. The parking lot beside the building is practically full of cars. The image below illustrates just how close the Oasis was to the bathing beach.

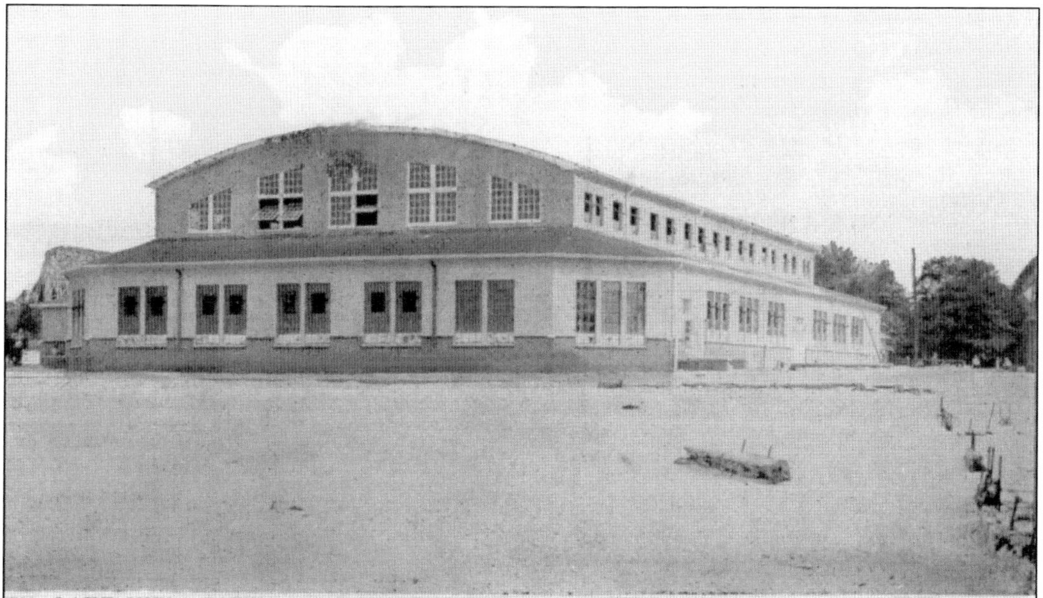

4702—LAKE VIEW CASINO, WASHINGTON PARK, MICHIGAN CITY, IND.

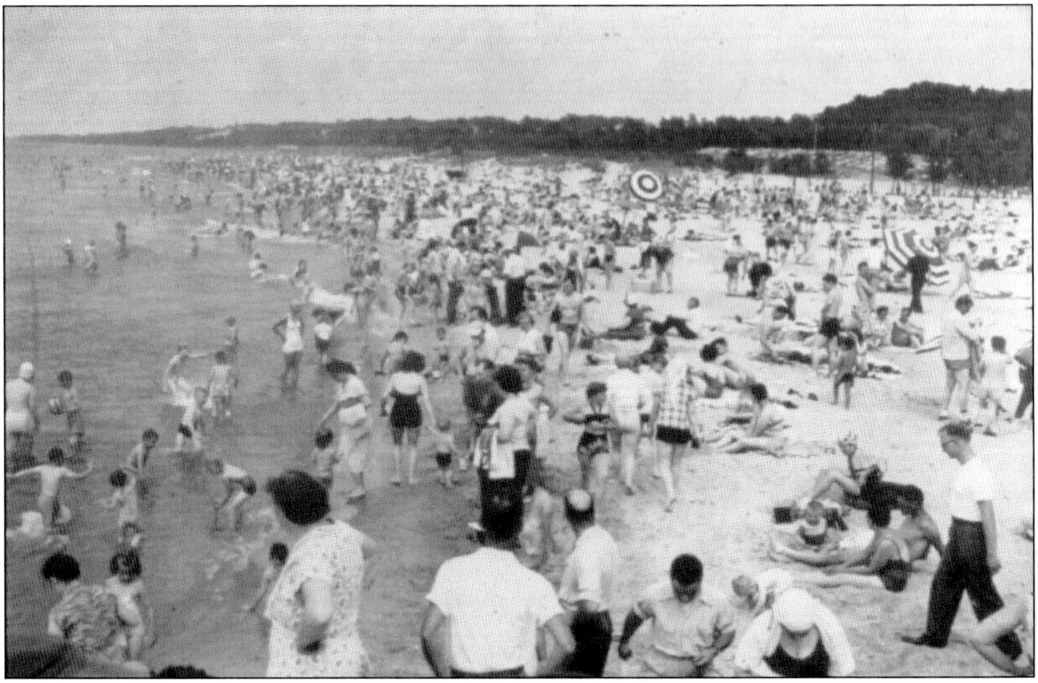

Harold Barr also managed the Oasis during its heyday in the 1930s and 1940s. In an issue of *Billboard* magazine, Barr explained how business began to drop off in 1949. The big band era was ending, and Barr tried to compensate by placing pinball machines and games inside the building in an effort to draw the younger crowds that once frequented the hall. This was just one of many things that signaled the end of the constant celebration on the lakefront.

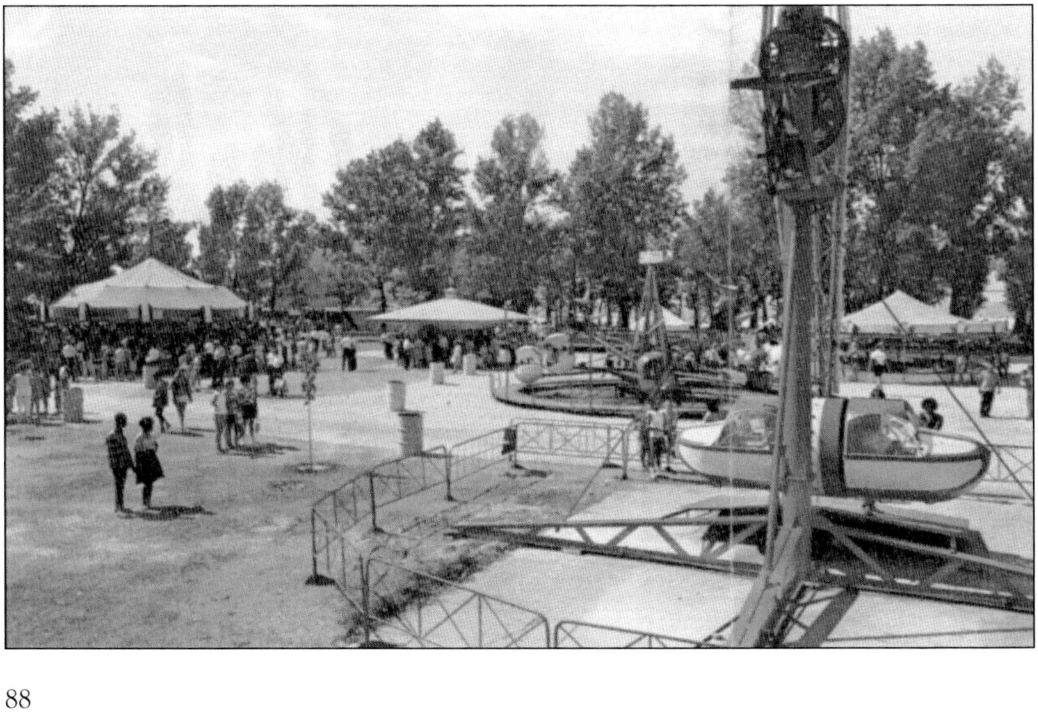

Six

When the Music Died

Several factors conspired to herald the end of amusements in Washington Park. Many people have their own theories, but, officially, age and neglect ended things on the lakefront. However, that was not entire story. Washington Park's amusement sector could have outlasted any one of the factors that ended in its demise, as other amusement parks all over the country had done successfully. The problem that truly ended amusement in Michigan City was much bigger than shoddy maintenance and old equipment. Although these were the factors that ultimately did close the amusement era of the park, problems had begun long before that.

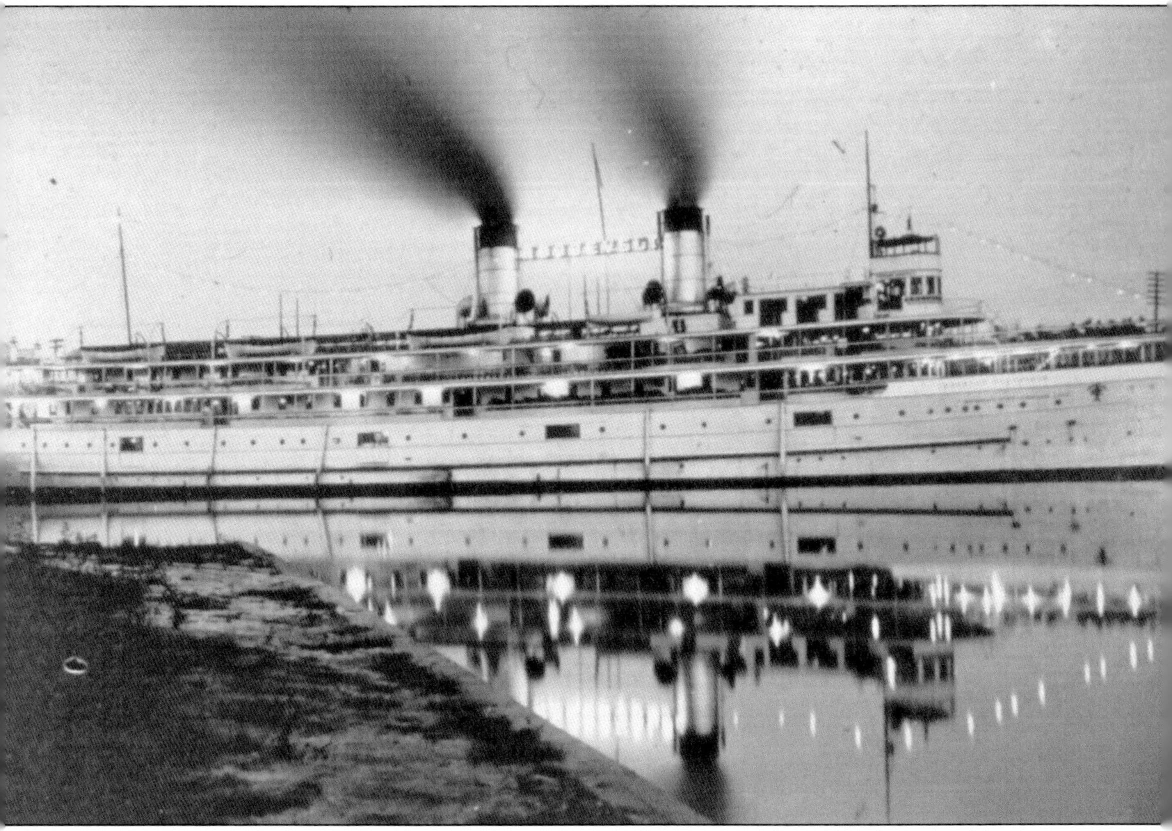

The first event occurred early on. Although it made just a ripple in the demise of the amusement park, it was enough to get the ball rolling. In the early 1900s, excursion boats brought people to Michigan City in droves. They unloaded the visitors at the docks along Trail Creek and then returned to Chicago for more. The excursion boat was not only quicker than a trip around the lake, it was believed to be safer.

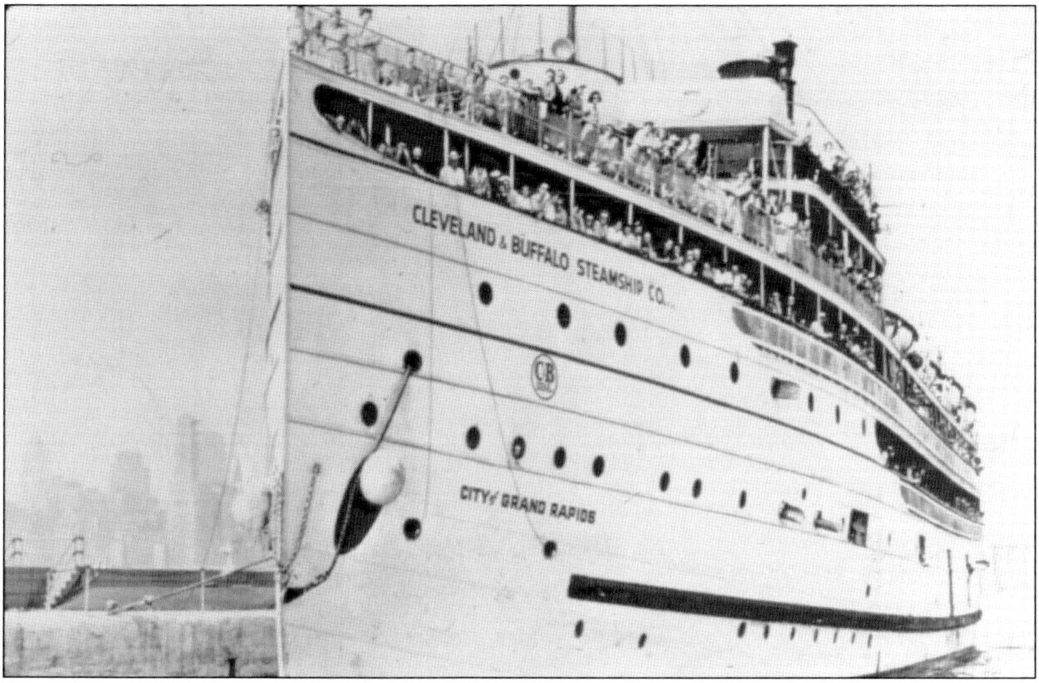

Safety, however, became an issue between 1910 and 1920, when several very serious and fatal shipwrecks caused visitors to either seek other ways of getting to the park or entertainment options in Chicago; the *Eastland*'s wreck was one of them. Pictured is the *City of Grand Rapids*, another steamer that made regular trips between Chicago and Michigan City. The ship was often full as it is in the photograph.

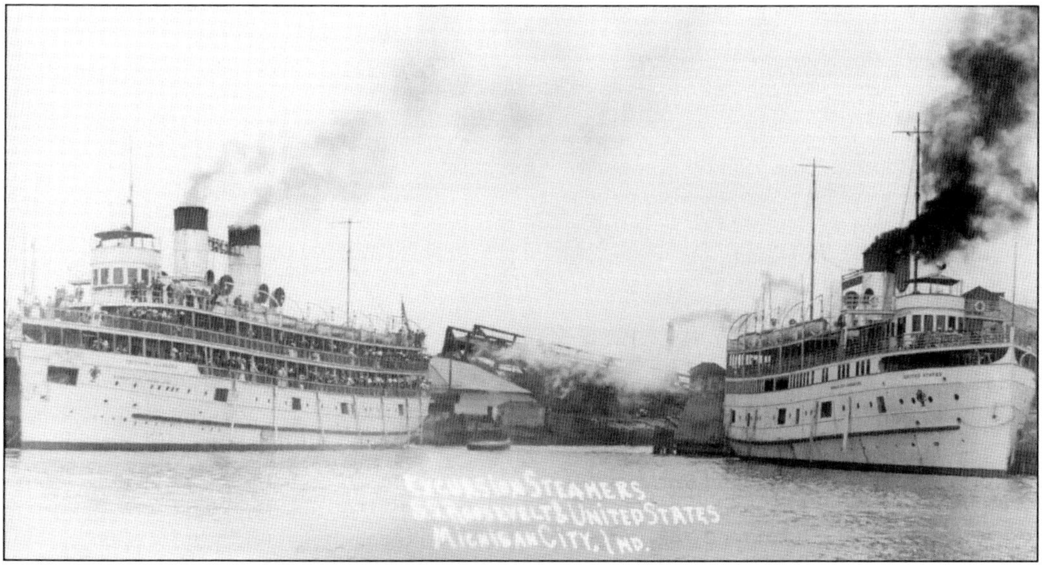

Another steamer crashed into the Franklin Street Bridge, impeding the direct route to Washington Park. The excursion boat business did pick up again, bringing more boats that called Michigan City their "port of call," according to Bob Kaser and Henry Lange's *Lakefront Legacy*. The shipwrecks caused a ripple but did not stop the amusement park, though the slowdown had begun. (Courtesy of Mike and Kathy Fleming.)

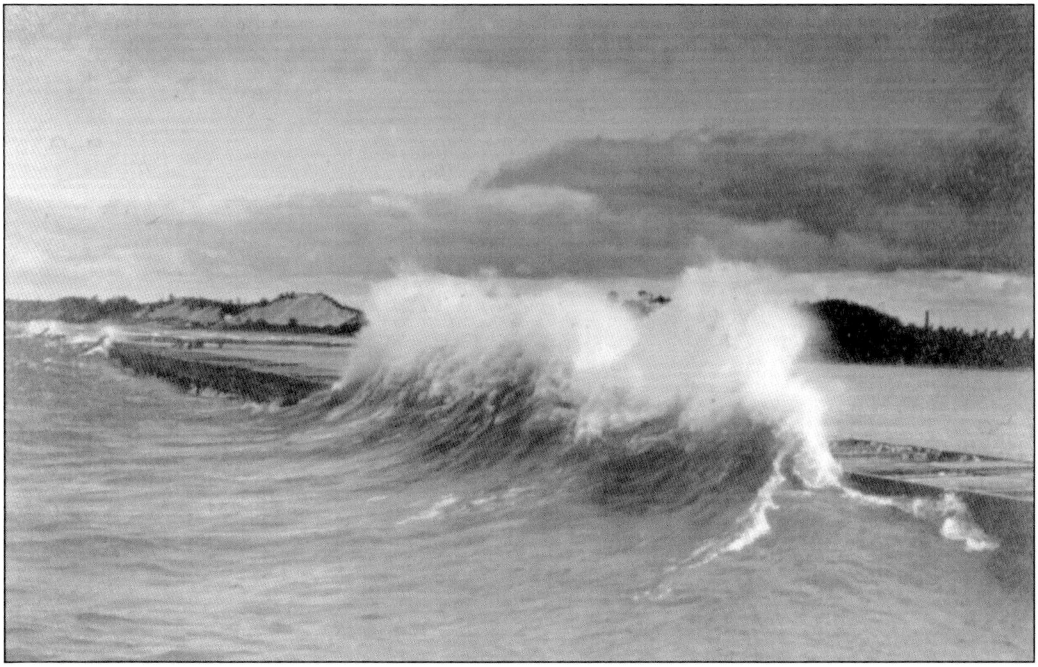

Another contributing factor in the demise of the amusement park was the fire that lit through the park in 1915, captured in the image below. Several structures were damaged or destroyed, but the city took steps to recover them. Narratives recorded by citizens of the city and filed at the Michigan City Library's genealogy department describe going to the park in the 1920s and riding the amusement park rides. This shows that the park did recover somewhat, but without proper documentation the extent of that recovery is unknown. The damage caused by the fire was another ripple. In truth, the small factors leading to the end of amusements in Washington Park were like the waves of Lake Michigan, eroding the shore until the ground was weakened enough to cause summer homes on the lake to collapse.

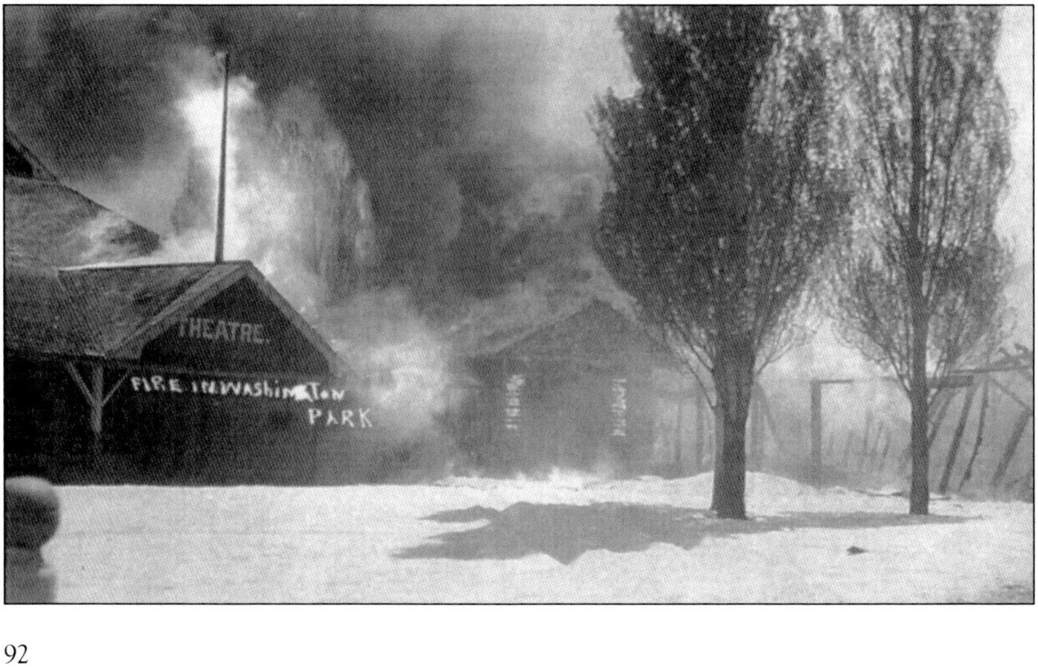

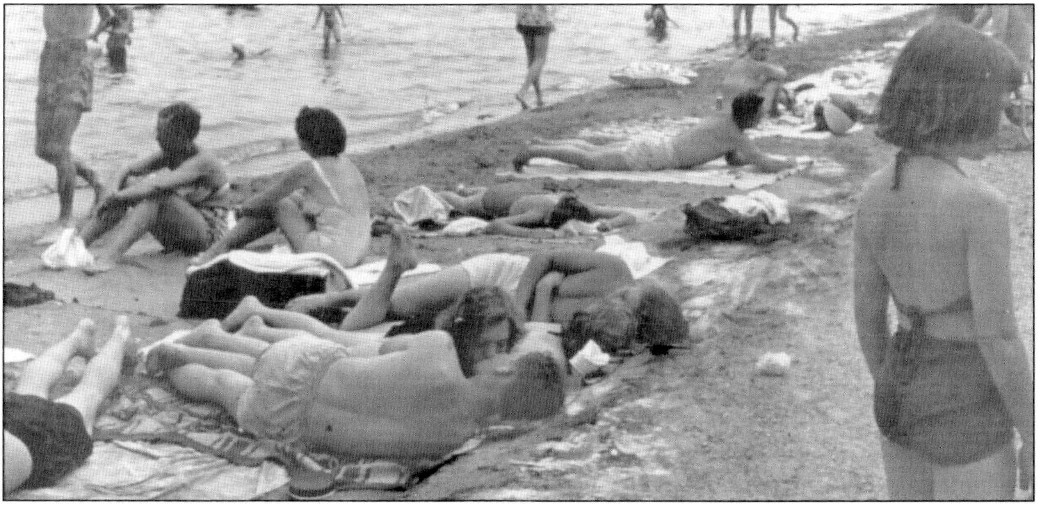

A major factor in the park's demise was the inability to adapt the offering to the changing times. This is best illustrated in the demise of the Oasis. The era of the big band and swing dancing came to a close in the mid-1900s after World War II. When veterans returned and people began to spend money again, the ballroom was not the preferred pastime. These more modern photographs illustrate that change of the times.

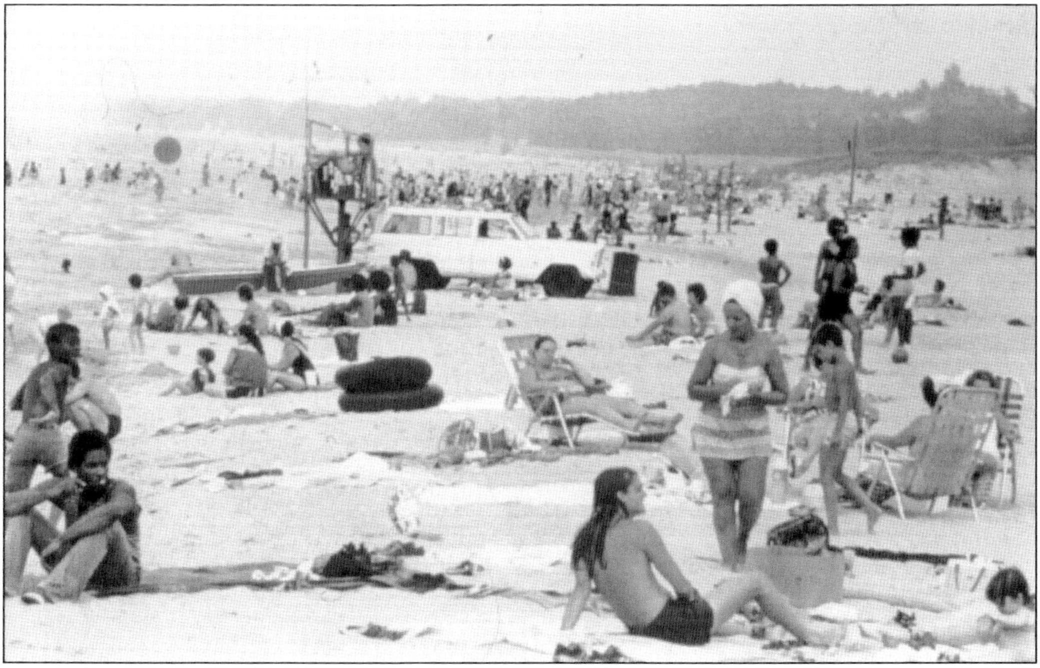

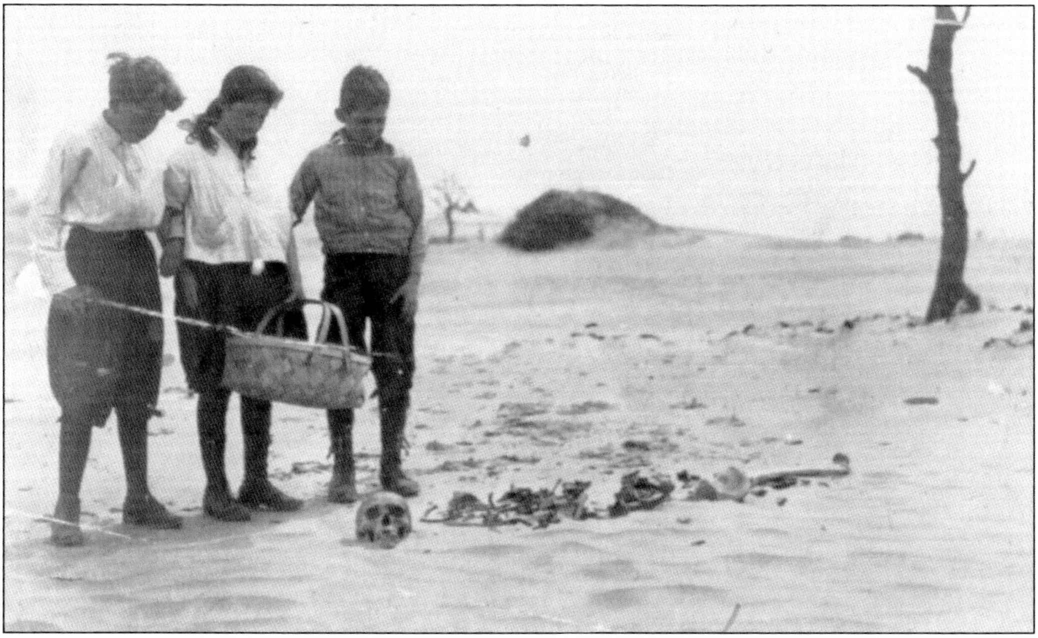

Harold Barr and the park department tried to alter the building to make it a game center for the children, but the effort came too late. Although the Oasis would remain open until 1962, its popularity had passed. Kiddieland and other amusements lasted a bit longer, but they too eventually succumbed. The most common complaints were that the rides were too old and outdated. Failing to keep up with the trends in the entertainment business is like the kiss of death. Business began to dry up, like this skeleton left on Washington Park's beach in the image above. (The skeleton washed up on the beach and was discovered as pictured; its origins are unclear.) The photograph below shows the Oasis a year before it closed.

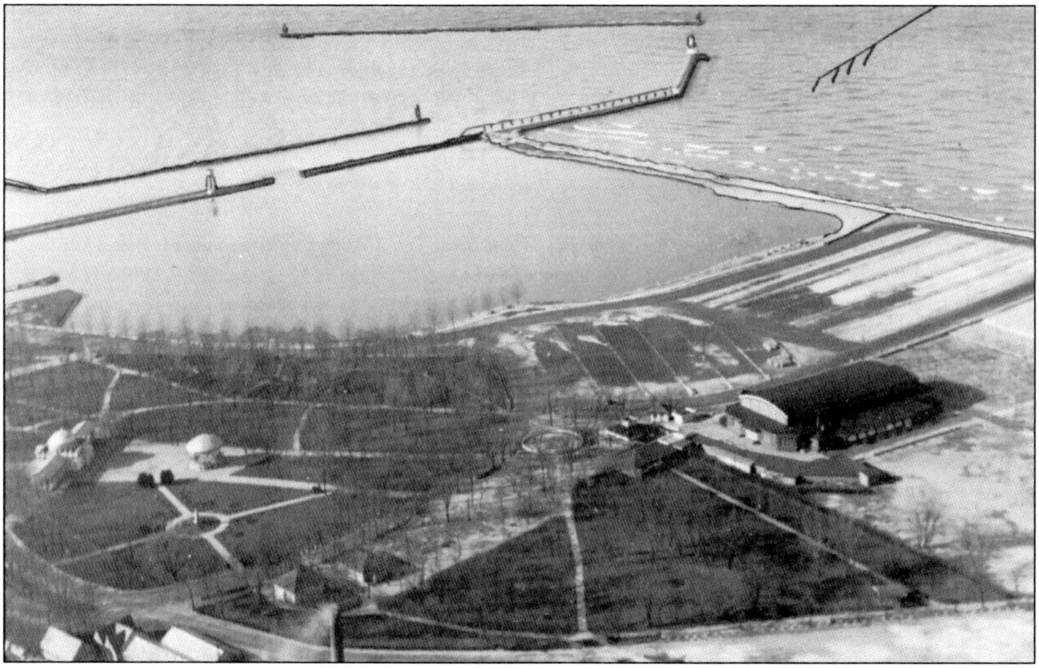

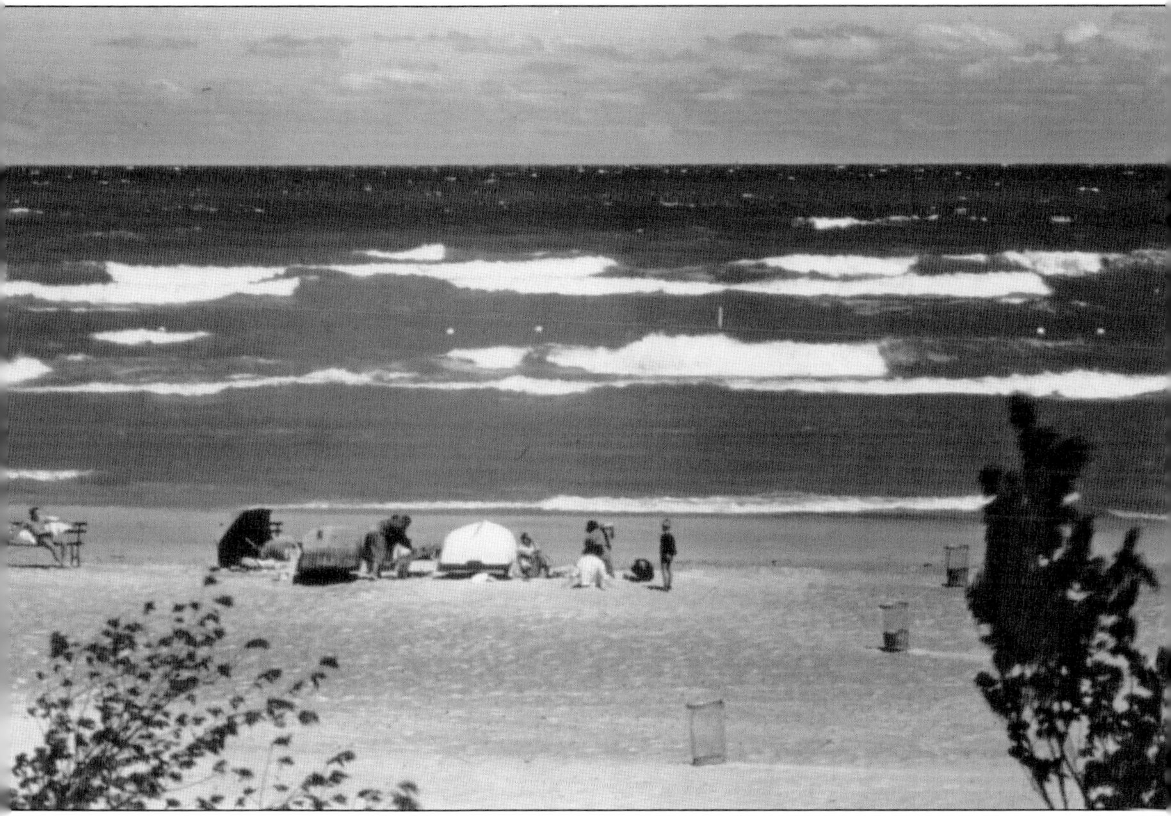

The problem was not that Barr and the park were not trying. The manager had plans to make the Oasis into a roller rink and reinvent the amusement offerings. The wave that overtook Lakeview Amusement was a legal technicality.

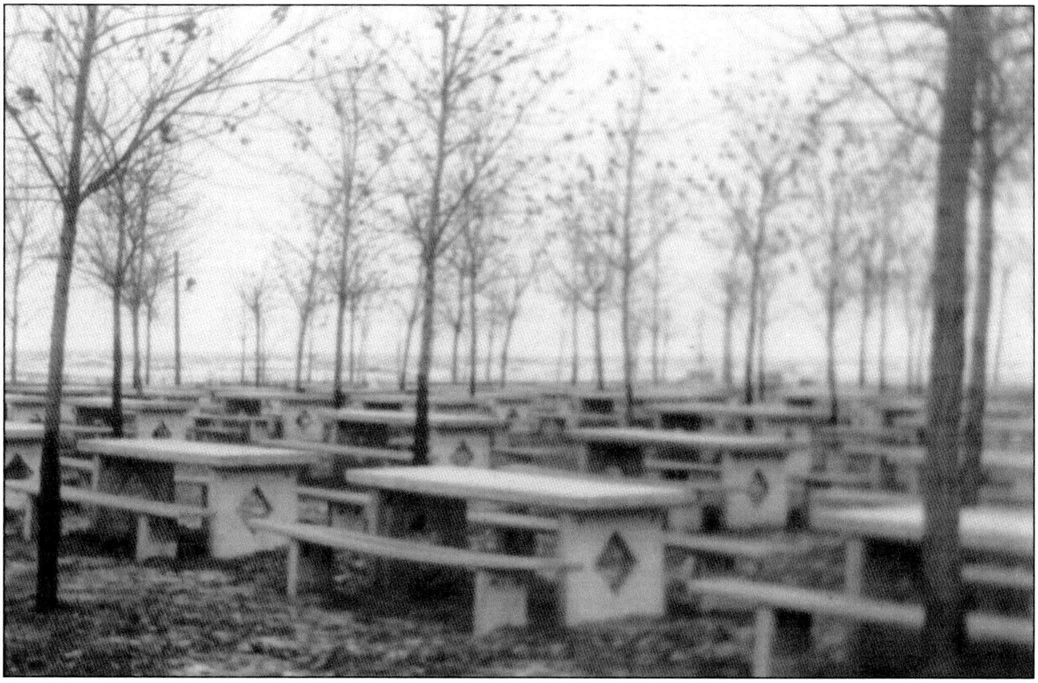

In 1961, community activist Roger McKee led a public crusade against Harold Barr's use of parkland for an amusement park. McKee's argument was that Washington Park's land was public property, and public property could not be leased for private use. It did not matter that such a lease had been in place in some form for the past 60 years or more. Pictured here are concrete tables that Barr made and placed in the park in the 1940s. It was just one improvement designed to draw and maintain crowds in Washington Park.

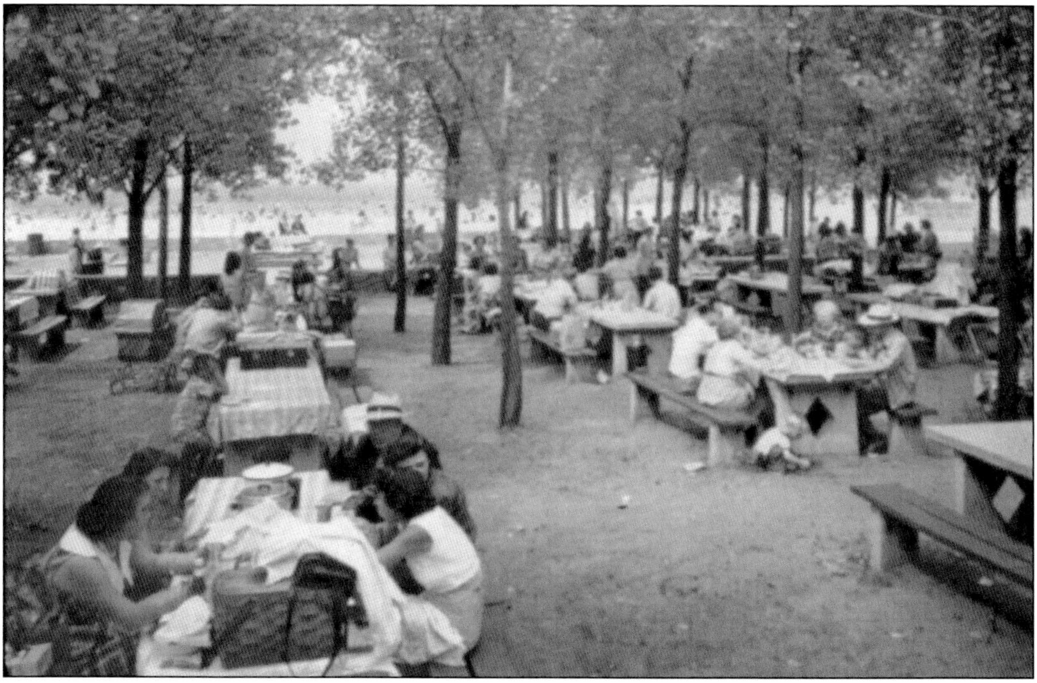

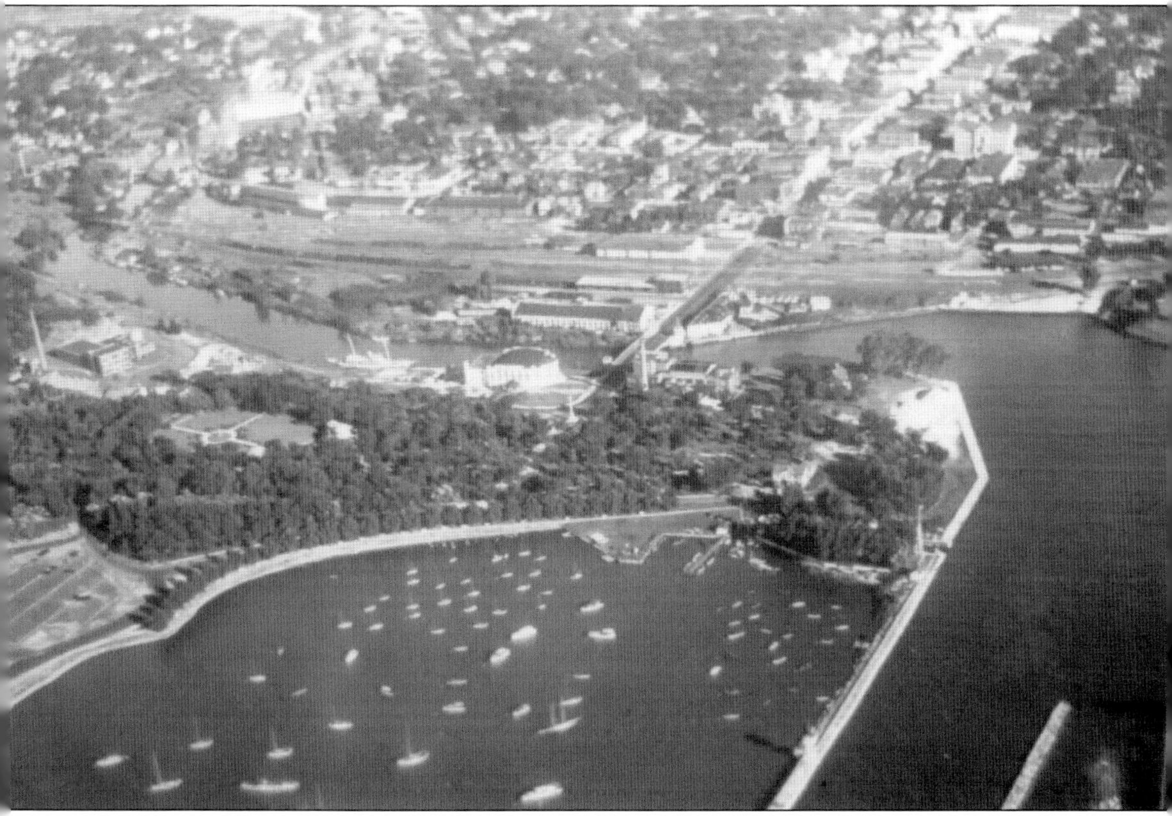

McKee's fuel came from a 1955 act that created a parks and recreation department that not only oversaw Washington Park, but every public park, golf course, and tennis court in the city. A previous act in 1933 created a park department and gave it jurisdiction over Washington Park and the zoo. This aerial view of parklands also includes the marina. During the same time period, the park department attempted to assert authority over pleasure boating in Michigan City as well. In 1962, the court dispute ended, not in favor of the park department.

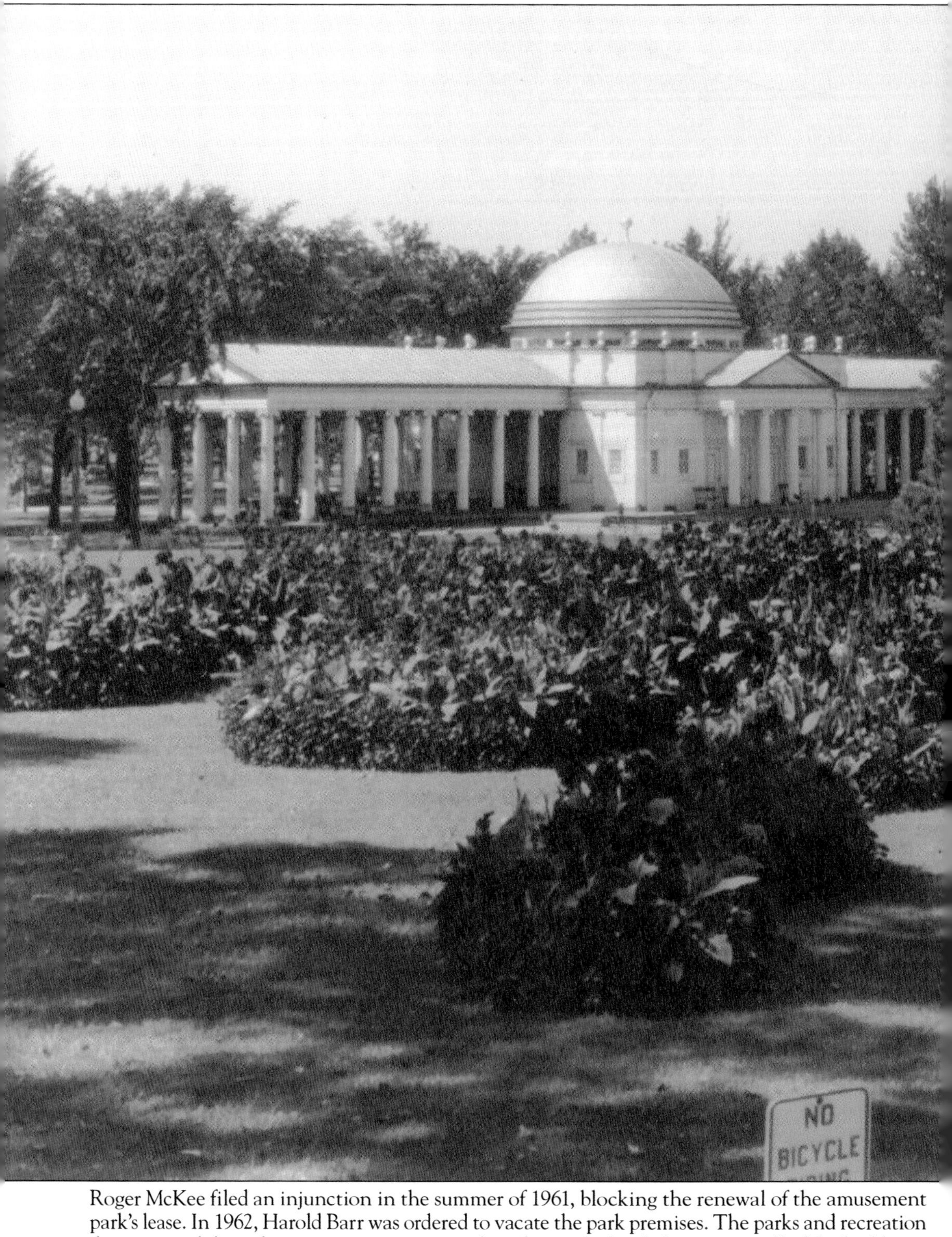

Roger McKee filed an injunction in the summer of 1961, blocking the renewal of the amusement park's lease. In 1962, Harold Barr was ordered to vacate the park premises. The parks and recreation department did ponder continuing operations but ultimately decided to remove all of the buildings,

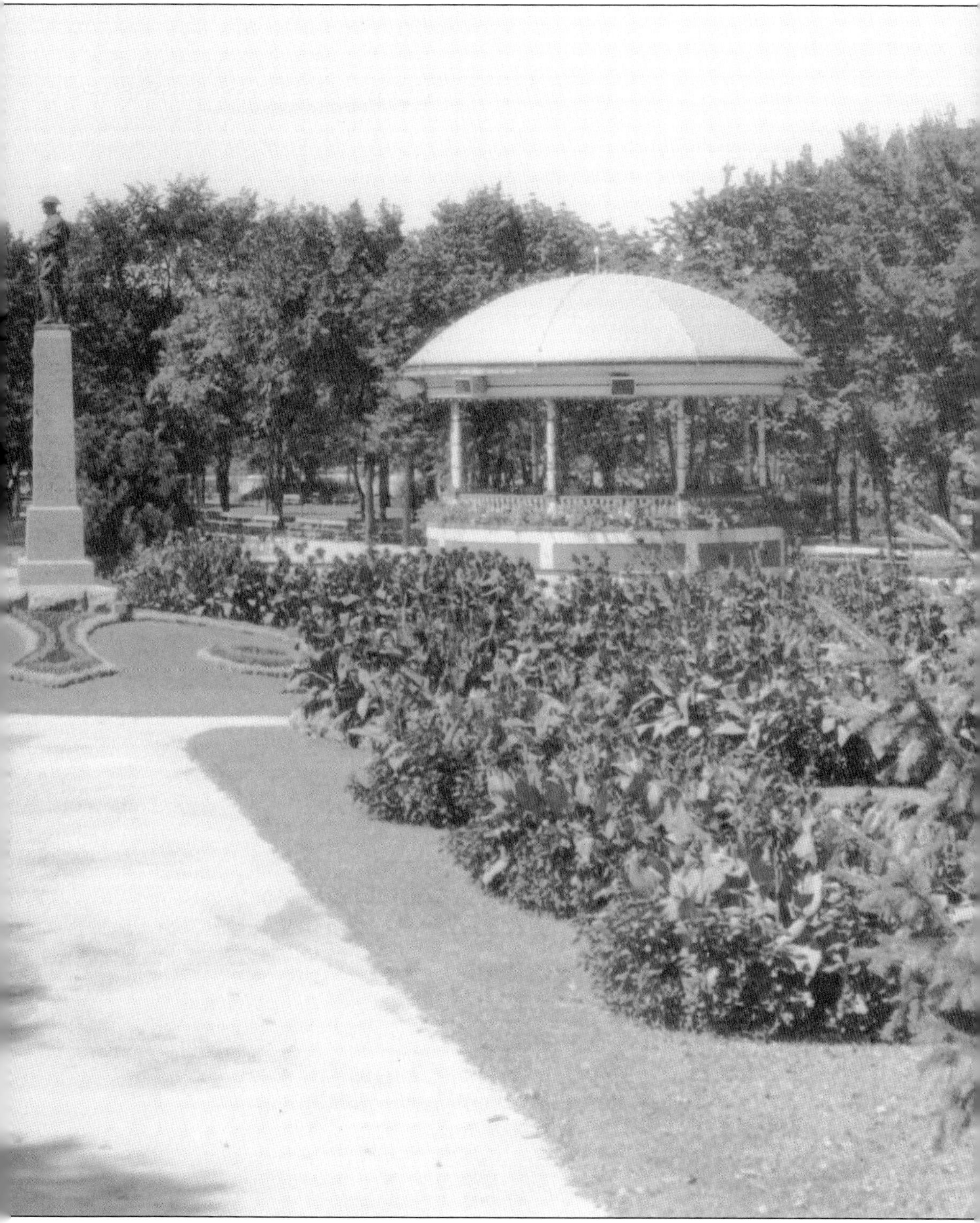

since they were too neglected and required an expensive overhaul. Furthermore, the department now had the immense job of taking care of all public parks and facilities, so there was no room for running an amusement park. Images like this one would only exist in picture and memory.

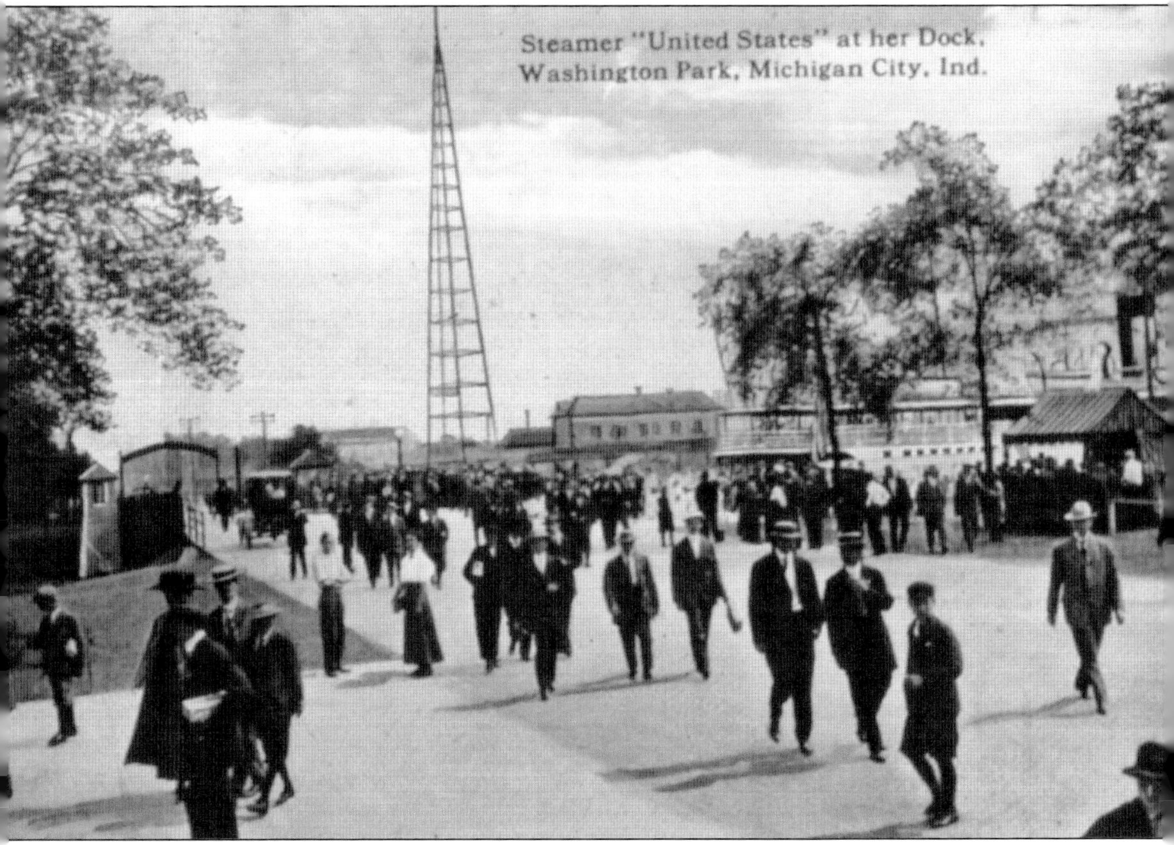

The park did get another person to run the facility. The Washington Park Amusement Company did try to keep the rides running, but that attempt ended in a lawsuit. The legal battle stretched on for years, but the amusement park as created in the early 1900s died for good in 1962.

Seven

Back to Nature

Recovering from of an operation run for decades by Barr was not as easy as it seemed. The park department was left with equipment, buildings, and materials that it could no longer use. The park superintendent at the time, James Cook, wanted to turn the Oasis into an indoor amusement facility, but that never materialized. The agency ended up removing the building, and equipment was left behind. Meanwhile, other structures, like the peristyle donated by John Barker in the late 1800s, were in desperate need of repair as well; there were issues with rot, among other things. No one had been allowed into the facility for quite some time, and a contractor who was consulted to make repairs recommended that the building be demolished. By the beginning of 1970, the peristyle was no longer. The Questers, a community group that currently maintains the structure, renovated the bandstand in 1973.

The park department slowly began removing the remnants of the park that the early founder envisioned. Traffic patterns were routed and rerouted in the 1970s and 1980s to give visitors the best scenic view without the bottlenecks. The structures built by the WPA, CCC, and FERA were maintained, especially the observation tower (renovated by a civic group in the 1980s), and benches, shelters, and walls were constructed at that time. The tennis courts have been removed, and today a splash pad sits in its place. With all the change, though, the garden formations and pathways created during the Depression can still be experienced.

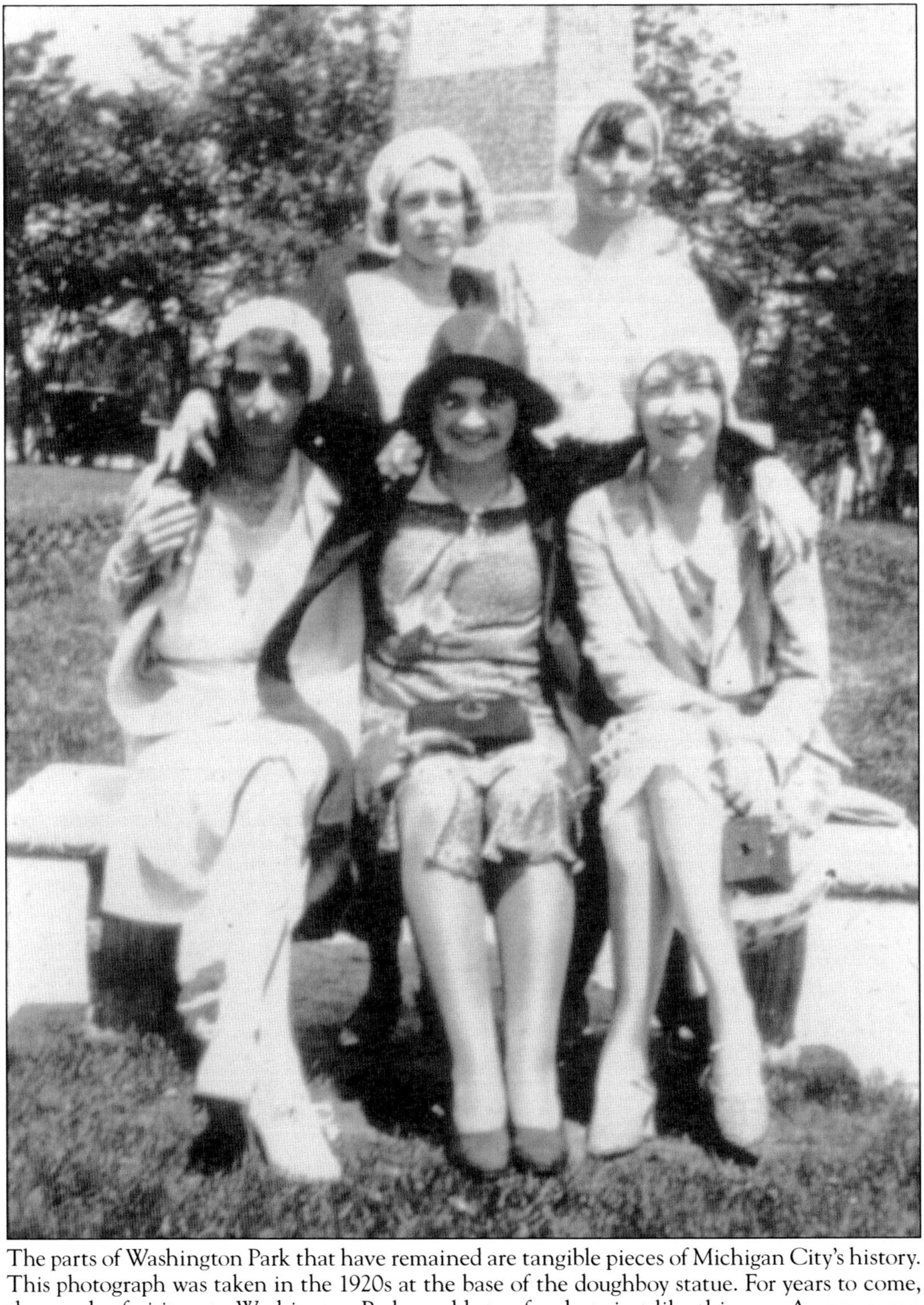

The parts of Washington Park that have remained are tangible pieces of Michigan City's history. This photograph was taken in the 1920s at the base of the doughboy statue. For years to come, thousands of visitors to Washington Park would stop for shots just like this one. A person can trace a history of a family by the images of smiling faces taken year after year in front of the monuments, statues, and structures in Washington Park.

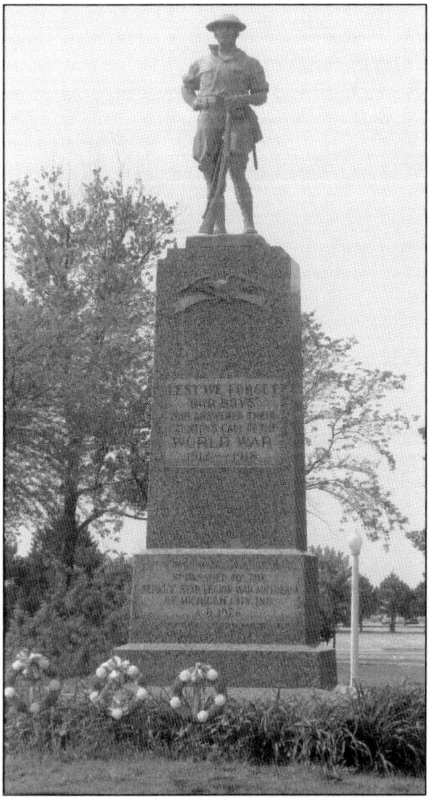

The landscaping that started in the 1930s was the highlight of Washington Park after the amusements were gone. In 2010, the America In Bloom project was in full swing in the park. Gardens like the one seen in the photograph below were reaffirmed as the ideal decoration in Washington Park.

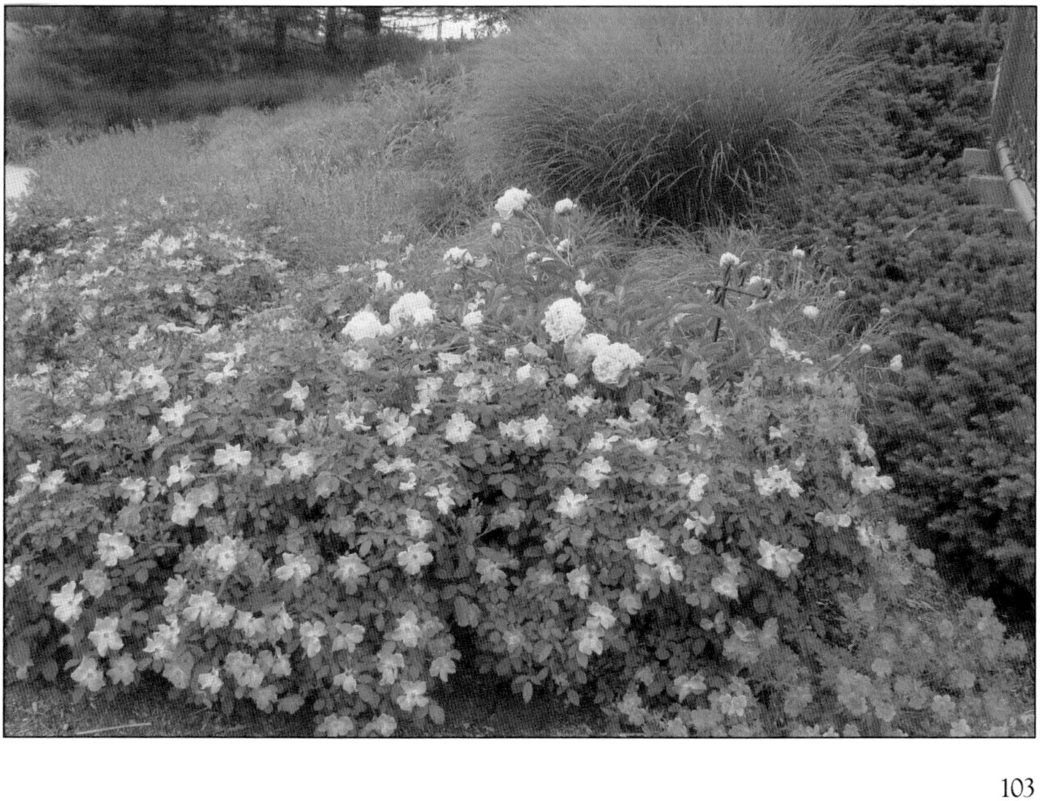

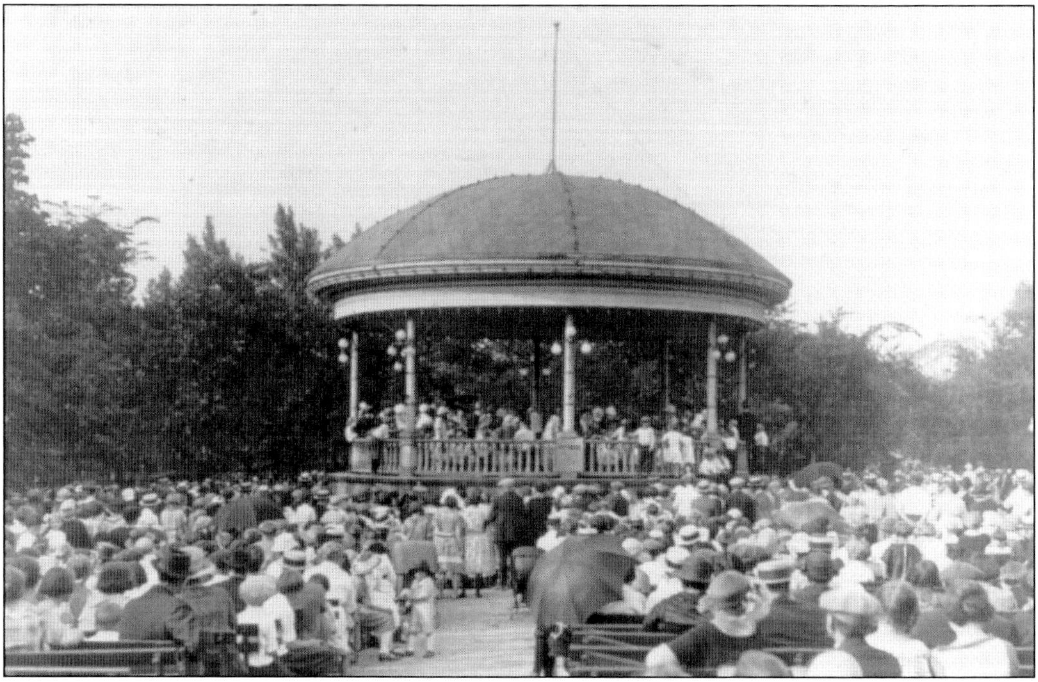

The bandstand shown here in the early years continues to be a functional showpiece in Washington Park. The benches are long gone, but the grasses surrounding the bandstand are great for picnicking. The amphitheater is now the center stage for performances.

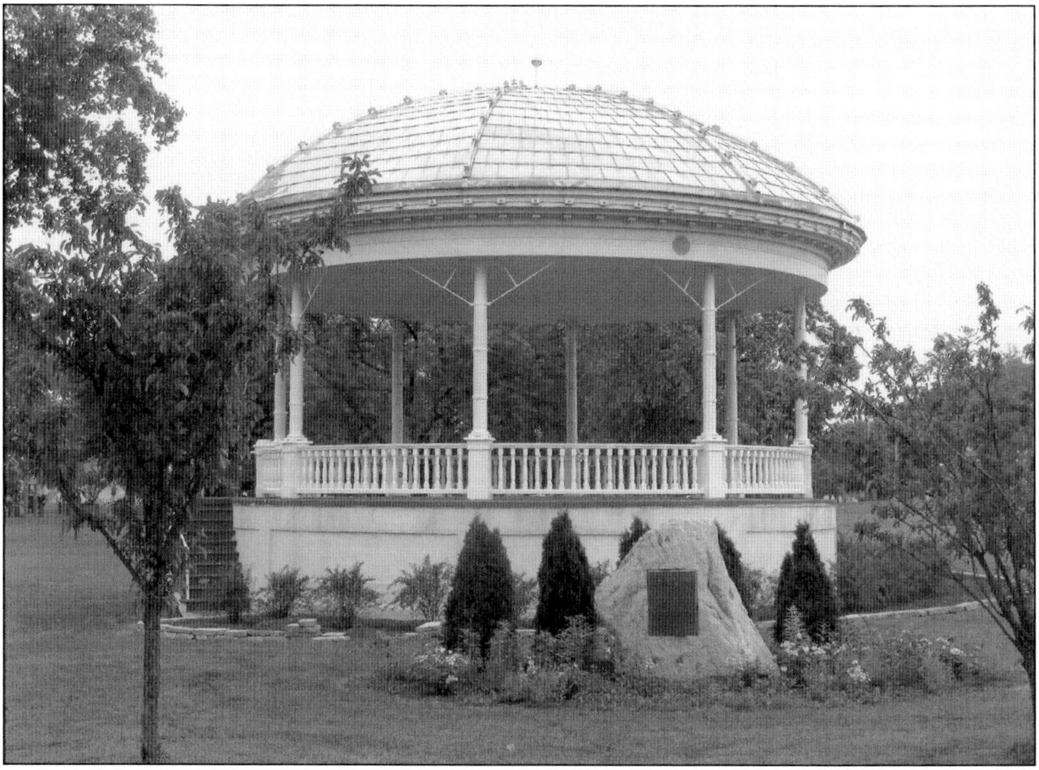

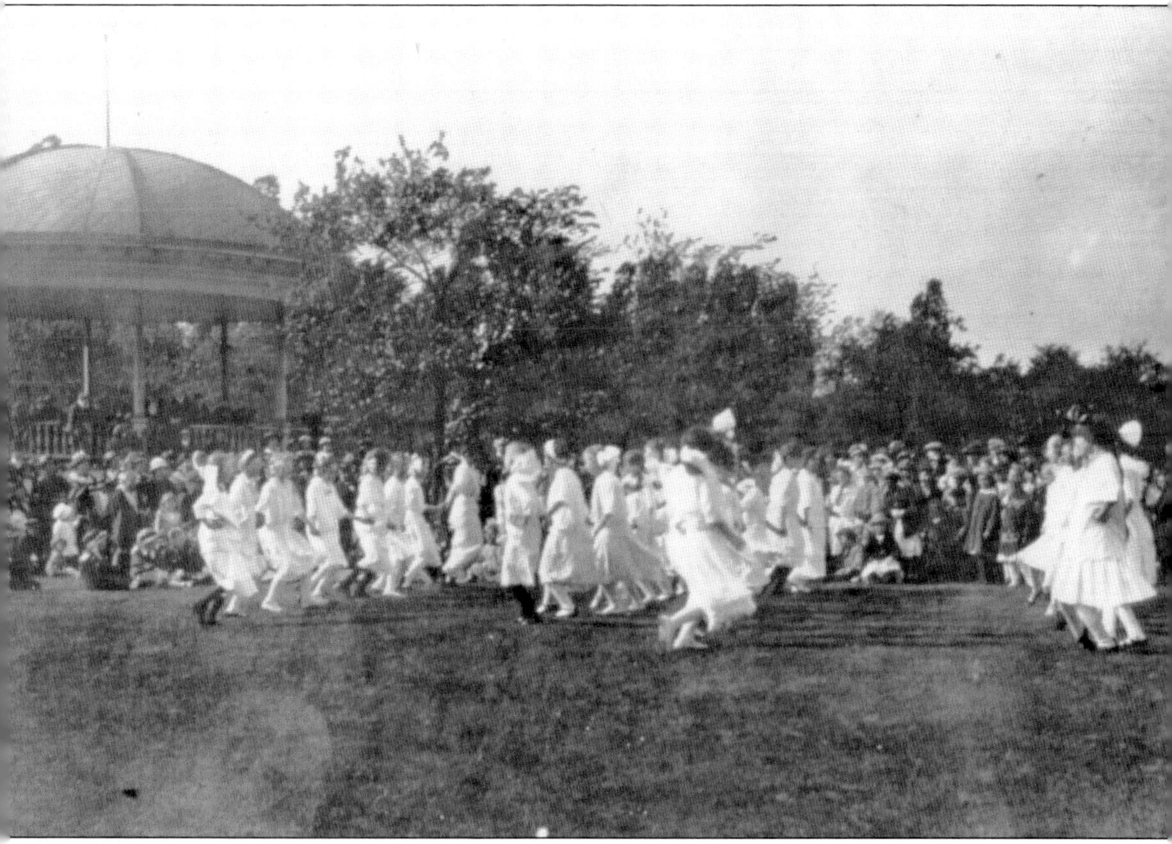

The old bandstand was a place the community could enjoy together at the lakefront. Before the amphitheater, the bandstand was the place for performances in the park. The close proximity of the peristyle simply made things more convenient.

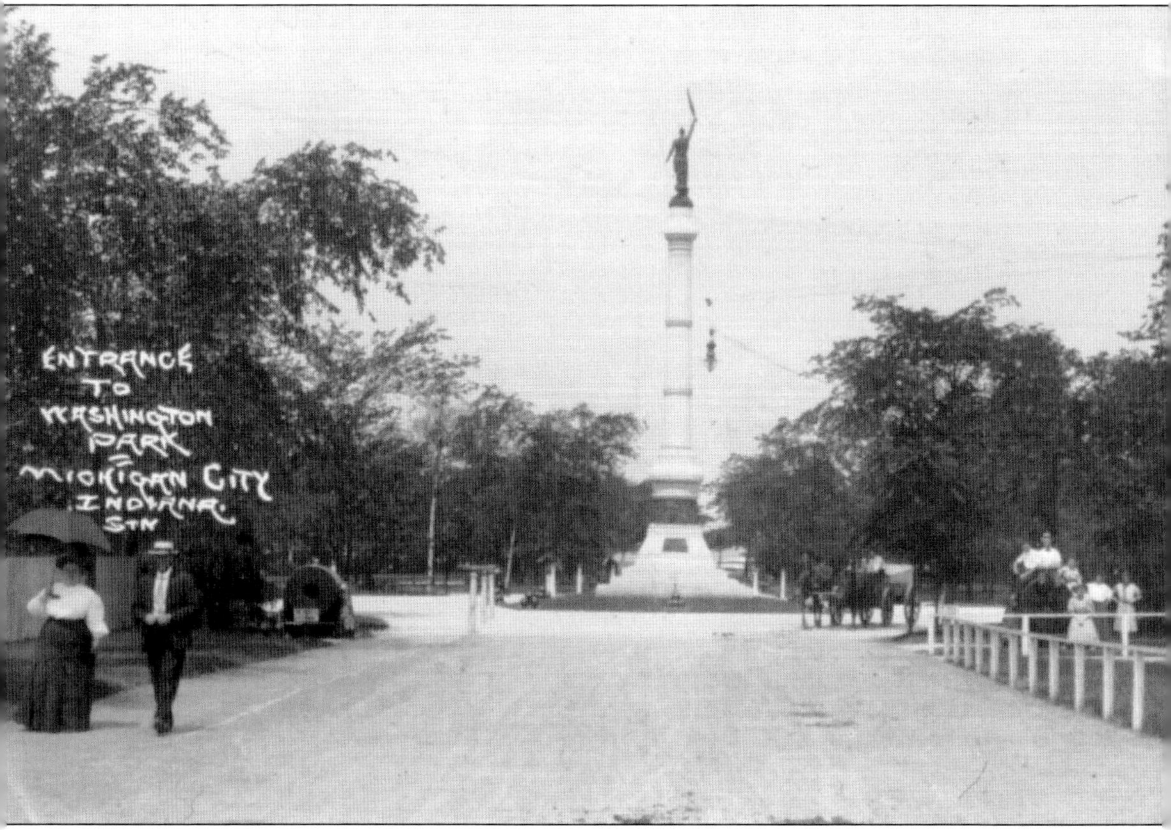

Another view of the entrance at the turn of the 20th century, the cannons in this photograph were melted down in 1942. The element of the park entrance that has not changed is *Victorious Peace* greeting visitors as they arrive. Today, cars replace the horse and buggy coming around the monument. Traffic patterns have also changed as well.

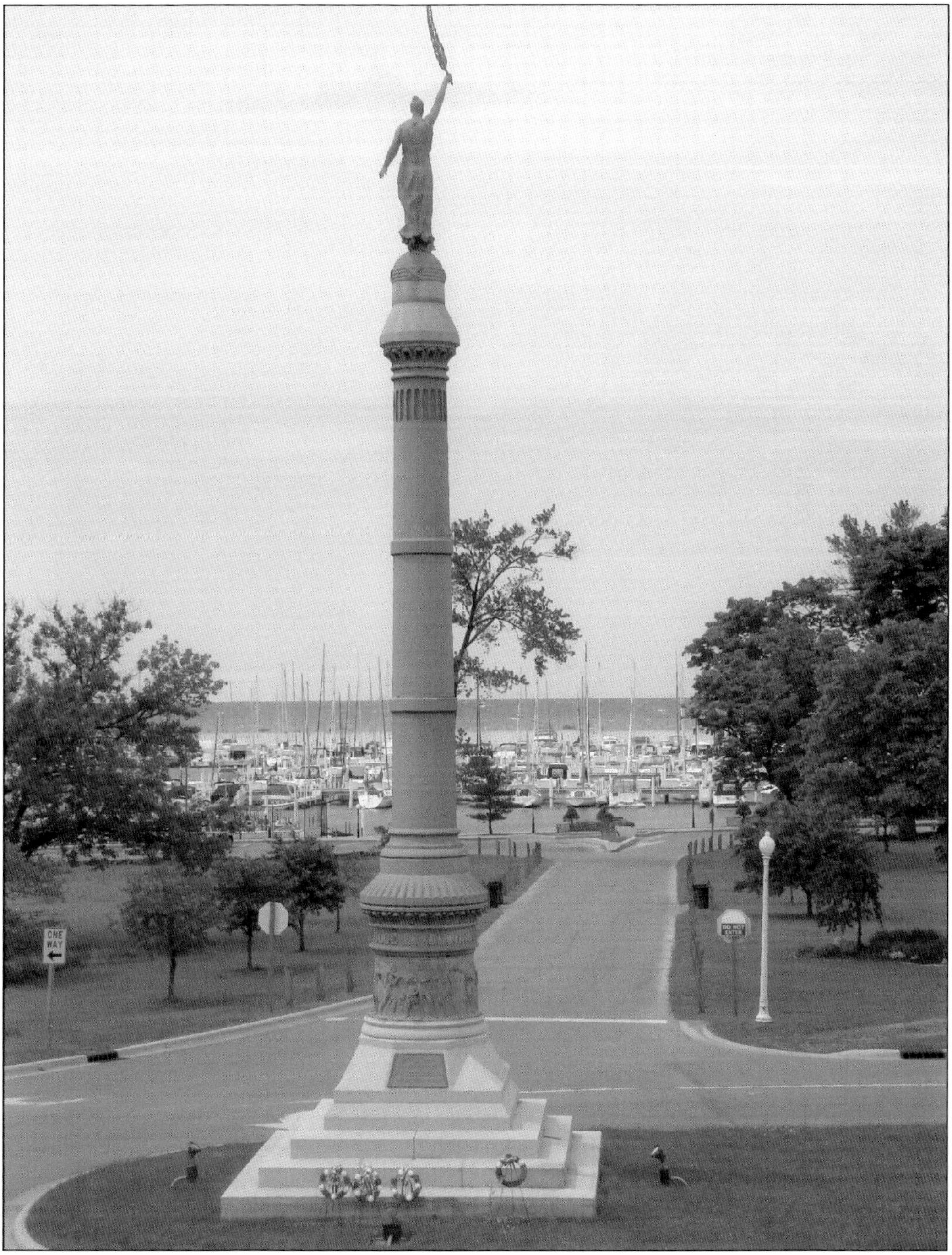

Today, the *Victorious Peace* monument in Washington Park stands with the lake and Washington Park Marina behind it. Gone are the cannons and entry stonework, but a new arrangement allows for a smooth, scenic route through the park. The statue is still the first thing one can see as he or she travels over the Franklin Street Bridge.

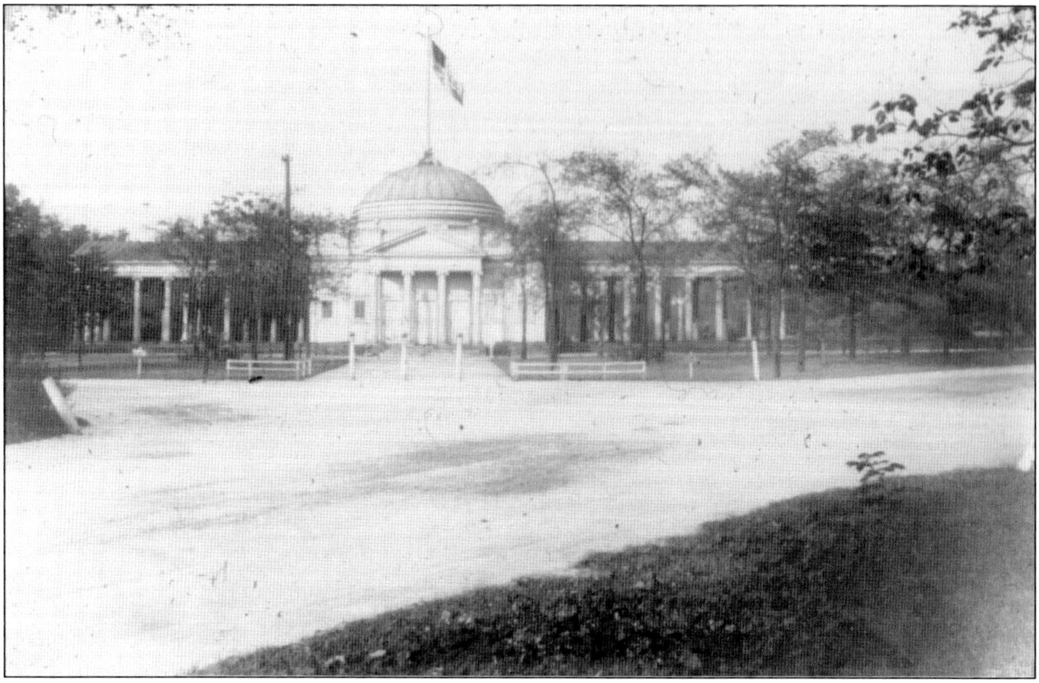

Most Michigan City residents and tourists have never laid eyes on a regal structure in Washington Park like the peristyle. There was a small effort to preserve the deteriorating building, but in the end the costs of repairs and upkeep were much more than the city and residents could afford.

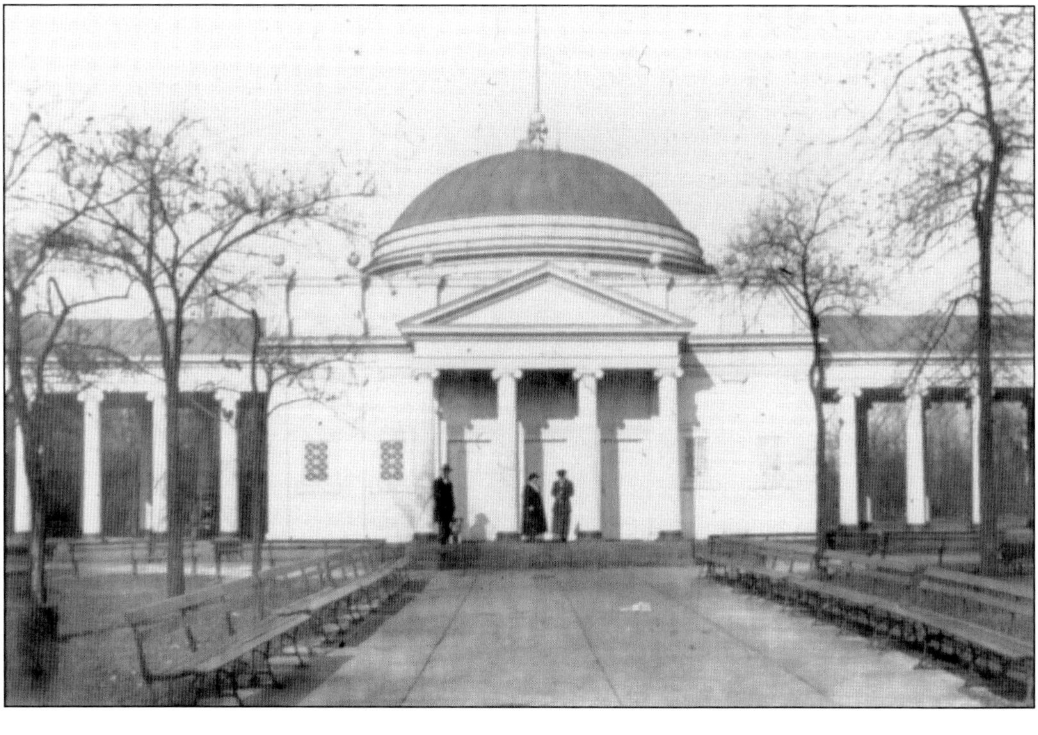

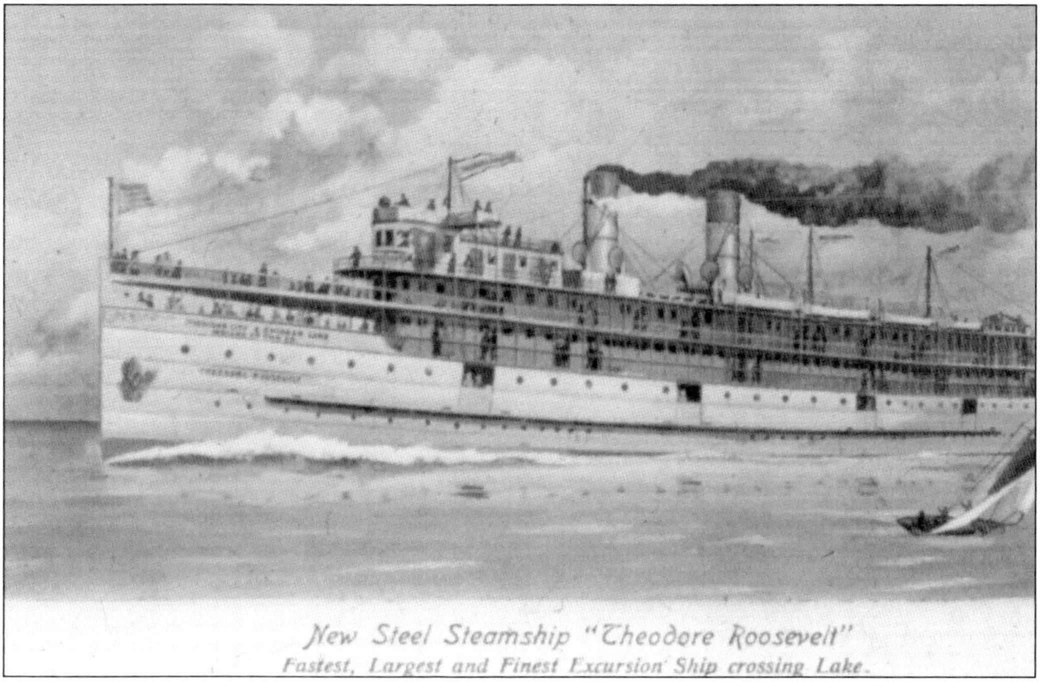

Another emblem of yesteryear that left the park was the steamers dropping off droves of passengers in the 1950s. Charter boats still exist today to ferry small groups back and forth, but they evoke only a very distant memory of the crowded steamers. Pictured here is the *Theodore Roosevelt*.

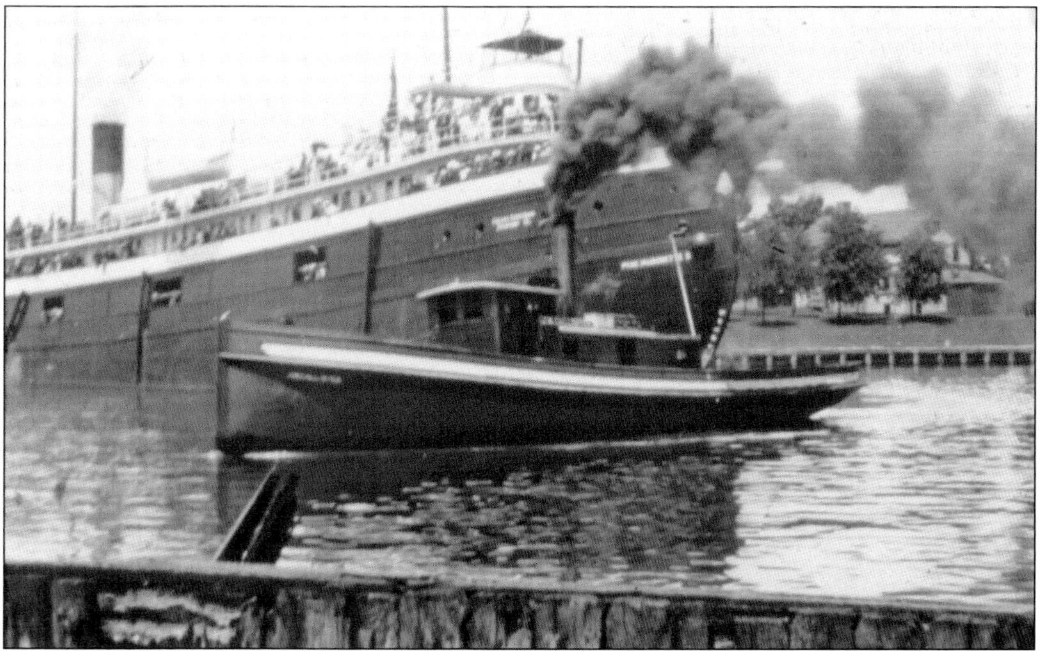

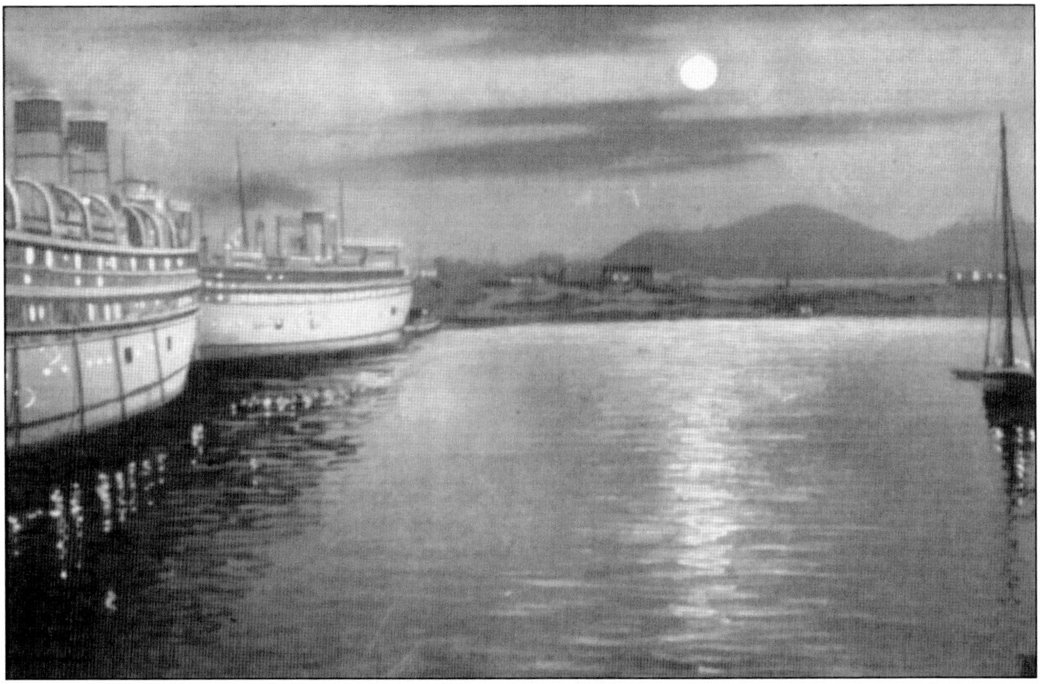

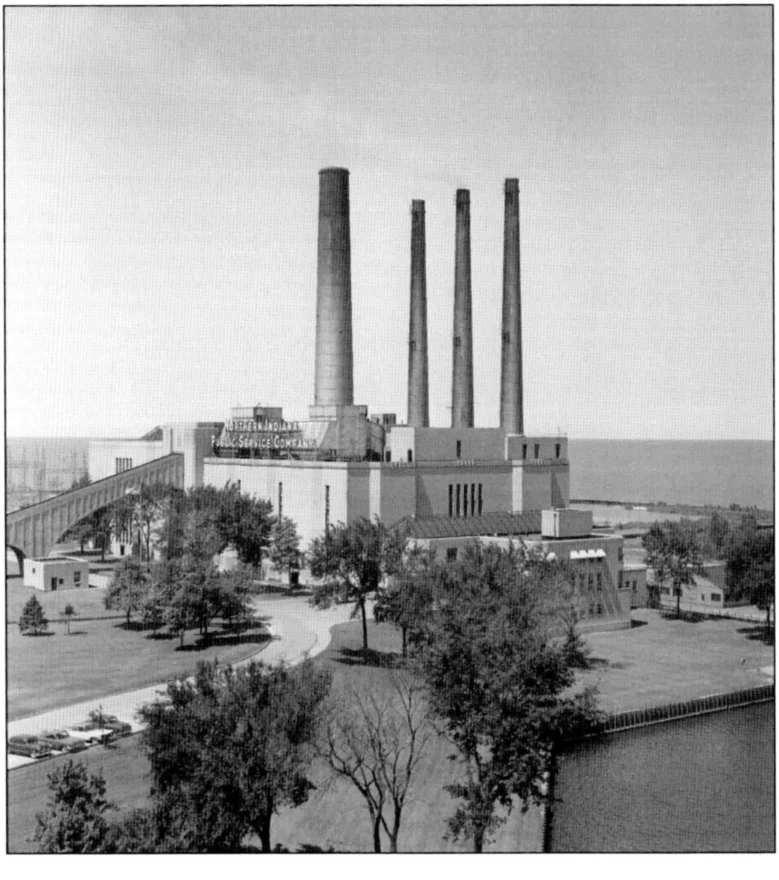

Steamers of the sizes seen above were once a common sight as they lined up along Trail Creek. They replaced the commercial ships, but smaller vessels now occupy the space. Today, the large Northern Indiana Public Service Company (NIPSCO) also occupies the tranquil skyline at night. In the image above, the Hoosier Slide's sister dune, Mount Baldy, is visible. By 1960, as seen in the image at left, the growing power plant had fully taken the place of the dune that once stood in the same location.

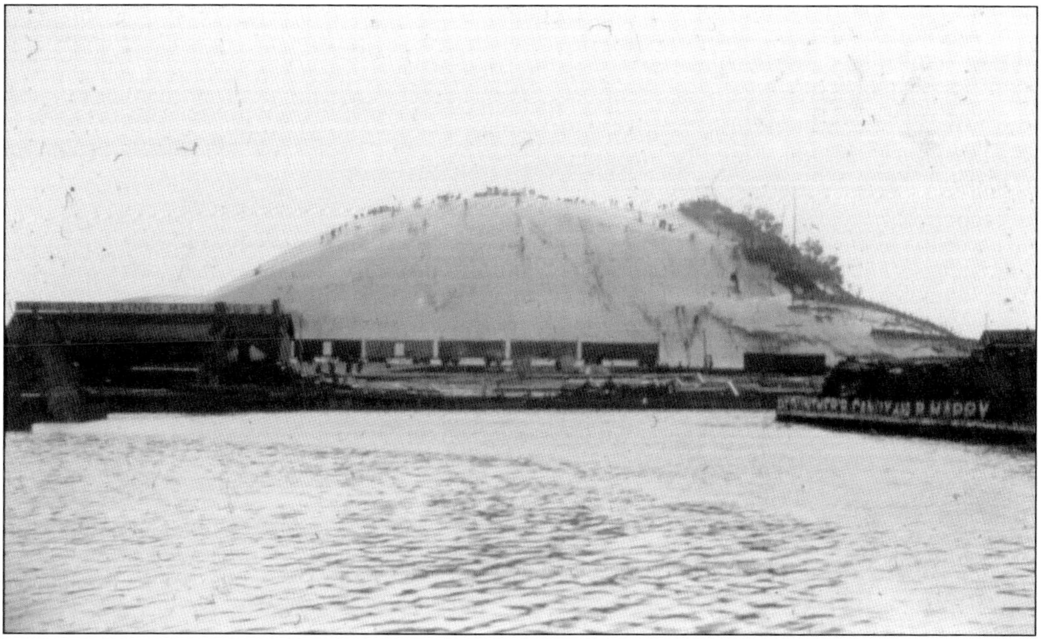

Hoosier Slide itself was carted away in the early 1920s to make glass. The NIPSCO power plant building now stands in its place.

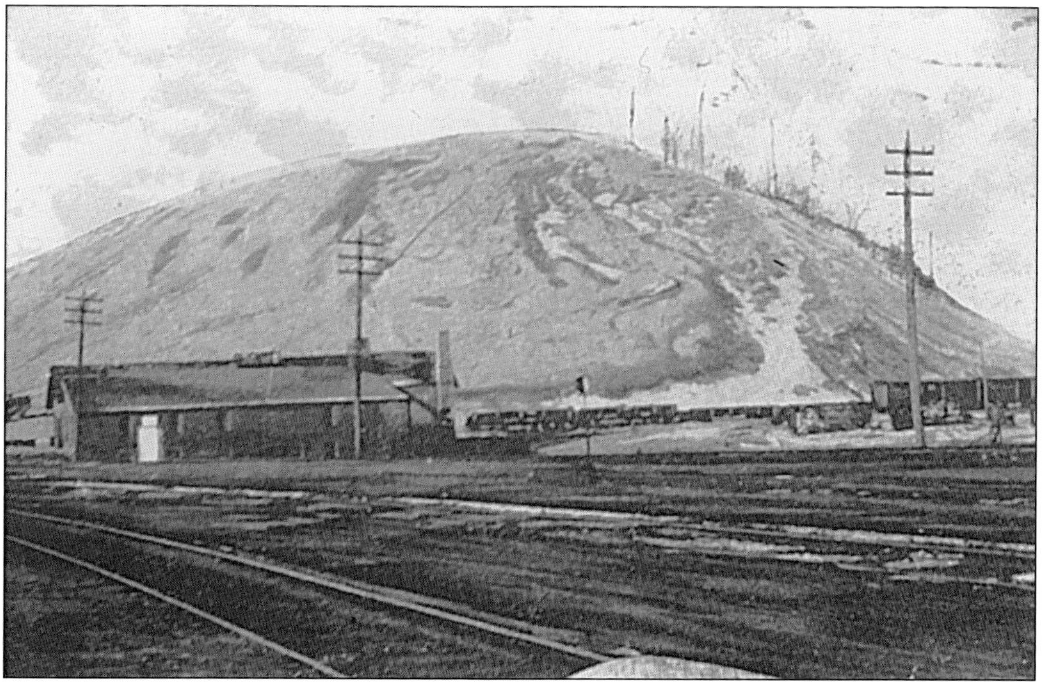

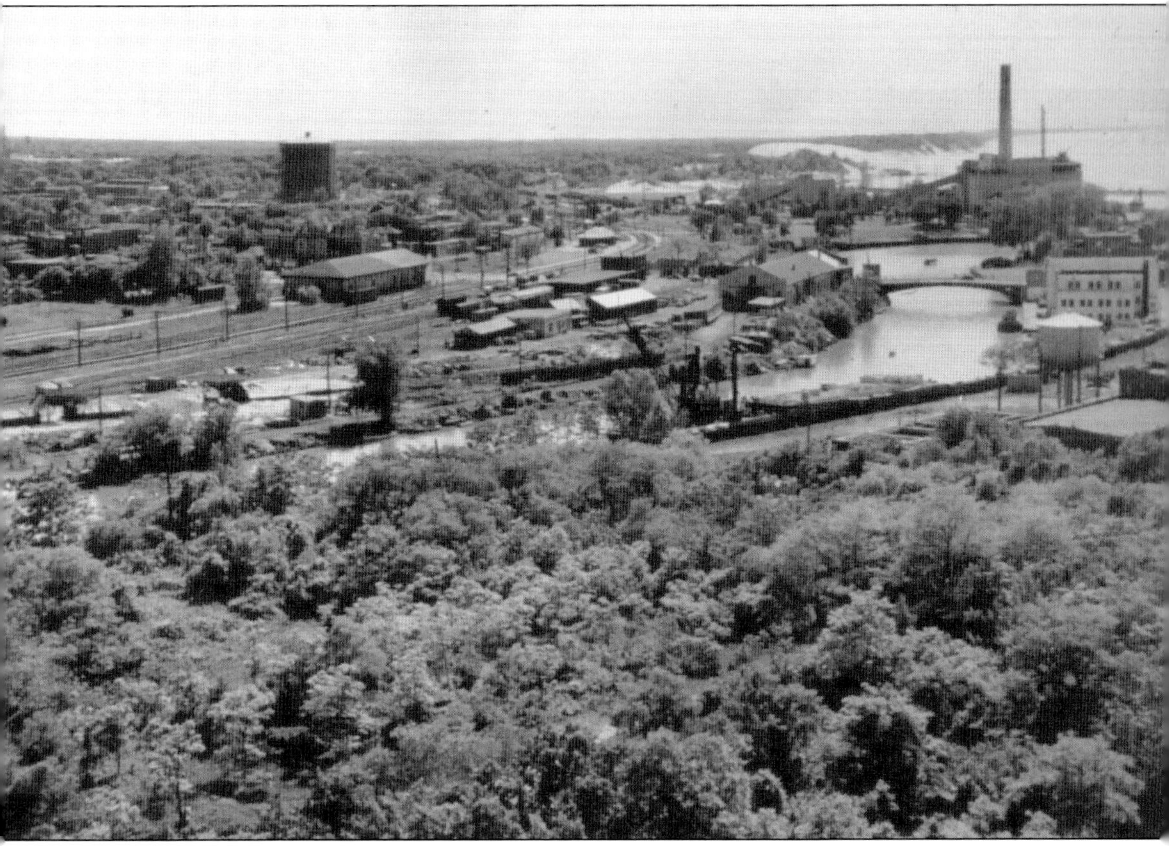

The new skyline is seen here with the power plant and shores of Trail Creek—without the presence of a steamship.

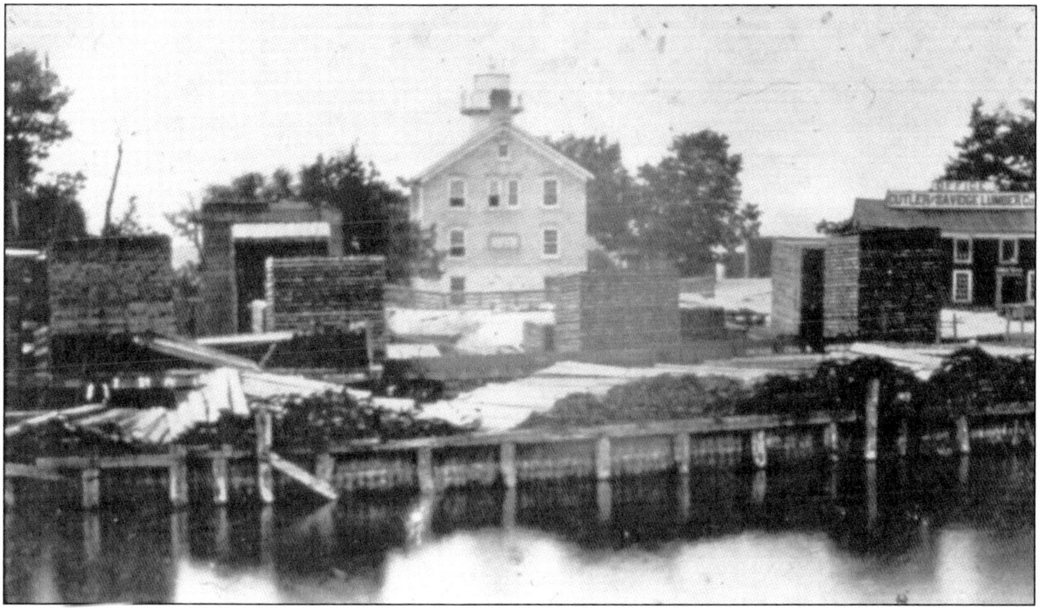

In this image from the late 1800s, the old lighthouse is surrounded by the lumber piles that littered the lakefront. Today, the building is a museum that houses much of Michigan City and lakefront history.

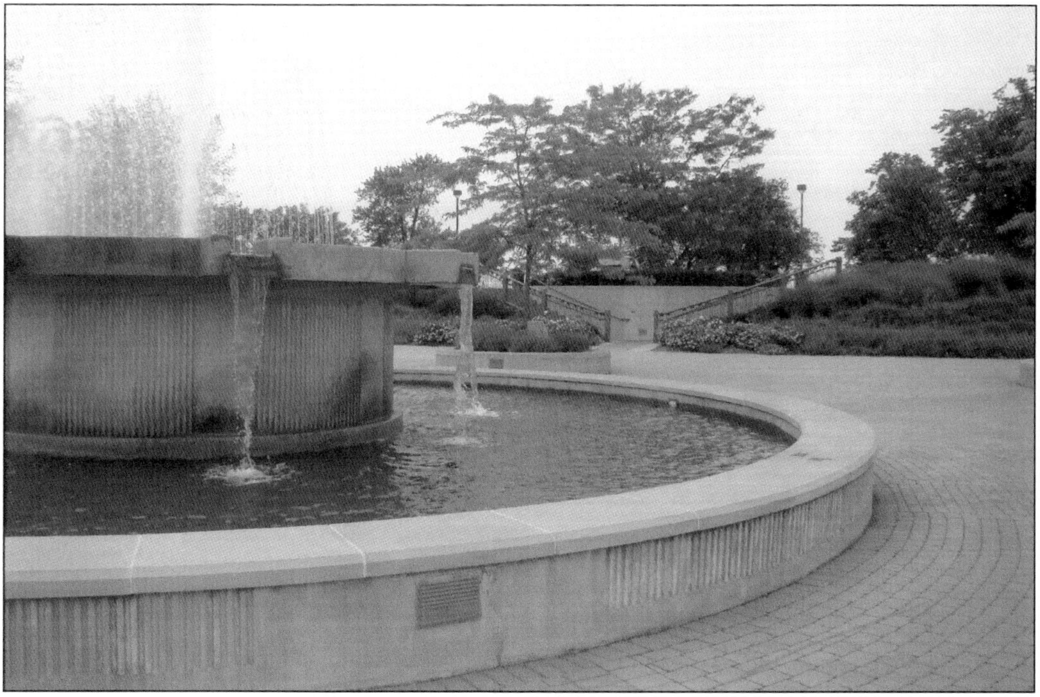

Adjacent to the Lighthouse Museum is Millennium Plaza, the area that was erected to commemorate the turn of the 21st century. It is located on the banks of Trail Creek between the Franklin Street Bridge and the Lighthouse Museum. The benches, fountain, monuments, and landscaping make the place a relaxing edition to Washington Park. It is also the desired place in Michigan City for weddings and public events. (Courtesy Michigan City Parks and Recreation Department.)

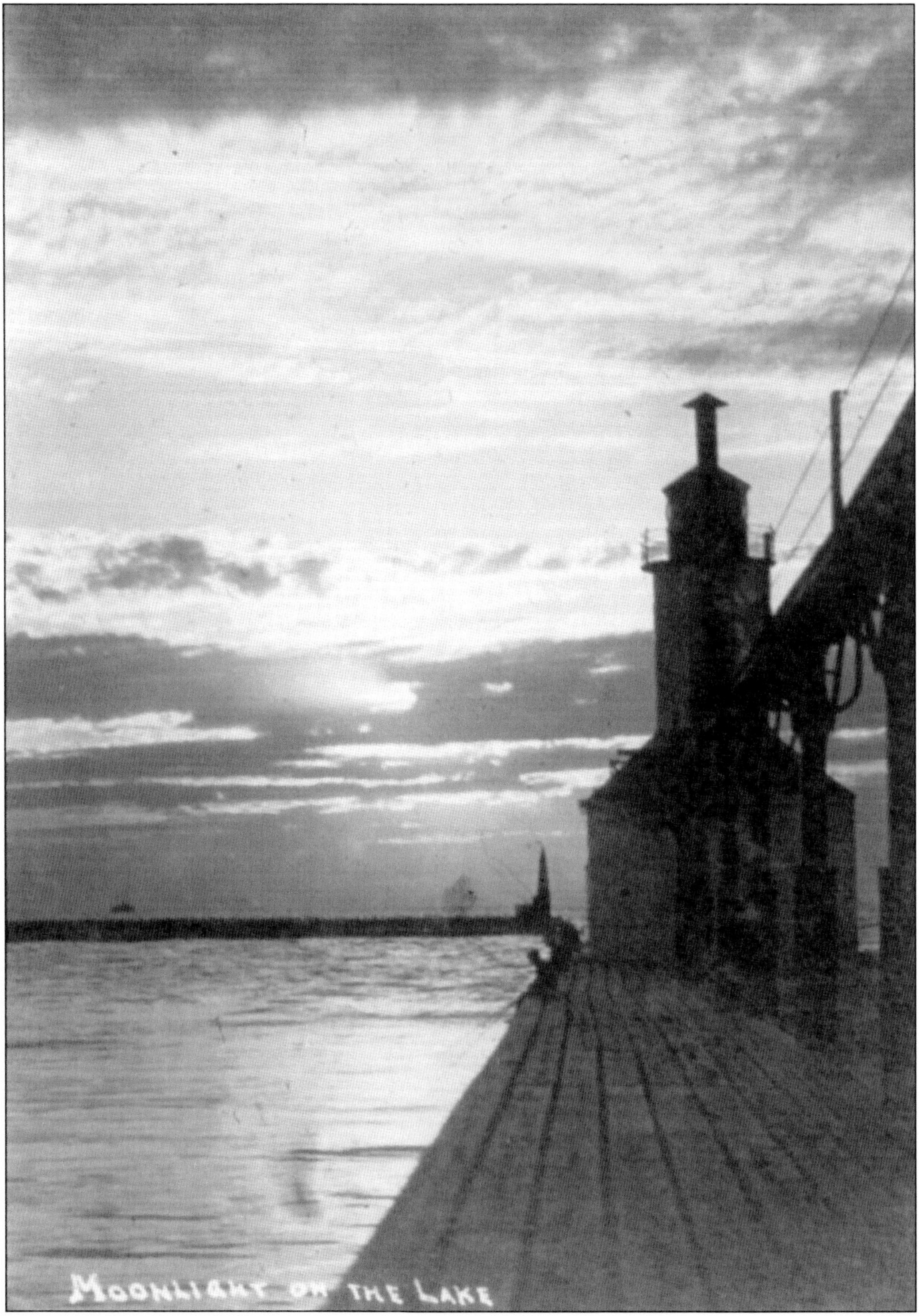

The catwalk and new lighthouse at the end of the pier that stand at the lakefront today are also remains of the past.

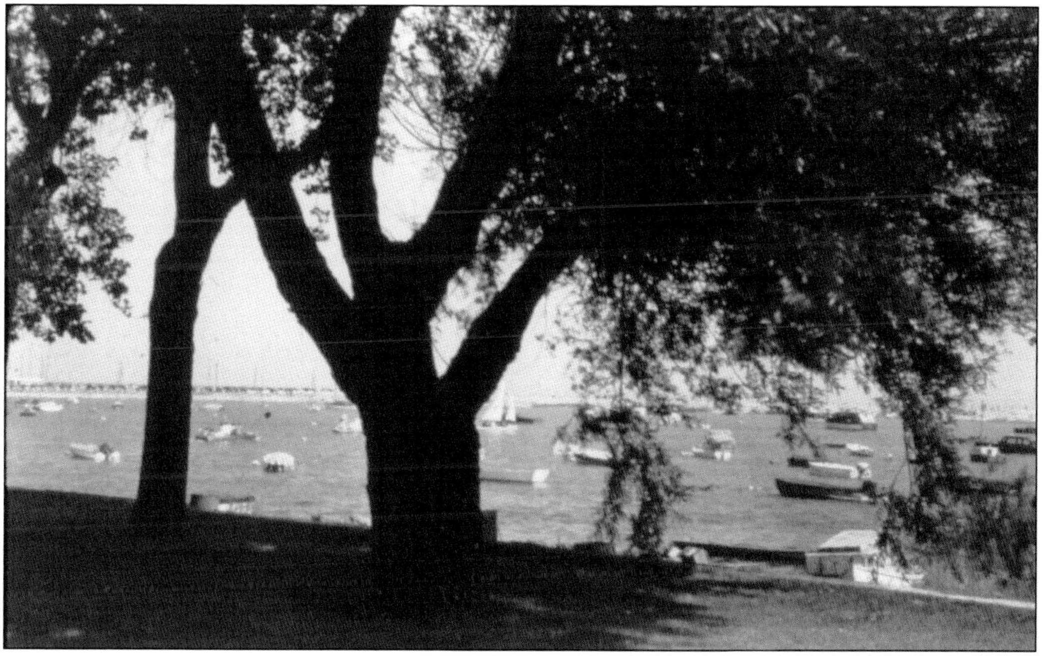

The marina, coming under control of a state-enabled agency in 1959, helped ring in the era of recreation in Michigan City. Pleasure boating had begun to take over the harbor beginning in the 1930s.

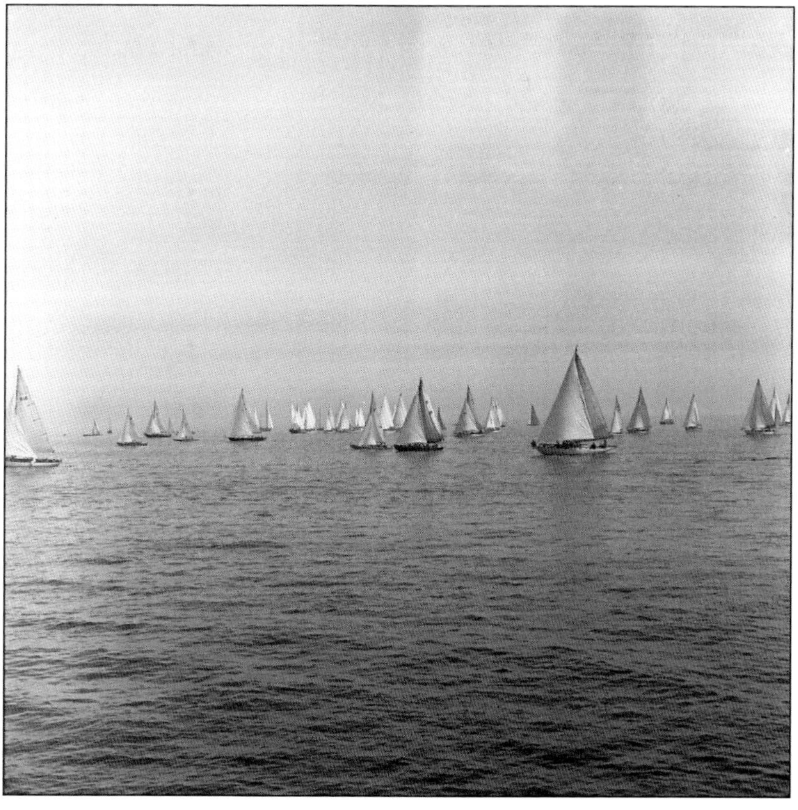

This 1960 photograph of the Columbia Yacht Race is one of many recreational boating events that were staged at Washington Park Marina. The area was and is still known for the proximity of the park, beach, and zoo, making Michigan City a popular place for boaters looking to dock for a night or two. (Courtesy Michigan City News Dispatch)

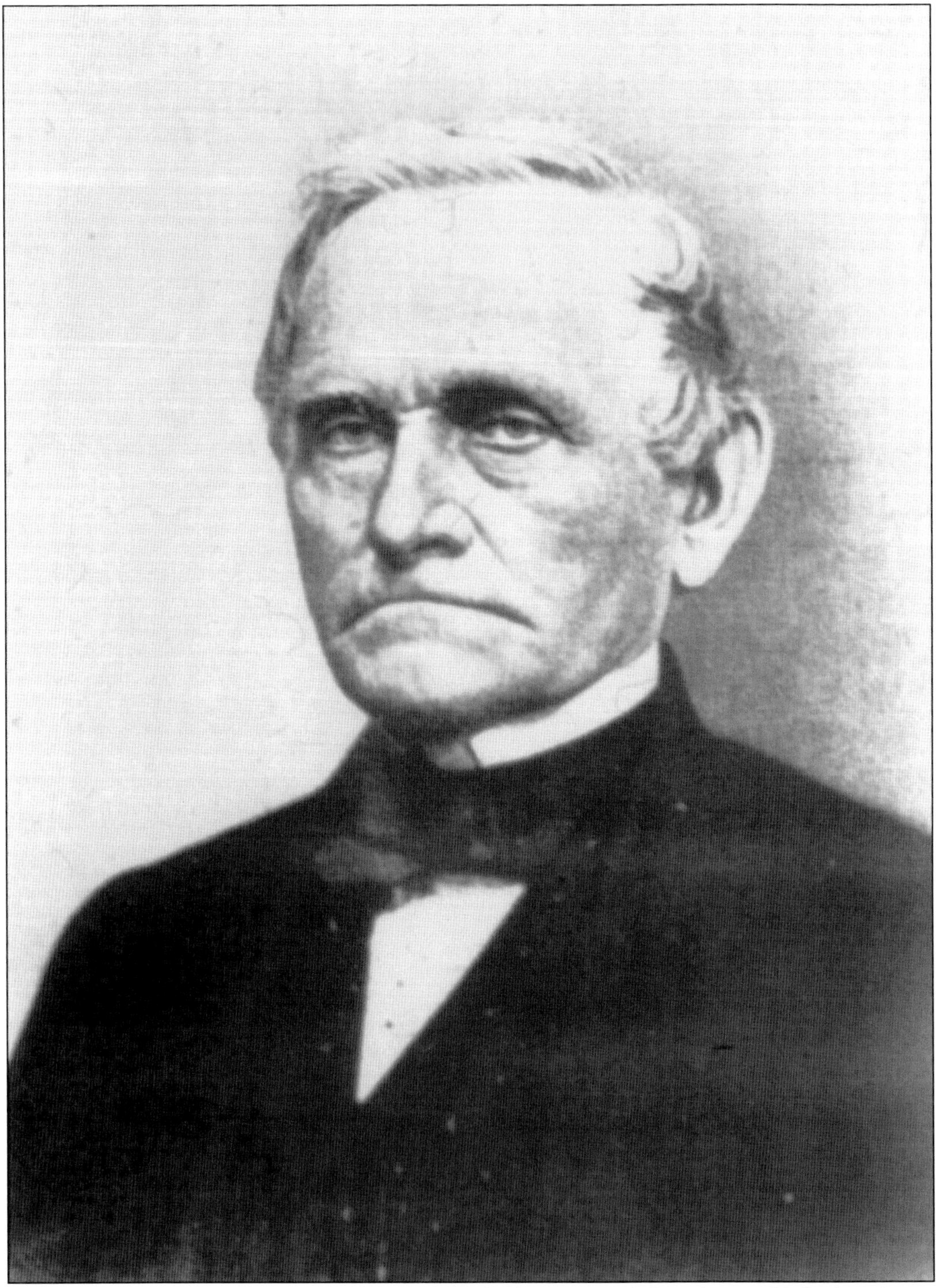

Speculators such as Isaac Elston, the man who bought the town and plotted it, established Michigan City with the hope that the place would become a commercial center on Lake Michigan. Instead, the town has become a tourist powerhouse. The amusements helped usher in the era of the tourist after the dream of a commercial port went unfulfilled.

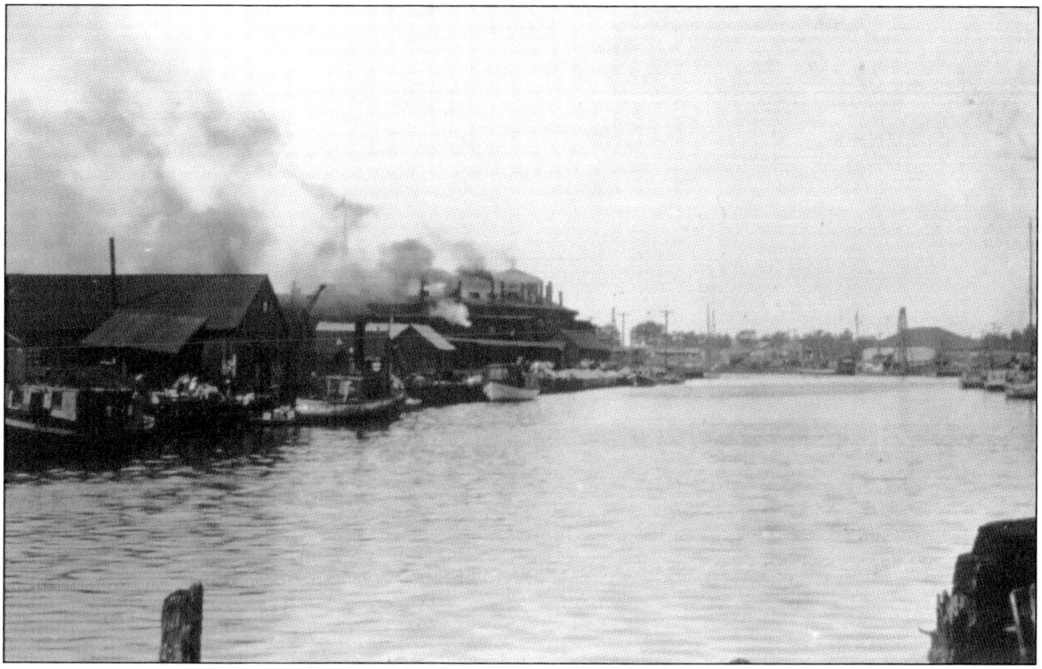

The marina assisted with the change, adding closure to a city's hope that the commercial traffic would end. These factories and cargo ships will never return to the lakefront.

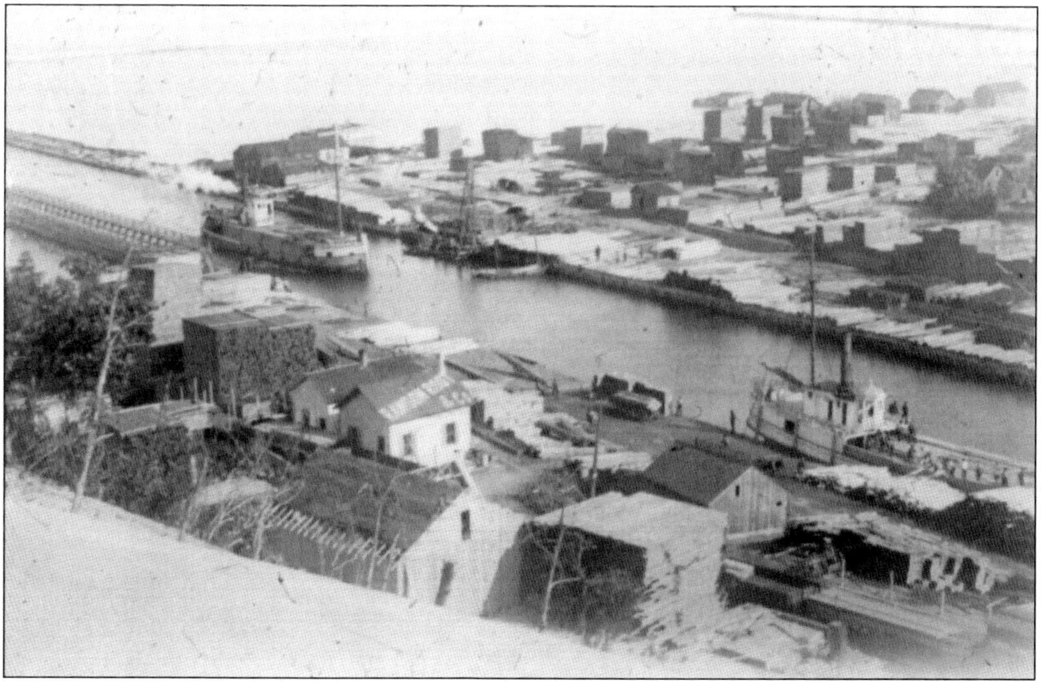

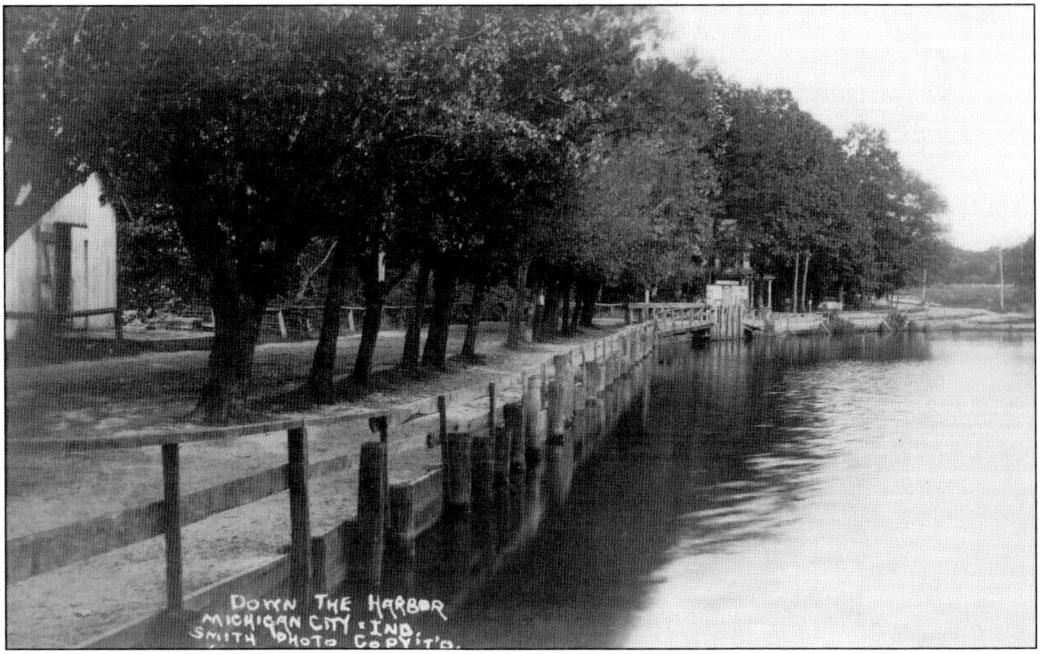

Trail Creek is now a serene stream suited for pleasure boating. Kayaks, canoes, yachts, and small fishing boats freely utilize the creek.

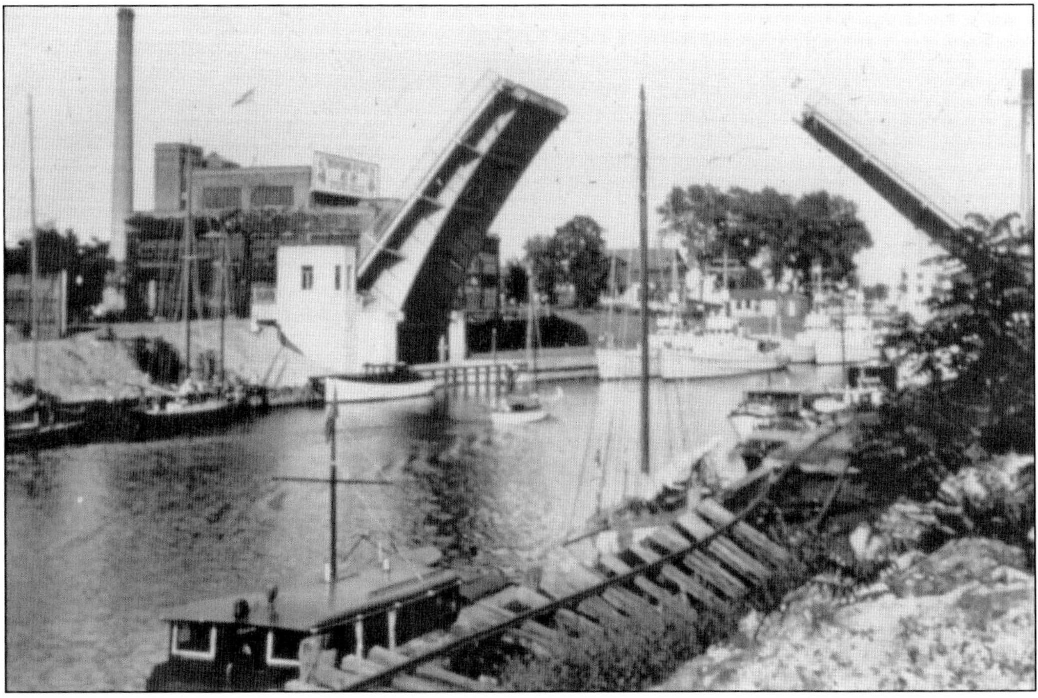

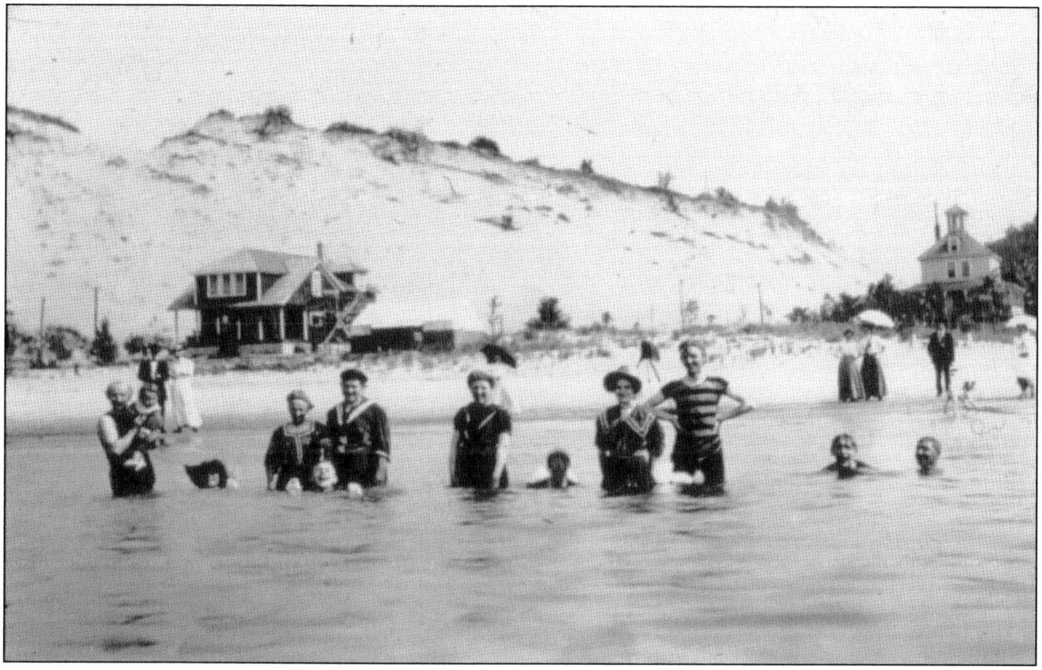

The beach has drawn people, even in the days of the amusement park. It has been and will remain an attractive activity for visitors to Washington Park.

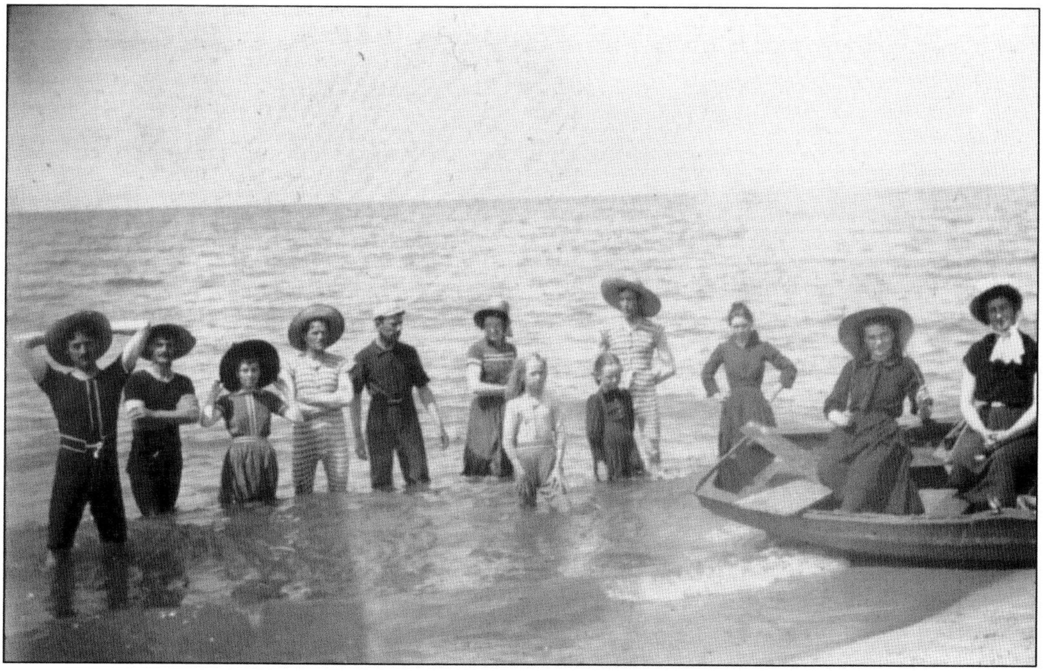

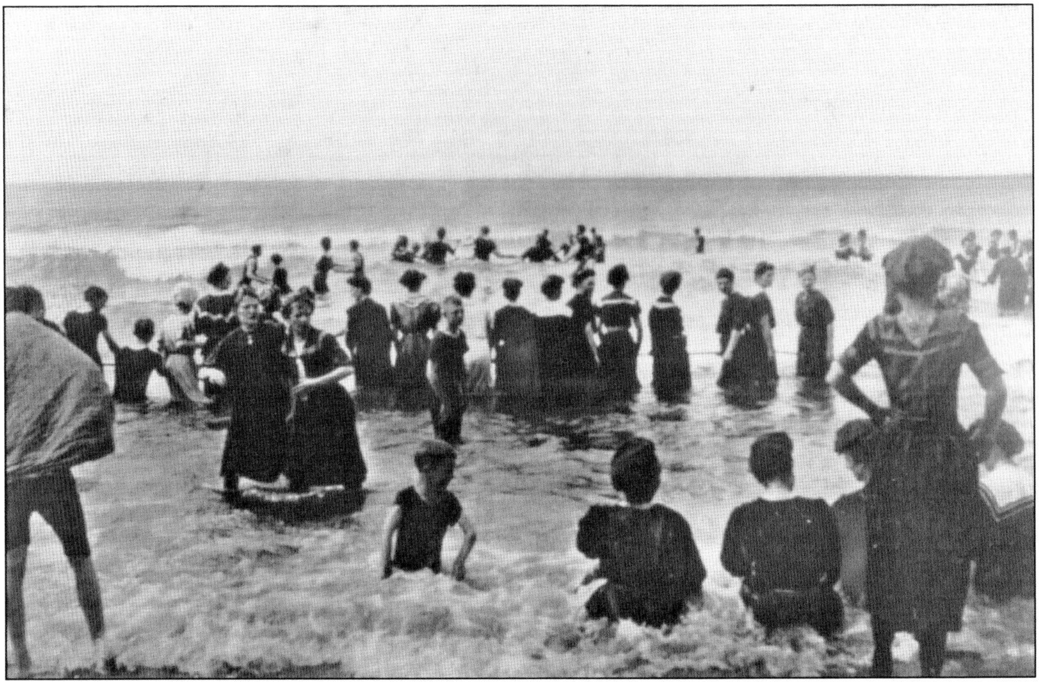

Even summer days in the early 1900s were spent cooling off in Lake Michigan by way of Washington Park. The naysayers who felt that the beach would never be a vital part of Michigan City were proved wrong. In the image below, the Michigan City lighthouse keeper spends a day at the beach with his family. (Courtesy of Mike and Kathy Fleming.)

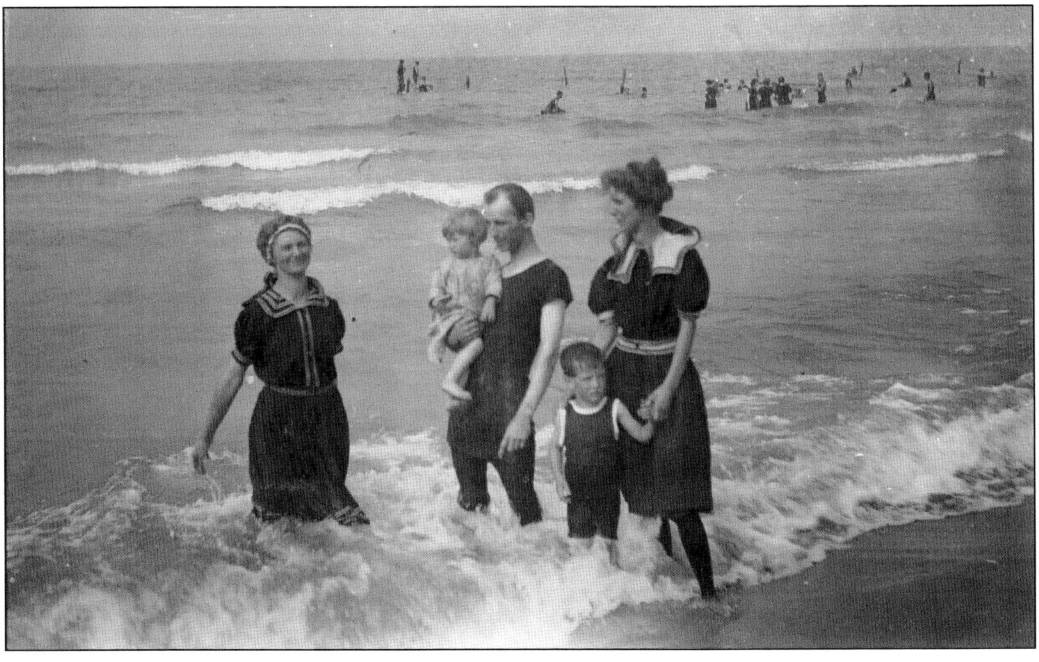

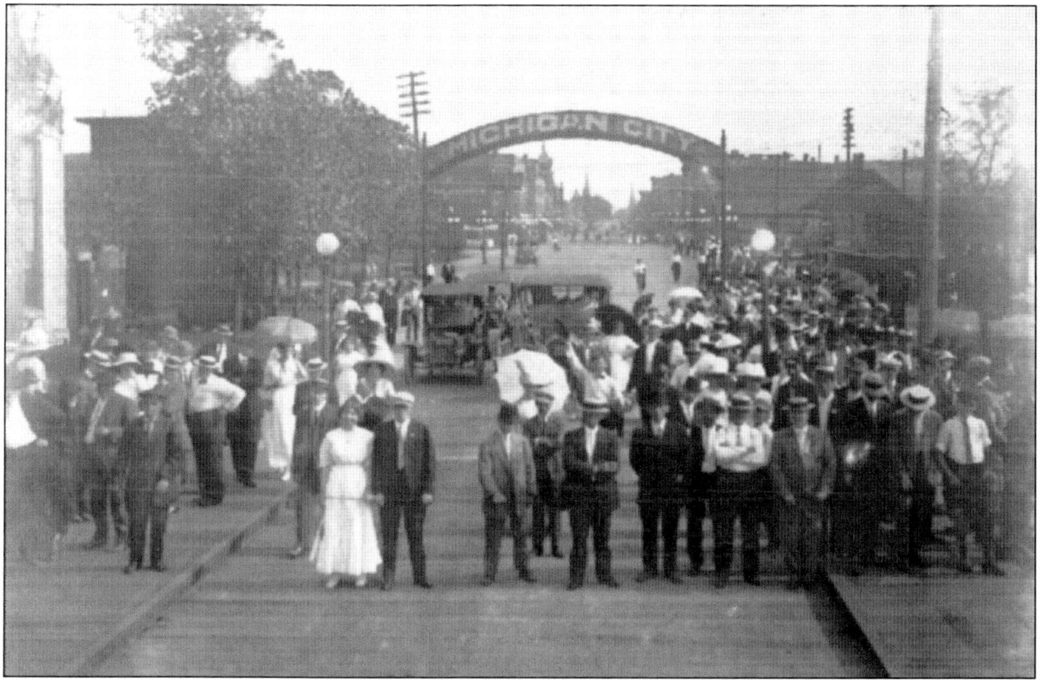

In fact, the entire city quickly came to rely heavily on the park and beach, as it still does today. It was very fortunate that Mayor Krueger pushed past the shortsighted plans of the community at the time to finagle the proper laws that led to Washington Park.

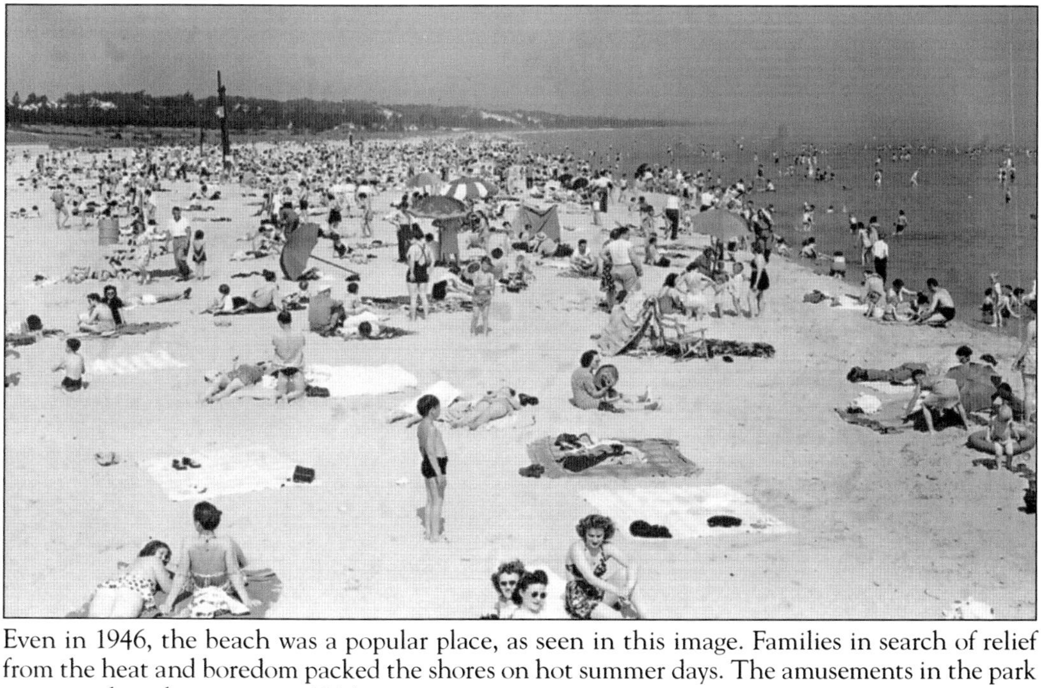

Even in 1946, the beach was a popular place, as seen in this image. Families in search of relief from the heat and boredom packed the shores on hot summer days. The amusements in the park were another alternative in 1946.

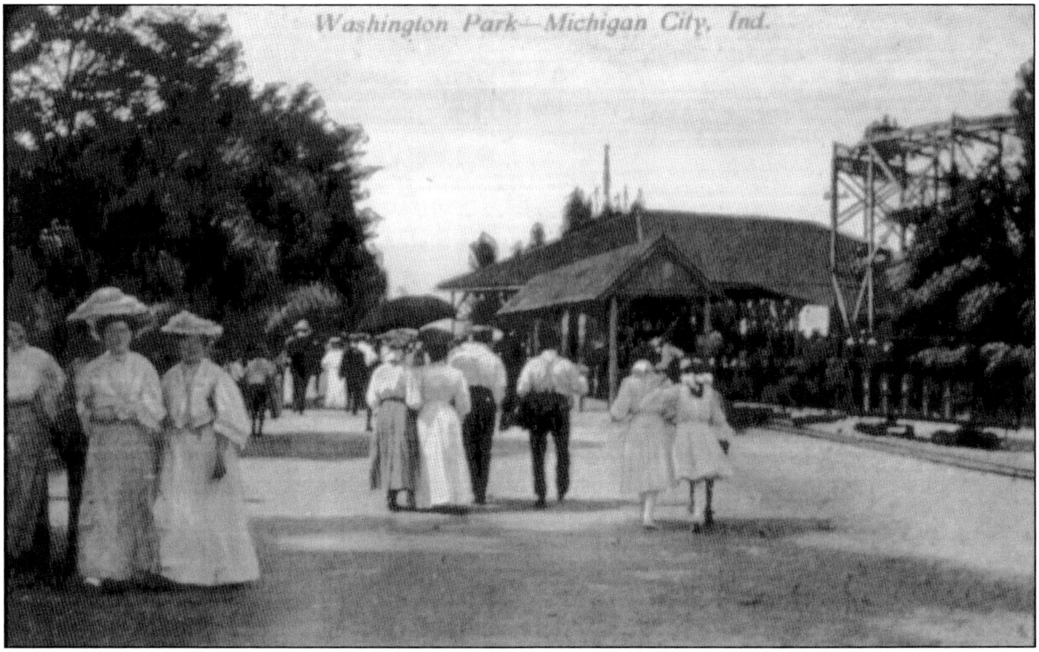

Without Krueger's foresight, photographs like the early 1900s view above of the concessions behind the wooden roller coaster would not have been possible. The beach would have never seen entertainment like that delivered by Washington Park Amusements.

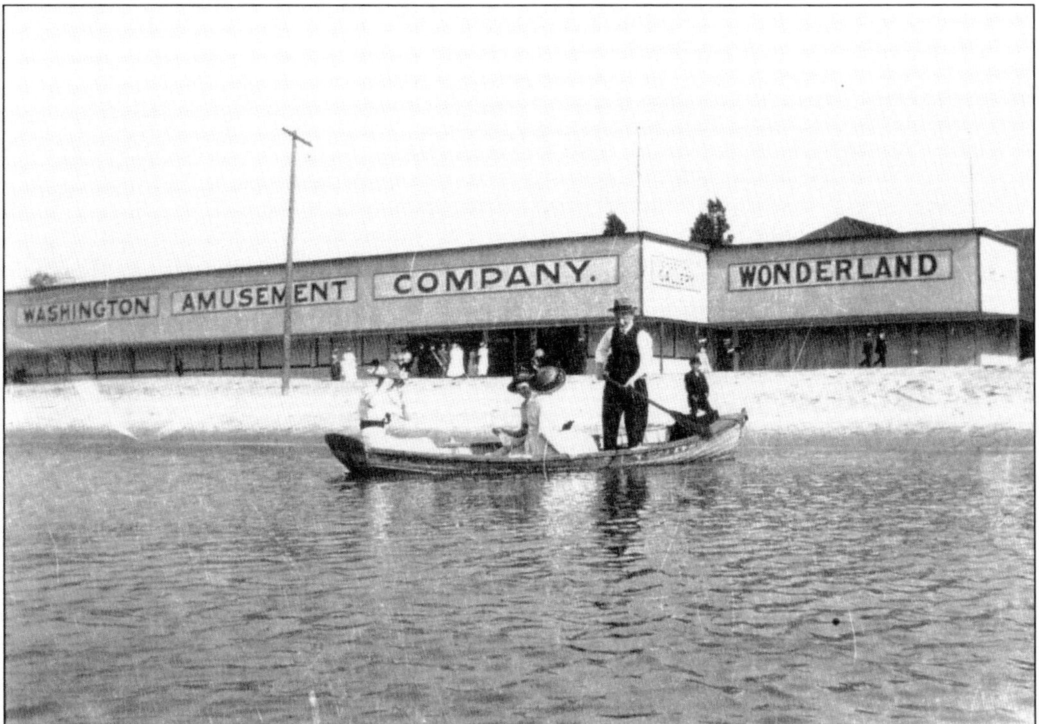

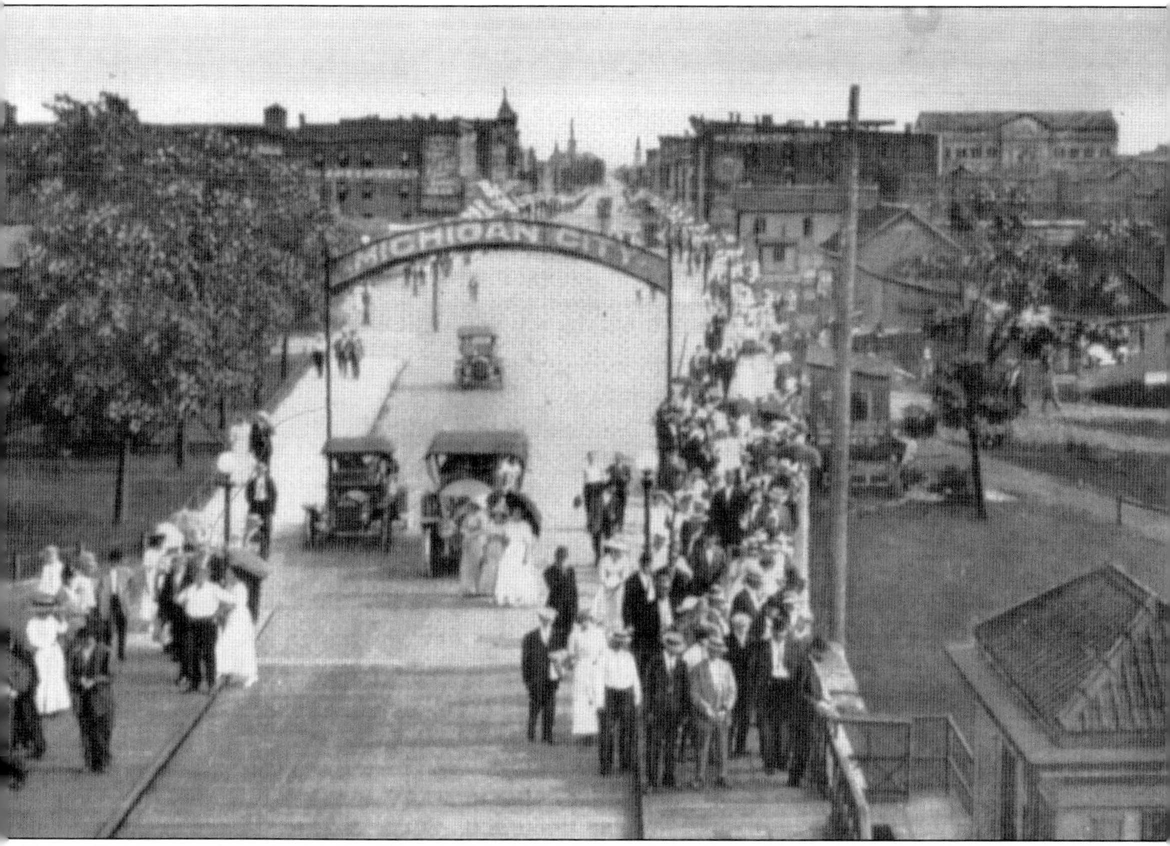

Even the square that Krueger sold to acquire the park has come back and left again. Franklin Street, pictured here in the early 1900s, closed to allow pedestrian access only but was reopened to cars and the square removed in the 1990s. And what about the town square that Mayor Krueger sold in the 1890s to acquire Washington Park lands? It returned years later as Franklin Square, located on Franklin Street. Unfortunately, the square does not exist today.

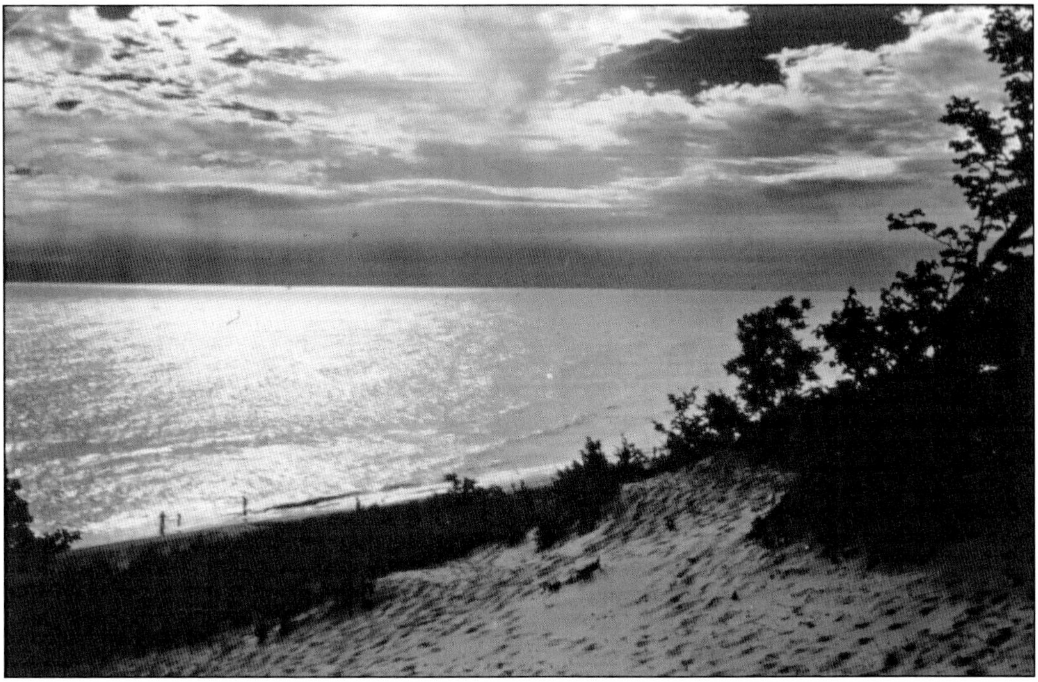

The photograph above, taken from Mount Baldy during the 21st century, resembles the type of environment that the early tribes and French traders may have found upon landing at the mouth of Trail Creek at the base of the Hoosier Slide in the early 1600s. Below is a view of a crowd at the beach in the early 1900s.

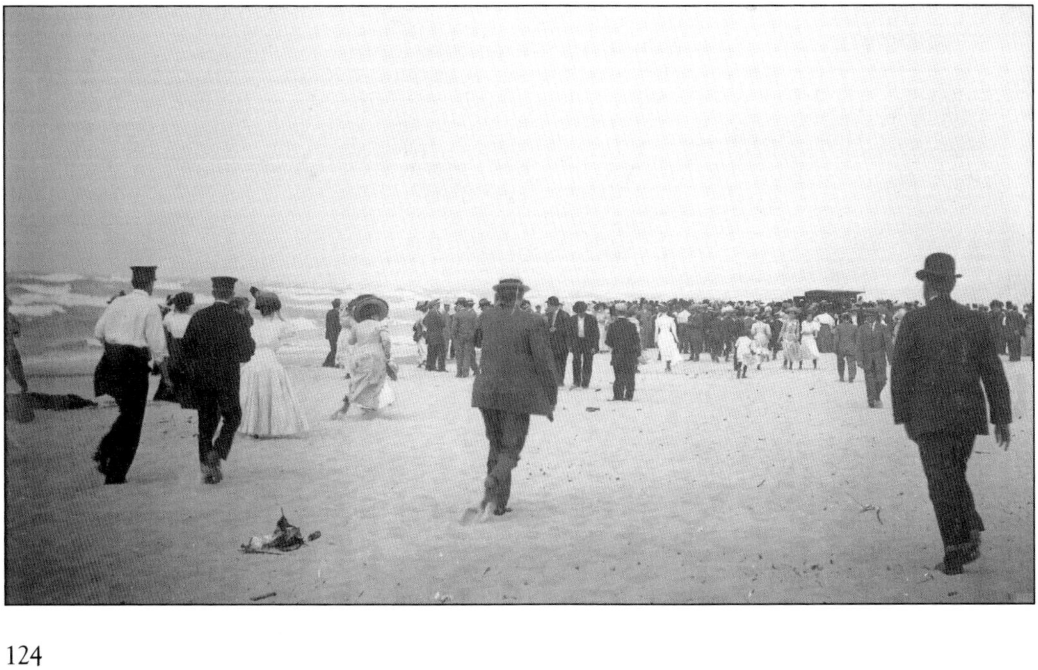

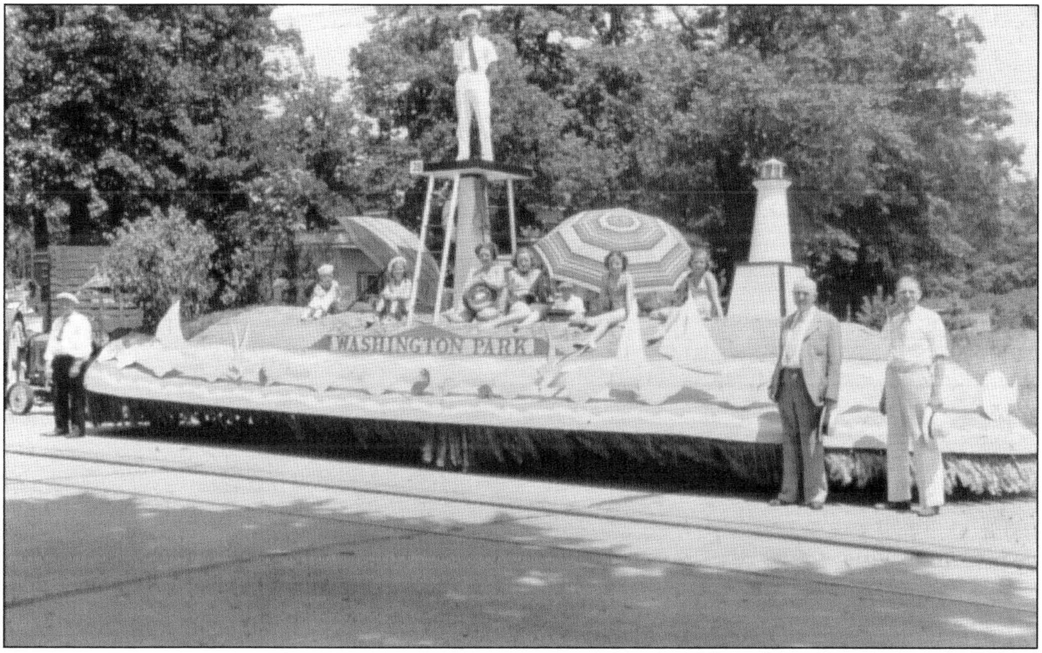

Washington Park's return to a natural environment is just one more incarnation in the long history of the area. New ideas and projects are slowly bringing the area back to amusements. The next 100 years may just see the return of the roller coaster.

Amusements like this Superboat Great Lakes Grand Prix race are staged at Washington Park, drawing tens of thousands of people and generating millions in tourist revenue. The area continues to thrive as an amusement center despite the absence of actual amusements. Boat races are another modern attraction that is a revival of an older pastime. This image of a 1960s boating event is evidence.

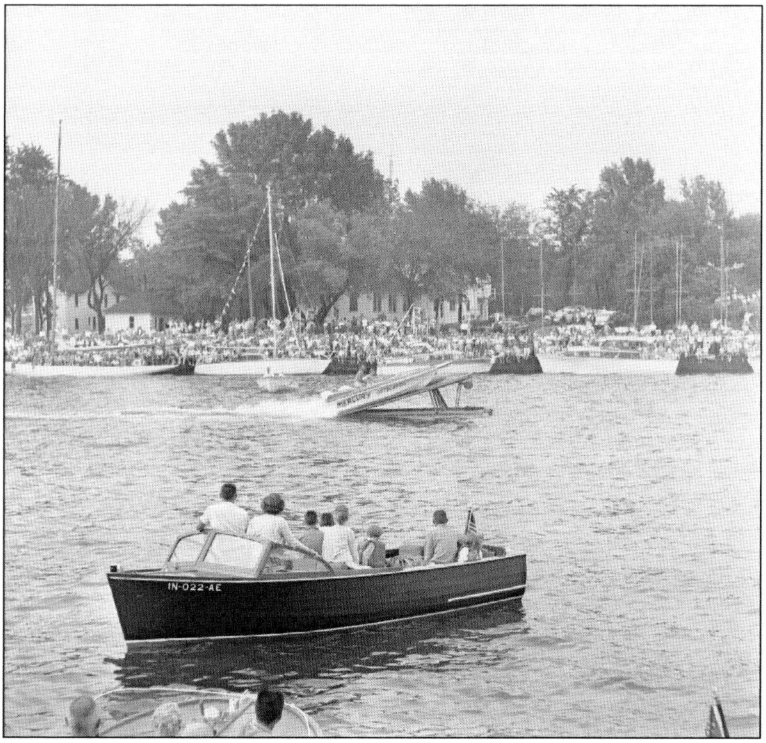

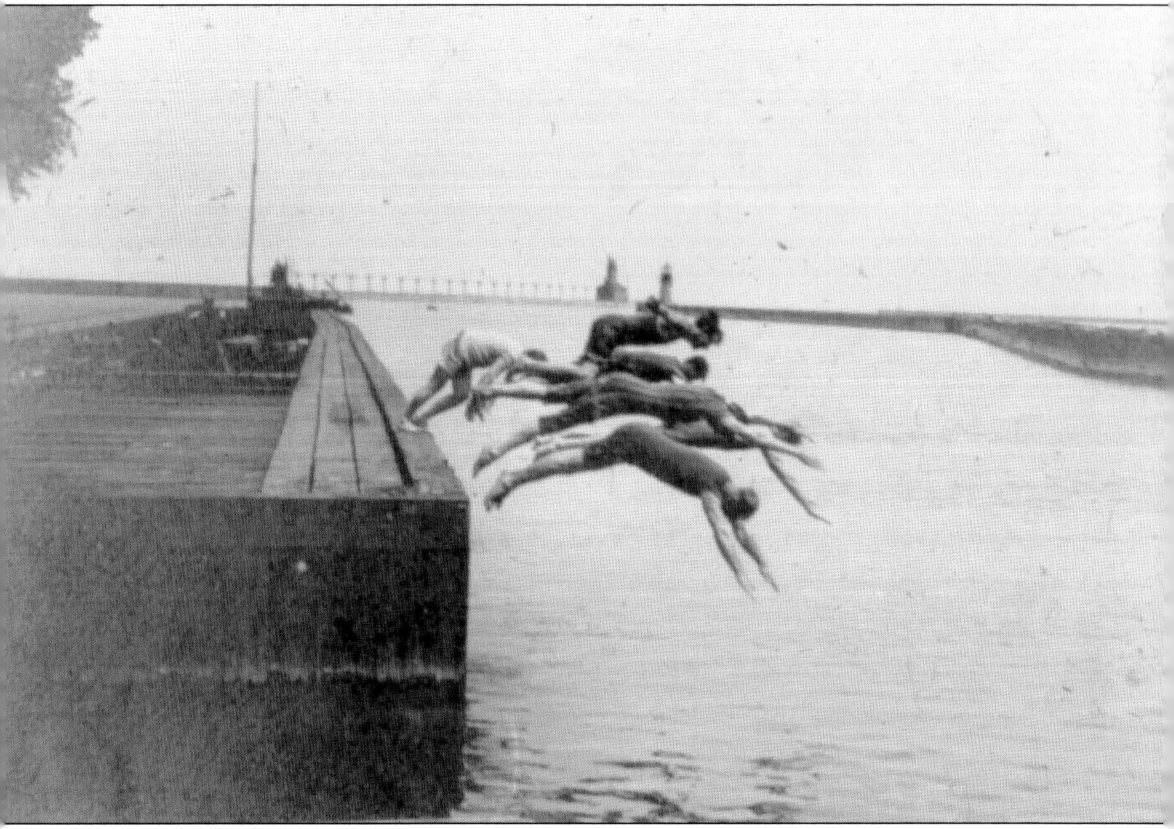

For now, Washington Park is all the recreation that the town of Michigan City needs.

Bibliography

A *Little Bit of History Series Book Three: Two Speeches of the Mayor Martin Krueger*. Michigan City, IN: Michigan City Historical Society, 1989.

"Barr Promotes Michigan City Moppetland With 3-Cent Days; Beautifying Park Started." *Billboard Magazine*. June 25, 1949.

"City Dads Throw Barr a Curve on Parking." *Billboard Magazine*. July 9, 1949.

Gruse, Dennis. *The Oasis: Three Decades of Big Band Sounds*. Michigan City Library Pamphlet Files.

Kaser, Bob and Henry Lange. *Lakefront Legacy*. Michigan City, IN: *Michigan City News Dispatch*, 1976.

Lange, Henry. "Anvil Chorus." *Michigan City News Dispatch*. October 21, 1978.

Michigan City Evening News. November 8, 1926.

Michigan City, IN. Woodland Hills, CA: Windsor Publications, 1965.

Munger, Elizabeth M. *Michigan City's First Hundred Years*. Michigan City, IN: Self-published, 1969.

Nicewarner, Gladys Bull. *Michigan City, IN: Life of a Town*. Michigan City, IN: Self-published, 1980.

Schafer, Mike. *Roller Coasters*. Osceola, WI: MBI Publishing, 1998.

Schultz, Fern Eddy. "Michigan City's Oasis by the Lake." *Michigan City News Dispatch*. May 20, 2009.

"Washington Park." *Michigan City Evening Dispatch*. March 5, 1897.

"Washington Park Off 15%." *Billboard Magazine*. June 11, 1949.

"While Strolling Through the Park." *Billboard Magazine*. April 27, 1946.

"WPAC Trial." *Michigan City News Dispatch*. January 17, 1979.

www.laportecounty.net.

www.arcadiapublishing.com

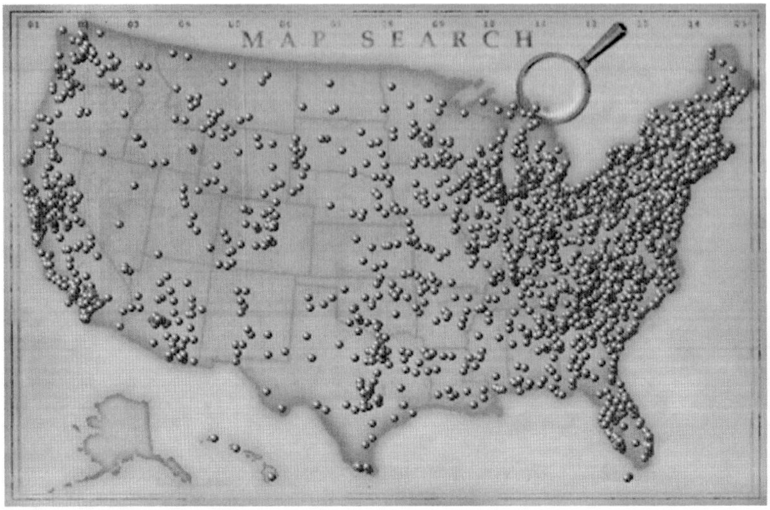

Discover books about the town where you grew up, the cities where your friends and families live, the town where your parents met, or even that retirement spot you've been dreaming about. Our Web site provides history lovers with exclusive deals, advanced notification about new titles, e-mail alerts of author events, and much more.

MADE IN THE USA

Arcadia Publishing, the leading local history publisher in the United States, is committed to making history accessible and meaningful through publishing books that celebrate and preserve the heritage of America's people and places. Consistent with our mission to preserve history on a local level, this book was printed in South Carolina on American-made paper and manufactured entirely in the United States.

This book carries the accredited Forest Stewardship Council (FSC) label and is printed on 100 percent FSC-certified paper. Products carrying the FSC label are independently certified to assure consumers that they come from forests that are managed to meet the social, economic, and ecological needs of present and future generations.

FSC

Mixed Sources

Product group from well-managed forests and other controlled sources

Cert no. SW-COC-001530

www.fsc.org

© 1996 Forest Stewardship Council

Find Your Place in History.